CONCEPT GEOGRAPHY

BOOK 3

SPENCER THOMAS

John Murray

Chancerel

Acknowledgements
Series Editor: Duncan Prowse
Editor: Catherine Dell
Researchers: Deborah Manley, Pat Foulkes
Illustrators: Cedric Knight, Alan Suttie, David Parkins, Donald Myall
Designer: Wendi Watson

The author wishes to thank all those who have helped in the preparation of this book, especially:
B.S. Hoyle, T. Hoare, R. Lawton, R. Colenutt, P. Daniels, T. Binns, G. Rowley, V. Robinson, P. Harriss, N. Suddaby, G. Elliot, T. Allan, P. Corrigan, B. Heinzten, M. Bradshaw, A. Browne.

Also available in this series:
Concept Geography Book 1 (ISBN 0 7195 4223 5)
Concept Geography Book 2 (ISBN 0 7195 4224 3)
Concept Geography Teachers' Book (ISBN 0 7195 4226 X)

© Twinburn Limited 1986
Reprinted 1987
All rights reserved. No part of this publication may be reproduced, recorded, transmitted or stored in any retrieval system, in any form whatsoever, without the written permission of the copyright holder.

Published by:
John Murray (Publishers) Ltd
50 Albemarle Street
London W1X 4BD

ISBN 0 7195 4225 1

Produced by:
Chancerel Publishers Ltd
40 Tavistock Street
London WC2E 7PB

Typeset by DP Press, Sevenoaks, UK. Colour by Scantrans, Singapore. Printed in Hong Kong

Photographs:
Cover: Buenos Aires and the Rio de la Plata shown in an image produced from electronic data returned to Earth by the Landsat Satellites. Buenos Aires is South America's second largest city, with a population estimated at over 11 million. The urban area shows up as the blue mass along the southern shore of the Rio de la Plata, which is over 50 km wide, but shallow and heavily silted. The Parana delta can be seen as the red area at the top left of the picture, with many distributaries flowing out through swampy wetlands unsuitable for agriculture. In the north, the Uruguay river joins the estuary. The northern shore of the Rio de la Plata is agricultural land in Uruguay. Wheat is grown in the west, maize in the centre and livestock in the east (top right of the picture). The red and blue patchwork to the south-east and south-west (bottom left and bottom right) shows the dairy and beef cattle farming on the fertile plain of the Argentinian pampas. Every effort has been made to trace the copyright holders of all the illustrations in this book, but the publishers will be pleased to make the necessary arrangements at the first opportunity if there are any omissions.

Aerofilms 62; Age Concern England 106; Air Flight Service 12; Airbus Industrie 87; ANT/NHPA 59; Associated Press 15, 27, 28, 36, 45, 46, 49, 55, 65, 75, 86, 97; Austin Rover 83; Australian Labor Party 53; AVX Ltd 77; Bangor Street Youth & Comm. Centre/Action Factory Community Arts 6; Barbados Board of Tourism 31; BP 39; British Antarctic Survey/A. Wootton 109; British Tourist Authority 90; Caithness Glass 10; Cambio-16 17; Camerapix 51; Colorific 19; Commission of European Communities 72, 77; Corrigan, G&P 57, 97; CSR (Sugar Division) 10; CWDE/IDA/Mary Hill 44; CWDE/World Bank/Ray Within 45; Daily Express 43; Darbourne and Darke (Architects); Dell, Catherine 22; Digital Equipment Co. Ltd; Eagle Star Group 85; Earthscan/G. Barnard 5; Earthscan/Mark Edwards 4, 5, 61; Electricité de France/M. Brigaud 42; Elf Aquitaine 38, 39; Embraer SA/Mars 41; Ferranti plc 84; Financial Times/Ashley Ashwood 79; Finnish Tourist Board 71; First Garden City Heritage Museum 20; Ford 83; Forestry Commission 65; Friends of the Earth/Duncan Baxter 43; Friends of the Earth/S. Boyle 4; Friends of the Earth/Wave Energy Group 5; Geological Museum (British Museum) 25; GeoScience Picture Library 5; Gould Electronics 4; Government of Ontario 98; Harland & Wolff plc 76; Herald & Weekly Times Ltd, Melbourne 37; Highlands & Islands Development Board 64; Hilling, David 88; Hoechst UK Ltd 41; Humberside Industrial Publications 91; Hutchinson Library 19, 27; Inmos Ltd 84; Intel 12, 13; International Coffee Organization 100; International Defence and Aid Fund 94, 95; Israel Government Tourist Office 97; J. Allan Cash 22, 24, 34, 35, 39, 50, 66, 70, 90, 93, 96; Labour Party 67; Livingston Development Corporation 20; Lloyds 33; London Regional Transport 21, 90; Mansell Collection 31, 54, 87, 92, 94; Marx Library 96; Mitsui 46; NEC 47; Novosti Press Agency 7, 74; Oxfam 45, 61; Photosource 15, 17, 67, 72; Prowse, D 46, 81; Reflex/Piers Cavendish 81; Reuters 33; Rex Features 48; Rolls Royce Ltd 84; Rowntree Mackintosh 100; Ruhrpark/Foto Lohoff 28; Saskatchewan Tourism 81; SBAC/Arthur Gibson 85; Scottish Development Agency 20, 21; SCDC Publications 73; Shell Photographs 88; Shelter 68; Simson, D 100; Simson, J 81; Singapore Tourist Promotion Board 89; Society of Motor Manufacturers and Traders 29; Solavolt International/NASA 108; Southern Newspapers plc 83; Spanish National Tourist Office 31; Springhill Farm 23; Stock Exchange 33; Swedish Pulp & Paper Association 8, 9; Tea Council Ltd 87; Tennessee Valley Authority 105; Thames Water 6; Thomson Holidays/Doug Goodman 31; Thomas, Spencer 21, 56, 107; Topham Picture Library 23; TRRL (Crown copyright reserved) 84; US Geological Survey 36; Volkswagen 82; Wilderness Society 59; Windmill Hill/St. Martins Property Group 85; Hydro-Electric Commission, Tasmania 84, Unilever plc 41; Geest 101; Saudi Arabian Information Centre 103; RSPB/John Marchington 103.

Contents

Locations
Renewable energy 4
Water – supply and demand 6
Close to raw materials 8
Close to the market 10
The advance of technology 12
Earthquake belts 14

Cycles
Urban growth and decay 16
Megalopolis, USA 18
New and renewed cities 20
Agriculture in the EEC 22
Building mountains 24
Restless oceans 26

Time/distance
On the outskirts 28
The tourist industry 30
The information industry 32
Moving with the seasons 34
Natural disasters 36

Relationships
The politics of oil 38
Trans-national companies 40
Nuclear power 42
Aid for development 44
Manufacturers to the world 46

Patterns
Migration of labour 48
Holiday economics 50
Catching votes 52
River patterns 54

Landscapes
Microclimates 56
Conservation matters 58
Desert takeover 60
The use of land 62
National forests 64

Regions
Two nations 66
Cosmopolitan Britain 68
Nations within nations 70
The European ideal 72
The Soviet bloc 74
Aid to the regions 76

Networks
Supply and demand 78
Staple foods 80
Economies of scale 82
The road to prosperity 84
Changing world trade 86

Hierarchies
Development and change 88
A roof over their heads 90
Primate cities 92
Separate development 94
Planning the economy 96

Morphology
Skyscraper cities 98
Plantation agriculture 100
Deciding how to farm 102
Tennessee's new deal 104
The third age 106
One world 108

Index 110

Renewable energy

> Renewable energy sources can only be exploited economically in certain locations

As the world runs short of traditional **fossil fuels** – and remains uncertain about nuclear power – there is growing interest in **renewable** sources of energy, such as the sun, wind and sea. These renewables are inexhaustible and non-polluting, but they do have disadvantages.
■ Geographical limitations: the optimum area for exploiting solar energy is within 31° of the equator; a long, tapering bay suits tidal power.
■ Unreliability: a wave machine needs choppy seas just as an aerogenerator requires a steady wind.
■ Diffuseness: to produce the same amount of electricity as a conventional power station, a windfarm needs to cover 30 times the area.

Yet, despite these drawbacks, renewables supply an increasing amount of the world's energy.

Falling water

Water power, exploited since earliest times, was harnessed in the mid-19th century to generate electricity. Today, **hydro-power** produces 25 per cent of the world's electricity, but only 2 per cent of the UK total. HEP's share is unlikely to increase as the best sites have all been utilized.
■ High mountainous areas in wet latitudes constitute the best HEP locations. Here heavy relief rainfall and melting snows provide abundant water.
■ The creation of storage reservoirs to keep the water supply constant may involve 'drowning' a valley, thus destroying farmland, settlements and scenic features.
■ Pumped storage schemes are costly, but more efficient and less damaging to the environment. Water, flowing from an upper to a lower reservoir, powers turbines during the day. At night, when demand for electricity is least, water is pumped back from the lower reservoir to the upper one for re-use.

Sunshine all around

The sun sends more energy to the Earth in an hour than the whole world consumes in a year. Even cloudy locations have a surplus of **solar energy**: the total falling on Britain in a year is a hundred times greater than the country's energy needs.
■ The sun's power can heat buildings directly. In northern Europe and America, many houses are now designed with large double-glazed windows and good insulation to make the most of natural warmth.
■ Collectors (panels) boost the sun's contribution. Solar panels, installed on roofs are widely used for heating water in Mediterranean and other hot lands.
■ Solar cells, commonly made of silicon, convert sunlight into electricity. Modern technology, from pocket calculators to satellites, increasingly uses solar power.
■ Many tropical LDCs are installing solar-cell (**photovoltaic**) systems to generate electricity in remote, rural locations.

Above: *Village television run by solar generated electricity in Niger. The photovoltaic array is on the right. Solar cells are pollution-free, contain no moving parts, require little maintenance and last up to 20 years; but the initial manufacturing cost is high.*

Above: *The world's largest solar energy generating station is in the Mojave Desert, north-east of Los Angeles. There, 1818 massive, angled mirrors reflect sunshine onto a special boiler on top of an 88-metre high tower. The concentrated solar energy (equivalent of 300 suns) heats water inside the boiler to almost 540°C and a pressure of 105 kg/cm^2, providing enough power to drive a 109-tonne turbine generator.*

Left: *Pitlochry is one of nine hydro-power plants using the waters of the River Tummel and its tributaries in the Grampian mountains. 46% of Britain's hydro-electricity is generated in Scotland.*

Above: Making biogas in the village of Akbarpur-Barota, India. Water is added to dung in a concrete pit; the mixture ferments and produces methane. The gas, stored in the holder behind, is piped to better-off households.

Plant power

Organic matter, known as **biomass**, is the most common source of energy. Worldwide it supplies 14 per cent of primary energy needs, but as much as 43 per cent in LDCs.
■ In LDCs wood and animal dung are the main forms of biomass. However, the over-exploitation of forests for firewood has caused an energy crisis currently affecting one billion people (rising to three billion by 2000). Dung is more valuable as a fertilizer than as a fuel, yet it is still burnt.
■ A more efficient use of biomass is **biogas**. A simple process converts dung and other organic waste into methane gas, suitable for cooking, heating and lighting. The leftover sludge makes rich manure. Biogas digesters are now widely used in China and India.
■ Biomass is also used in developed countries. In Nottingham, for instance, incineration of domestic waste supplies heat to 15,000 homes.

Above: The Wairakei geothermal power station generates 5% of New Zealand's electricity. The exploitation of geothermal energy can conflict with tourist interests, as it results in less surface activity (steam, boiling mud, geysers) for visitors to see.

Above: Californian wind farms take full advantage of west coast topography: mountain passes become natural funnels, drawing cool air from the sea to warmer inland valleys during the summer.

Space-age windmills

The wind is inexhaustible and, in many locations, relatively reliable. For centuries, it powered corn mills and water pumps until windmills were replaced by steam power. In the 1970s, prompted by the energy crisis, wind-power technology began to be updated and redeveloped.
■ Today's windmills are **aerogenerators**: wind turbines designed to produce electricity. In California, 10,000 turbines now supply around five per cent of the state's electricity. Denmark aims to wind-generate 10 per cent of its electricity by 2000.
■ Large wind machines, producing over one megawatt of power have not yet been proved. Instead thousands of smaller turbines are grouped together in **windfarms**. Such concentrations have a marked visual impact on the environment and are thus sited in remote areas.
■ Wind turbines, possibly located offshore, could generate 20 per cent of UK electricity. Aerogenerators are being tested in Scotland.

Hot rocks

The earth's interior heat is a usable power source, but so far supplies only 0.1 per cent of the world's energy needs – largely because deep drilling costs are so high. It is most economically exploited in active volcanic areas, where superheated water rises to the crust and even breaks through in **geysers**.
■ Countries as far apart as New Zealand, Iceland, Japan, France, Hungary and Italy already use geothermal energy.
■ In some places, notably Iceland, heating systems tap underground hot water direct.
■ Elsewhere, as in New Zealand, natural steam power drives turbines to generate electricity.
■ Research into Britain's possible sources of geothermal power is taking place in Cornwall, but underground temperatures (50–60°C) are too low for power generation.

Ocean power

The sea's limitless power, available in some measure to every country with a coastline, remains largely unharnessed. There are three possibilities for tapping it.
■ Tides: a barrage, incorporating turbines, across a tidal estuary generates electricity from the incoming tide. It traps the water behind it, thus allowing generation from the outflow as well. The only tidal power station in operation, across the Rance in Brittany, produces the world's cheapest electricity. In the UK the Severn estuary is an ideal location for a tidal power barrage.
■ Waves: there are various ways of converting waves into electricity. To date, the world's only wave power station is in Norway, near Bergen.
■ Temperature: the temperature difference between warm surface water and colder depths has energy potential, which is being researched.

Below: A wave machine being tested on Loch Ness. The calm water behind the device indicates that energy has been extracted. With its long coasts and rough seas, Britain could generate 30% of its electricity from wave power.

1 What is renewable energy?
2 What are the obstacles to developing it on a large scale?
3 Which sources of renewable energy are most appropriate to: a) developed countries; b) LDCs?
4 Which renewable energy sources are suitable for: a) urban areas; b) rural areas?
5 Assume you are advising the government on future policy. Would you recommend developing renewable or non-renewable sources?

Water-supply and demand

A resource can be transferred from a place where it is in plentiful supply to a place where it is in demand.

Britain's water supplies

Water is in demand because it is a basic necessity of life.
- It is needed for personal consumption, for agriculture, for industry and for leisure.
- Demand for water is rising constantly. Fifty years ago each person in Britain consumed 125 litres of water per day; today that figure is 340 litres; it is estimated that by 2000 demand will double.

Below: *Fishing on the Walthamstow Reservoir north-east of London. Recreational use of rivers, reservoirs, and lakes managed by Water Authorities includes angling, boating, sailboarding, bird-watching and water-skiing.*

- These figures include industrial use, which consumes more than half of all water used. It takes 450,000 litres of water to make one car; 190 litres to produce a Sunday newspaper.

In a country like Britain with a temperate climate, water appears to be in plentiful supply.
- There are 91 million litres available per person per day. But only 6.6 per cent of the water that falls on the earth is used; the rest is lost by evaporation and run-off.
- But there is a surplus in some parts of the country and a shortage in other parts.
- As demand rises (Americans already consume twice as much water as Britons), more conservation and better management are required to guarantee adequate supplies.

Water management

Water management in England and Wales is the responsibility of ten Regional Water Authorities.
- Water Authorities charge water rates to each household to pay for their services. In many countries water is metered like gas and electricity so people pay for the amount they use; meters are also available in Britain.
- Authority boundaries are based on the catchment areas of major rivers, thus an entire river basin is under one management.
- Most of the water from the north and west comes from surface flows; in the south and east it is from natural underground reservoirs called aquifers.
- For the future various plans are under consideration such as refilling depleted aquifers and building barrages across estuaries like the Wash, which could provide water for a million people.

Left: *As part of its pollution-control programme, Thames Water operates a laboratory launch. Fish and water organisms are trawled up from the river bed for analysis; if tests show pollution, this is then investigated.*

Water Authorities of England and Wales (with population and annual precipitation)

- Northumbrian 2.6 m, 879 mm
- North West 6.9 m, 1217 mm
- Yorkshire 4.6 m, 833 mm
- Severn–Trent 8.3 m, 773 mm
- Welsh 3 m, 1334 mm
- Anglian 5 m, 611 mm
- Thames 11.5 m, 711 mm
- South West 1.4 m, 1194 mm
- Wessex 2.3 m, 864 mm
- Southern 3.9 m, 794 mm

1 Which parts of England and Wales have a surplus of water?
2 Which parts have a deficit?
3 Use your atlas to identify estuaries suitable for water-storage barrages.
4 Why are the principal UK water sources in the north and west?
Class activity: Divide the class into two groups: a) farmers in a Welsh valley, which is about to be flooded by a reservoir; b) residents of Birmingham who need water for their homes and industries. Debate the motion: 'Water management must be for the good of the majority'.

Below: *This advertisement for Thames Water summarizes the various responsibilities of a Regional Water Authority. Thames Water, the country's largest Authority, manages the water cycle in a 13,000 km² area based on the Thames basin.*

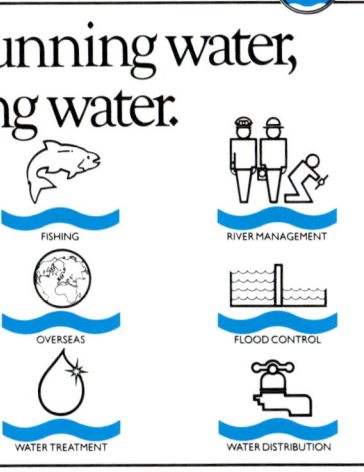

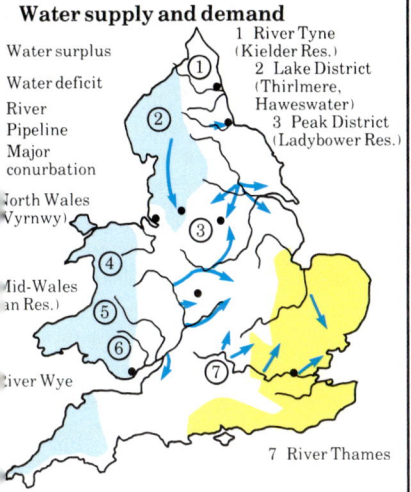

Irrigation for Soviet farms

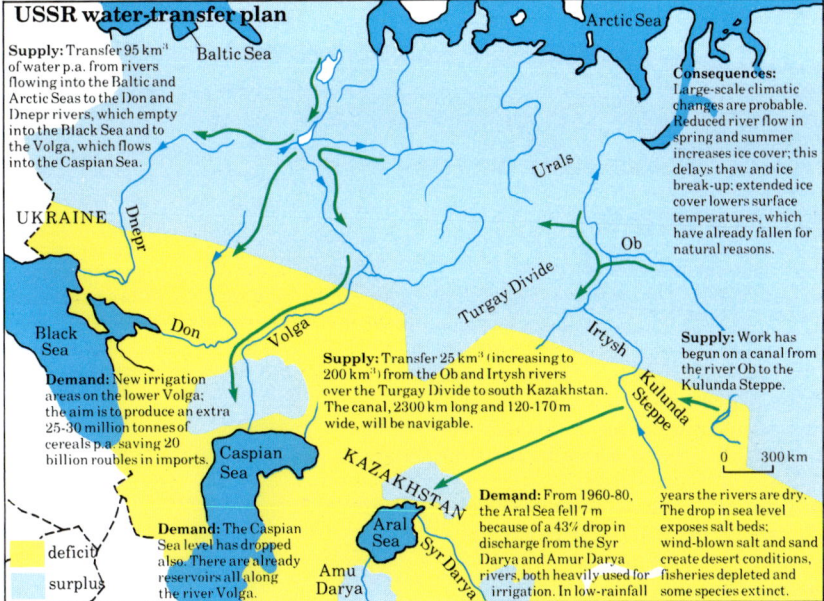

One of the biggest problems facing the Soviet government is the country's inability to feed itself.

- Large numbers of people work on Soviet farms (23 per cent of the population compared with 2.8 per cent in the USA). Yet, with 75 per cent more land cultivated than the USA, the USSR only manages 80 per cent of US agricultural output.
- Soviet agriculture is mostly based on government-run, collective farms, which are large but inefficient. Under three per cent of farmland is in private hands, yet this sector produces 25 per cent of farm output.
- The Soviet authorities have always favoured large, state projects. In the 1970s, agriculture took a quarter of all state investment funds.
- In the last decade, Soviet planners hoped to solve their problems by providing extra water for irrigation in the dry south and east.

Water from the north

Southern European Russia, Kazakhstan and Central Asia account for some 75 per cent of the Soviet population and 80 per cent of the agricultural and industrial production. Yet only 16 per cent of the river flow is in this area. Major rivers, except the Volga, flow north. Annual precipitation decreases from the north-west to the south-east. In Central Asia it is less than 300 mm p.a. Government projects focused on diverting surplus water from north-flowing rivers to the south where there is a deficit. In 1986, however, these transfer schemes were re-assessed and some were abandoned because of technical problems and escalating costs.

Left: *Canal construction in the Kyzyl Kum desert in Kazakhstan. This project has now been completed and the reclaimed land is being used for cotton cultivation. In the USSR, both cotton and rice production depend on irrigation.*

> 1 Why is irrigation essential to the USSR?
> 2 Which parts of the USSR have surplus water?
> 3 Under the water-transfer plan, which areas are to be irrigated?
> 4 How is water to be transferred to these areas?
> 5 What problems are involved in transferring water from one part of the USSR to another?

Close to raw materials

Some industries have to be located near the source of their raw materials.

Europe's timber yard

The forests of Scandinavia are a major source of sawn timber and wood pulp.
- The main market for Scandinavian forest products is Western Europe. Developed countries require enormous quantities of timber for construction purposes and paper for printing and packaging.
- Logs are bulky and expensive to transport. So timber is mostly processed as close as possible to its source: the forests.
- The natural coniferous forest of Scandinavia is called **taiga**. It covers over 70 per cent of Finland and 50 per cent of Sweden.
- Trees are mainly Scots pine, Norwegian spruce, fir and laurel. These trees are adapted to the climate. They have thick bark to shield them from wind and cold; cones to protect seeds; needles to prevent loss of moisture; long shallow roots for stability in thin soil; downward-sloping branches so that snow slides off easily.

Sweden's green gold

Sweden is the world's third largest producer of timber (after Canada and the USA). But with a population of only 8 million, the home market is small. Over 90 per cent of wood pulp and 70 per cent of paper is exported.

Below: *The warm North Atlantic drift and prevailing westerly winds make Scandinavia's climate mild for its latitude. Lower and drier areas of Sweden and Finland have better soils and climate for forests than Norway, which is wetter and more mountainous.*

Climate and vegetation in Scandinavia

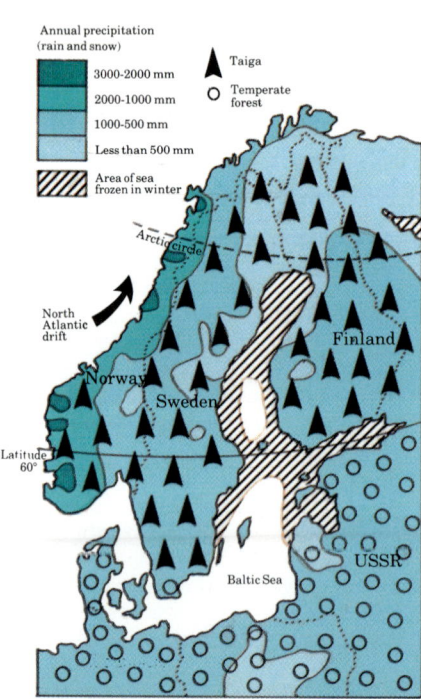

Timber processing

Swedish pulp, paper and board industry

■ Paper/board mill
■ Pulp mill

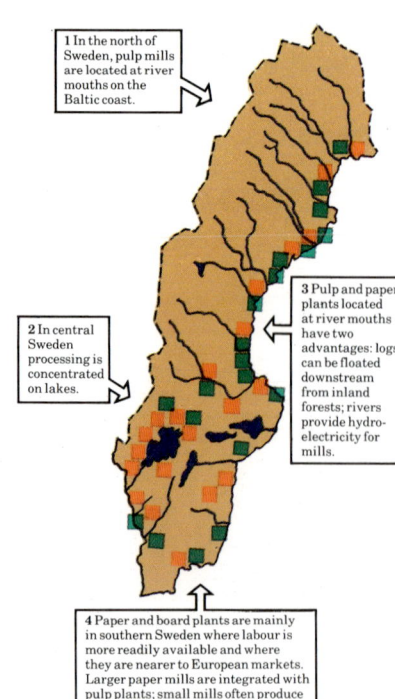

1 In the north of Sweden, pulp mills are located at river mouths on the Baltic coast.

2 In central Sweden processing is concentrated on lakes.

3 Pulp and paper plants located at river mouths have two advantages: logs can be floated downstream from inland forests; rivers provide hydro-electricity for mills.

4 Paper and board plants are mainly in southern Sweden where labour is more readily available and where they are nearer to European markets. Larger paper mills are integrated with pulp plants; small mills often produce specialist products.

Below: *Rivers are still the most important means of transporting logs. There are over 32,000 km of public floating-ways, employing 40,000 people to handle 150 million logs a year. Most sawmills and pulp mills are located on lakes and rivers.*

Cement for Niugini

Above: *Nursery for conifer seedlings: in Sweden trees are scientifically cultivated like any other crop. There is a reserve of timber as more trees are planted than cut. Three-quarters of Sweden's forests and all the pulp and paper industry are privately owned.*

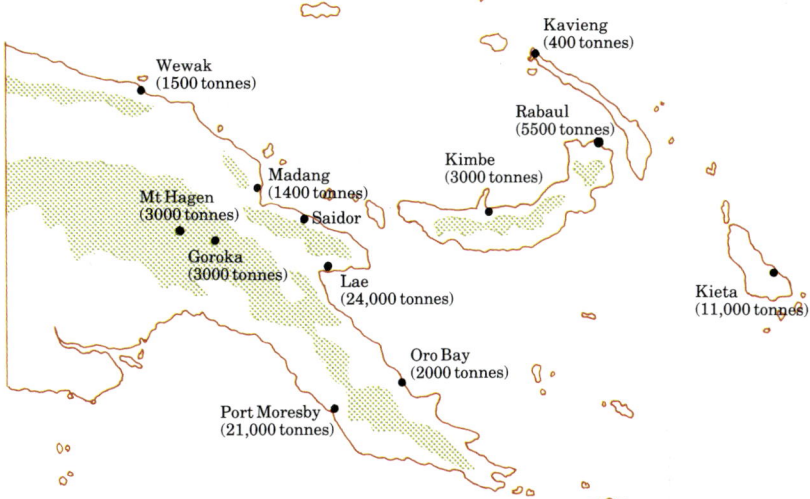

Niugini cement consumption

Above: *Today logging is a year-round activity. But traditionally timber felling was a winter job, when people could not work their farms and when logs could be moved easily over snow to frozen rivers. As the rivers thawed in spring, logs were floated down to mills.*

1 Why is timber a crop? Why is it such an important crop in Scandinavia, especially in Sweden?
2 Why are most sawmills and pulp mills located on rivers, lakes and along the coast?
3 Name the main products processed from timber.
4 Why is it more beneficial for Sweden to process timber into these products than to export trees?

Cement is made by grinding three parts of chalk or limestone with one part of clay or shale, then crushing and roasting the mixture in a kiln. Limestone is the main raw material. It is bulky, plentiful and cheap, but expensive to transport in relation to the final value of the cement. As a result manufacturers tend to locate cement works near chalk or limestone quarries. Cement, too, is bulky and transport costs are high, yet cement is a basic requirement of any economy and most countries aim to supply their own needs.

■ Niugini (Papua New Guinea) has a population of three million; most of the economy is at subsistence level. Internal transport networks are poor, largely because the country is so mountainous. Niugini's entire cement requirement of 60,000 tonnes a year is imported; yet Niugini has widespread limestone deposits. To replace imports, a local cement industry is being planned. There are three alternatives:

■ A 200,000-tonne per year rotary kiln plant at Saidor, built by a foreign-owned company in partnership with the government. Rotary kiln plants are the most modern, most efficient and most expensive. They are used in all developed countries and produce 95 per cent of the world's cement. They run on coal or oil: Niugini has neither. A rotary kiln plant would supply all Niugini's needs and leave a surplus for export.

■ Two vertical kiln plants, one at Lae and the other at Port Moresby. Vertical kilns are simple and cheap to construct and maintain. They can run on charcoal which could be supplied by a sawmill at Lae. Cement distribution from the two plants would be by coastal shipping.

■ Five vertical kiln plants, one in each of Niugini's main centres of population: Port Moresby would have a 35,000-tonne plant; Lae, Kieta, Rabaul and Kimbe would each have a 10,000-tonne plant. Local distribution would be by road and coastal shipping.

Class activity: The Niugini government has six main aims. Use them to decide which of the three alternatives the government should adopt:
a) expansion of the national economy and government revenue;
b) import replacement;
c) government control in certain sectors of the economy;
d) decentralization of economic activity spread evenly throughout the islands;
e) meeting local government expenditure from local sources;
f) encouraging small-scale artisan industry and improving the job prospects of women.
1 With the government's aims in mind, decide which type of kiln should be used, vertical or rotary, and why.
2 Decide where the cement plants should be located. Give your reasons.

LOCATIONS

Close to the market

Some industries have to be located near their markets.

A clear view of the market

Three hundred years ago the glass-making industry depended on the proximity of its main raw material, sand, and fuel for heat. This was because both are heavy and expensive to transport in relation to their value.

Today, the industry's end products – sheet glass and bottles – are fragile and need costly insurance in transit. So the modern glass industry is located near its markets.

■ The glass industry began on sandstone outcrops in the Weald of south-east England where the forests supplied wood for fuel. With the Industrial Revolution glass, like iron, migrated to the coalfields. In 1851 Pilkington's glassworks in St Helens was using eight tonnes of coal to make one tonne of glass. As concentrations of population and industry were also in the coalfields (with the exception of London), glass-makers were near their markets.

■ By the beginning of this century the demand for glass was expanding – especially in the food/drink and automotive industries. In the 1920s glassworks were opened in London, close to Crosse and Blackwell's plant, and in Birmingham, close to the HP Sauce factory. Another factory, also in Birmingham, supplied windscreens to West Midlands vehicle manufacturers.

■ Today glass is a highly automated and specialized industry, but the cost of transport is still a factor in location. For example, laboratory apparatus is made at Enfield in London; two thirds of scientific research takes place in the South-East.

Above: *Away from the main glass centres, there are some small factories employing traditional skills to produce decorative glassware – partly for the tourist market. Here, a craftsman at Caithness Glass in Wick, Scotland, is taking a gather of glass from the furnace.*

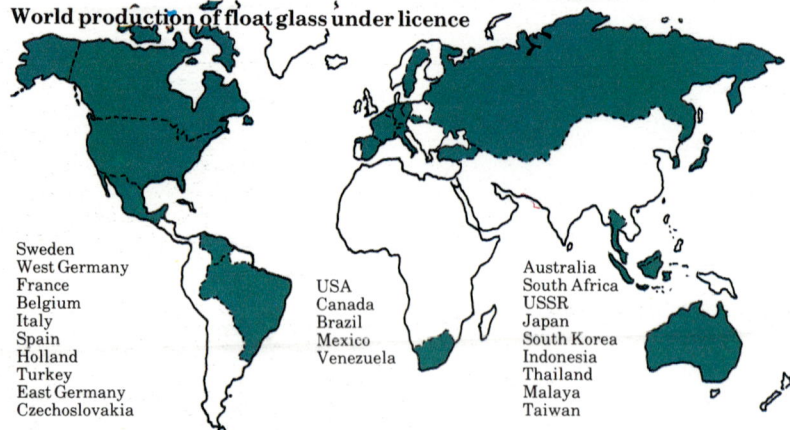

World production of float glass under licence

Sweden
West Germany
France
Belgium
Italy
Spain
Holland
Turkey
East Germany
Czechoslovakia

USA
Canada
Brazil
Mexico
Venezuela

Australia
South Africa
USSR
Japan
South Korea
Indonesia
Thailand
Malaya
Taiwan

Left: *Today, the market for flat glass is worldwide. The major manufacturers, Pilkington, patented float glass (a special flat glass process) in 1957 and concentrated UK production in St Helens. But they have licensed its manufacture in 24 other countries.*

Keeping the market sweet

Sugar is a cheap and bulky product that must be produced close to its market at every stage. Cane has to be grown near crushing mills; raw sugar, refined near consumer markets. Also, many products using refined sugar must also be processed near their markets.

The Australian sugar industry, concentrated along the north-east coast, supplies all domestic sugar needs and exports a large surplus.

Right: *A mill in North Queensland surrounded by cane fields. Sugarcane farmers must have a nearby market – a mill – for their crop since it deteriorates unless processed within 16 hours of cutting. Most of Australia's sugarcane is grown on small, privately-owned farms; the average farm covers 55 ha.*

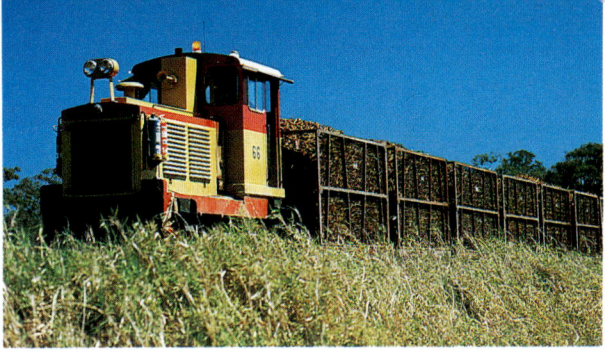

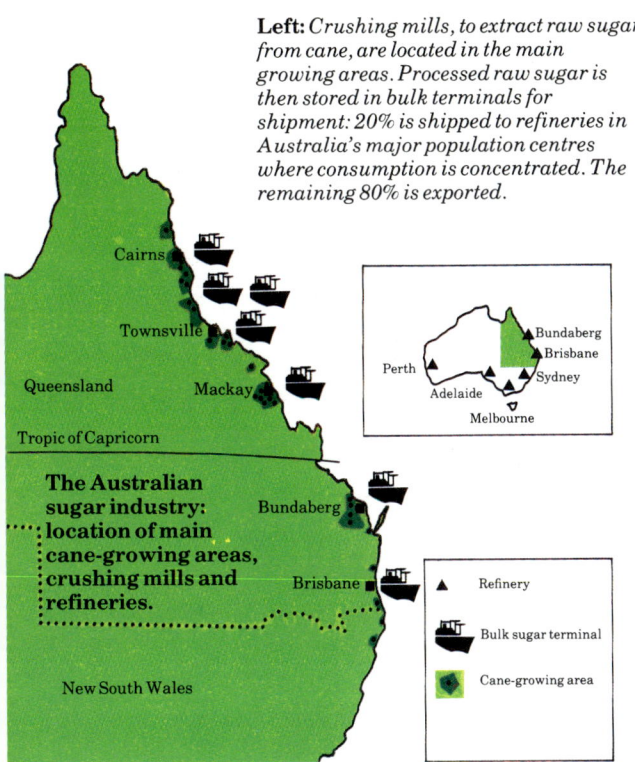

Left: *Crushing mills, to extract raw sugar from cane, are located in the main growing areas. Processed raw sugar is then stored in bulk terminals for shipment: 20% is shipped to refineries in Australia's major population centres where consumption is concentrated. The remaining 80% is exported.*

The Australian sugar industry: location of main cane-growing areas, crushing mills and refineries.

Above: *Cane is extremely bulky, but it must be transported to the mill quickly. Almost all – 99% – travels from field to mill on a 4000-km network of narrow-guage railways.*

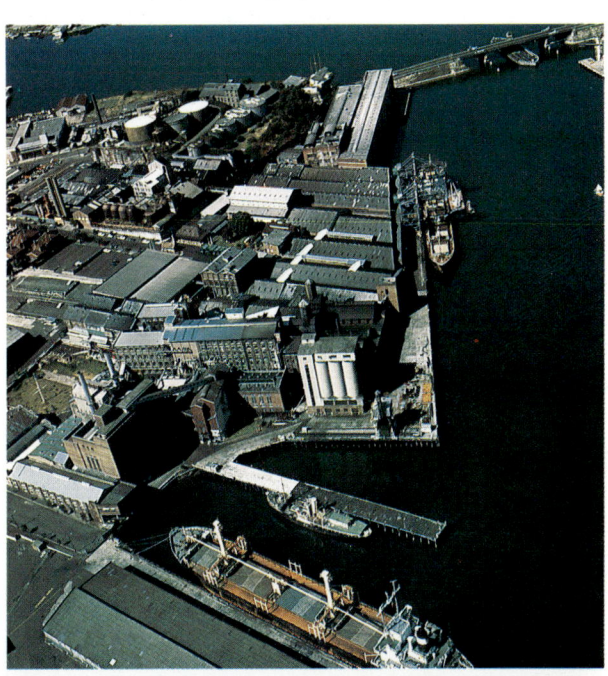

Right: *Sydney refinery, located on the quayside for easy access to raw sugar shipped in from Queensland, serves its local market. Three-quarters of refined sugar goes to food and drink manufacturers. As many of their products, like jam and beer, are bulky, glass-packaged and low-value, they, too, must be produced close to markets.*

Below: *Raw sugar storage in a bulk terminal. Australia exports 2.7 million tonnes of raw sugar each year. It is refined close to consumer markets in importing countries: Japan, Canada, Korea, Malaysia, China, USA, USSR, Singapore and New Zealand.*

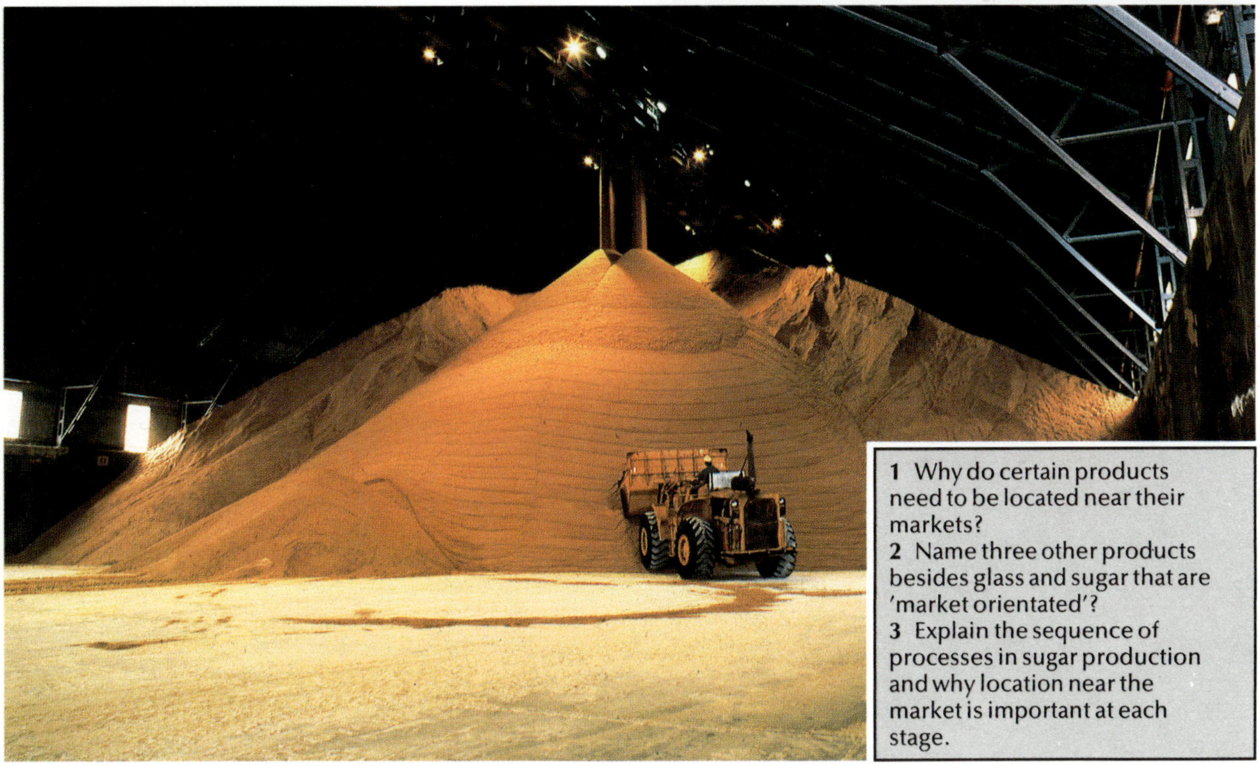

1 Why do certain products need to be located near their markets?
2 Name three other products besides glass and sugar that are 'market orientated'?
3 Explain the sequence of processes in sugar production and why location near the market is important at each stage.

The advance of technology

LOCATIONS

The people and skills required by an industry influence its choice of location.

Cherries to chips

In the 1930s Santa Clara County, California, was known as the Valley of the Heart's Delight. It grew cherries, apples and bumper crops of plums, which made it the prune capital of the world. Today, known as Silicon Valley, it is the world's hi-tech capital. This change has occurred because:
- Stanford University, in Palo Alto at the head of the valley, has been a centre of innovation since the turn of the century. Radio research at Stanford in the 1930s produced the valley's first modern electronics company: a professor persuaded two of his best students, William Hewlett and David Packard, to start their own firm rather than follow the brain drain to the eastern states. Hewlett-Packard now has annual sales of almost £3 bn. In the 1950s Stanford set up the first university science park, where research-based companies could develop. Today the park contains 55 firms, employing 17,500 people.
- The success of the pioneer companies encouraged entrepreneurs to set up their own businesses. Many new firms have started as spin-offs from existing companies. More than 100 companies have been founded by people who began with Fairchild, which in 1957 was one of the first microchip companies in Silicon Valley.
- Hewlett-Packard and Apple Computers both began in garages. Today most new high technology firms are launched with an investment of £1 m or more. The money is provided by venture capital companies, which are prepared to take a high risk in the hope of a quick gain on their investment.
- The electronics industry is based in Silicon Valley because of the concentration of special skills available in the area. Of the 200,000 people who work in Silicon Valley, over 12,000 are PhDs. Of America's 600 venture capital companies, 100 are in nearby San Francisco. There are over 3000 high technology companies in Silicon Valley.

Below: *Silicon Valley's pleasant environment was one of the factors encouraging growth. Ironically, much of that has now gone, as three to four new companies set up factories in the valley every week. California's Mediterranean-style climate remains an attraction.*

Right: *High technology companies tend to have open and comfortable offices. This goes with a relaxed style of management, in which everyone is encouraged to take part. It is the opposite of the strict hierarchies that operate in many older, large companies.*

Electronic migration

As high technology companies grow, research and development has to remain where scientists, engineers and entrepreneurs can meet constantly to exchange and develop ideas. Silicon Valley is not the only such place in the United States. Also, the actual production of high technology products does not have to be in expensive locations, like Palo Alto. Thus, once established, high technology companies can become mobile, 'footloose' industries.
■ In order to keep in touch with as many new ideas as possible, Silicon Valley companies began to set up offices in other research centres. Cambridge, Massachusetts, and Minneapolis, Minnesota, have rival universities and electronics industries. Europe, Japan and other countries now have smaller but useful research centres which attract high technology companies.
■ While retaining contact with centres of research, many of the talented people who make up the industry's main resource, prefer to live in environmentally attractive places. For this reason high technology companies often establish branches in non-industrialized regions. In the US the southern 'sun belt' states with their hot climate provide a popular location.
■ As the manufacturing costs in developed countries increased, high technology companies investigated low-wage countries as alternative sites for production plants. Taiwan, for example, offered many advantages: duty-free entry of components; low taxes; few pollution controls; labour at 15 per cent of US cost, with no trade unions. As well as these advantages, many newly-industrializing countries have a large workforce which can easily be trained for microchip assembly and other precision tasks.

The growth of Intel

The microprocessor manufacturer, Intel, was founded in 1968 by two executives from Fairchild Semiconductor. In less than five years it became obvious that the new company would have to expand beyond Santa Clara. The map shows how Intel grew.

Right: *Each of the chips on this bubble memory wafer stores four million bits of information, or the equivalent of 250 typed pages. Intel started manufacturing bubble memories in 1977.*

Intel's expansion

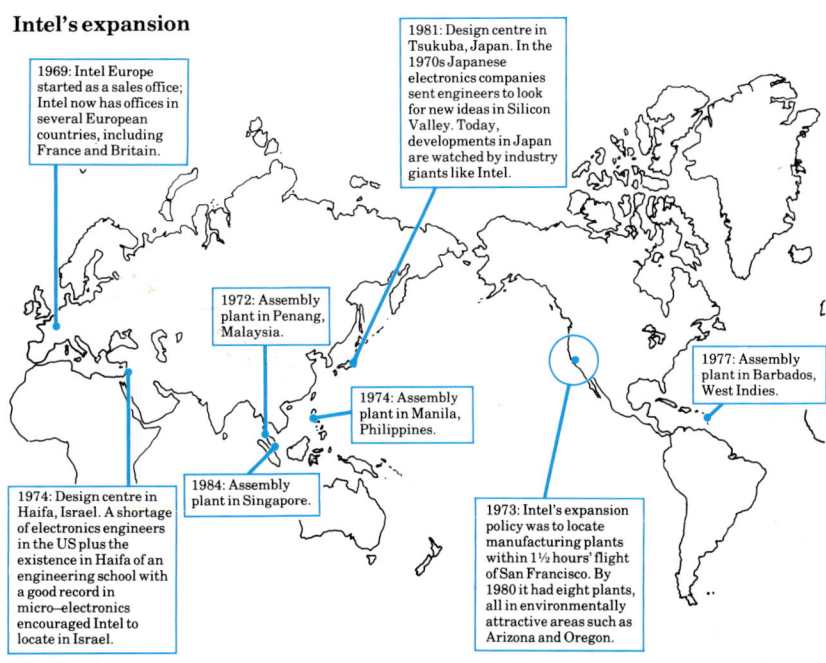

1969: Intel Europe started as a sales office; Intel now has offices in several European countries, including France and Britain.

1981: Design centre in Tsukuba, Japan. In the 1970s Japanese electronics companies sent engineers to look for new ideas in Silicon Valley. Today, developments in Japan are watched by industry giants like Intel.

1972: Assembly plant in Penang, Malaysia.

1974: Design centre in Haifa, Israel. A shortage of electronics engineers in the US plus the existence in Haifa of an engineering school with a good record in micro–electronics encouraged Intel to locate in Israel.

1974: Assembly plant in Manila, Philippines.

1984: Assembly plant in Singapore.

1977: Assembly plant in Barbados, West Indies.

1973: Intel's expansion policy was to locate manufacturing plants within 1½ hours' flight of San Francisco. By 1980 it had eight plants, all in environmentally attractive areas such as Arizona and Oregon.

Above: *A microcontroller shown on an inch ruler. Microcontrollers are used to regulate electrical appliances, from clocks to car instruments.*

Above: *Microprocessor assembly requires very clean conditions, with less than 100 particles of dust per cubic metre (cleaner than an operating theatre). This is Intel's assembly plant in Malaysia.*

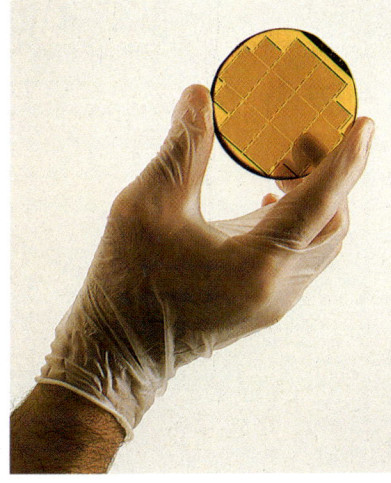

1 How has Santa Clara County, California, become the high technology capital of the world?
2 Why are highly-qualified personnel drawn to areas like Santa Clara and Minneapolis?
3 What are the attractions of LDCs for high technology companies? Why are these advantages disappearing?
4 Describe and explain how high technology industries differ from traditional 'heavy' industries. Consider: appearance; location; surrounding environment; working conditions; skills required.

Earthquake belts

> Certain physical processes are more likely to take place in certain locations than in others.

Shakin' Earth

Earth tremors can happen almost anywhere in the world, including Britain. In April 1984 Wales experienced its worst tremor this century and 5000 homes had their electricity cut off. But most of the world's severe earth tremors occur in well-defined earthquake belts.

- The belt around the rim of the Pacific Ocean accounts for 68 per cent of all earthquakes.
- The Mediterranean belt experiences 21 per cent of all earthquakes.
- The remaining 11 per cent mainly occur in belts of minor activity, such as the mid-Atlantic ridge and the East African Rift Valley.

The Earth has a certain amount of natural elasticity, which allows it to absorb small tremors. When movements are stronger, the Earth's crust fractures at its weakest points. This is why the main earthquake belts follow plate margins and the worst quakes occur in regions of recent mountain-building activity.

How earthquakes work

Earthquakes cause shock waves which travel through the Earth and along its crust. It is sometimes possible to see the ground ripple in waves up to 30 cm high. The upward movement is like a series of blows from a giant hammer.

Such rapid shaking, even through just one centimetre, is enough to wreck all buildings except those specially designed to withstand quakes. This is because earthquakes release several types of **seismic** (earthquake) waves, all travelling at different speeds and in several different directions at once.

Earthquakes originate at a point called the **hypocentre**, which may be deep underground. From there primary, and then secondary, body waves travel through the Earth.

The point on the Earth's surface above the hypocentre is called the **epicentre**, or focus. Surface waves, which spread out from the epicentre, are the most destructive.

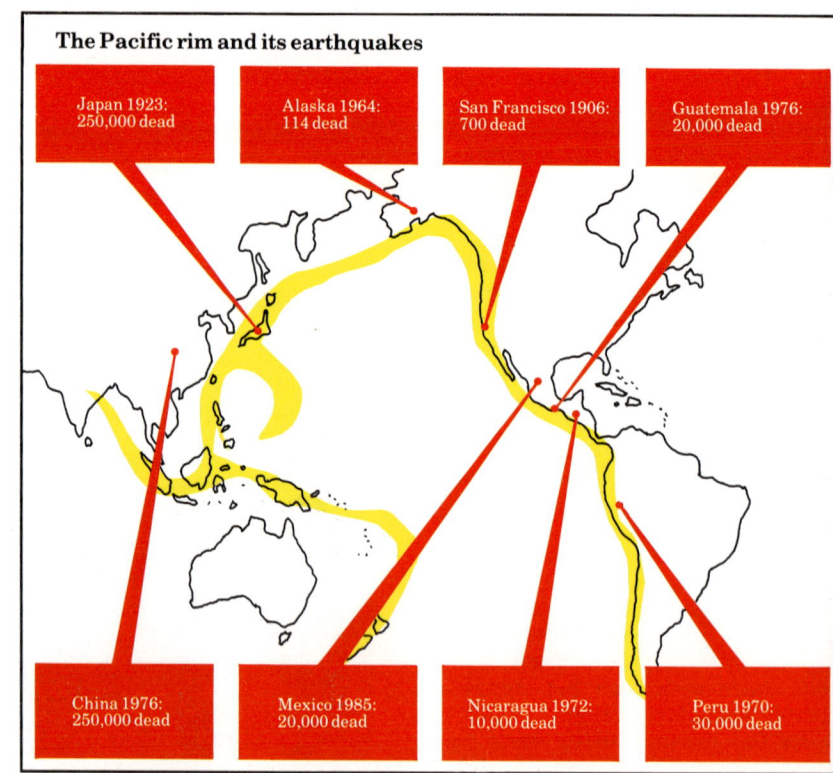

The Pacific rim and its earthquakes

Japan 1923: 250,000 dead
Alaska 1964: 114 dead
San Francisco 1906: 700 dead
Guatemala 1976: 20,000 dead
China 1976: 250,000 dead
Mexico 1985: 20,000 dead
Nicaragua 1972: 10,000 dead
Peru 1970: 30,000 dead

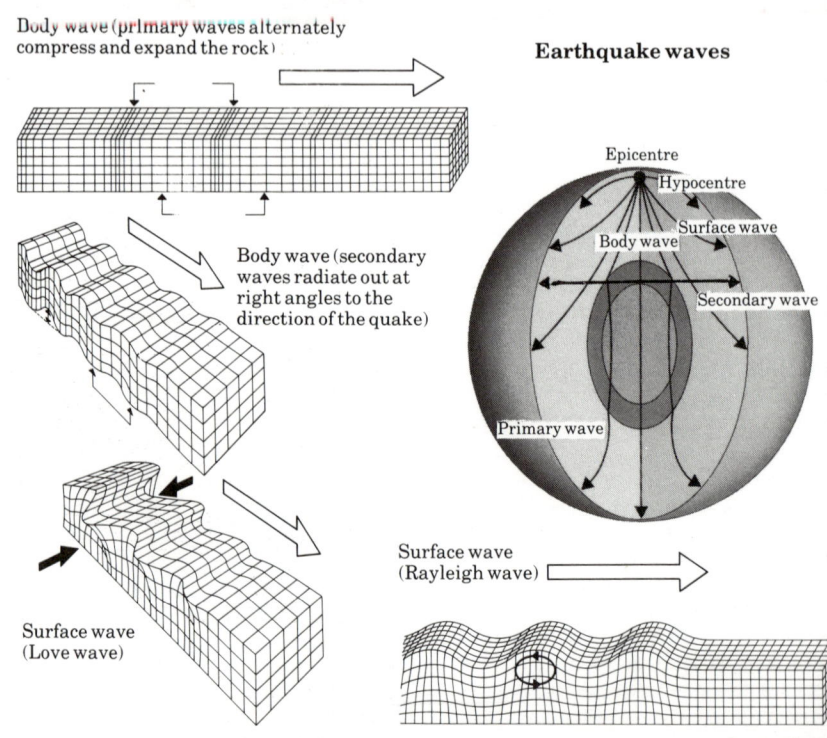

Earthquake waves

Body wave (primary waves alternately compress and expand the rock)

Body wave (secondary waves radiate out at right angles to the direction of the quake)

Surface wave (Love wave)

Surface wave (Rayleigh wave)

Measuring earthquakes

Using sensitive instruments called seismographs, scientists can record the amplitude of waves and the distance between them. This allows them to work out the exact position of the epicentre. There are two main measures of earthquakes:

■ The Richter Scale measures the amount of energy released in seismic waves. A Richter 2 quake is hardly noticeable while the strongest ever recorded (northern Japan, 1958) measured Richter 8.9.

■ The Modified Mercalli Scale measures the amount of damage caused by an earthquake, regardless of its Richter measurement. This enables comparisons to be made between historical and modern earthquakes.

Modified Mercalli Scale	
I Detected by seismographs	**II** Felt in tall buildings
III Felt inside houses	**IV** Doors and windows shake
V Glass and china break	**VI** Leaves and chimneys fall
VII People run outside	**VIII** Most houses fall
IX Roads break up	**X** Buildings all destroyed
XI Bridges fall; ground cracks	**XII** Total destruction; ground waves

Right: *In 1980 an earthquake of 6.8 on the Richter Scale and X on Mercalli Scale hit southern Italy. Almost 3000 people died and 500,000 were made homeless. Villages were devastated; roads, water and electricity supplies were cut. Here a sniffer dog helps locate buried victims. Italy is astride the Mediterranean earthquake belt.*

Below: *A major earthquake brings many problems other than collapsed buildings. Essential services – water, gas, electricity and sewage disposal – are disrupted; people, made homeless by the disaster, lack shelter, food and clothing; roads are blocked, communications cut; contaminated water and decaying bodies spread disease. In 1985, Mexico City was ravaged by a Richter 7.8 quake. This Mexican soldier stands beside a notice warning people to guard against disease by throwing away their gloves after touching a corpse.*

Saving lives

Using the methods of measurement and knowledge of earthquake behaviour, scientists are learning how to predict earthquakes. Only weeks before the 1985 Mexican earthquake, a scientific paper was published that might have saved thousands of lives. Its authors identified an area of seabed off the Mexican coast which had not experienced any minor quakes for a long period. In surrounding areas there had been many small tremors. This could – and did – indicate that a major earthquake was likely there.

There was a more successful prediction in China in 1975, when the city of Haicheng was evacuated 10 hours before a Richter 7.3 earthquake. Observations of ground water levels, and animal behaviour plus a series of small earthquakes – the foreshock – gave warning of the main disaster.

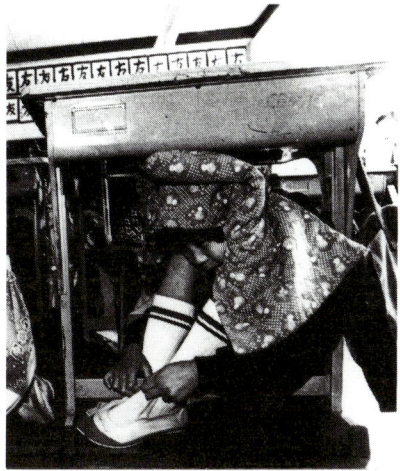

Above: *Japan, on the Pacific rim, prepares itself for future earthquakes with regular drills involving the emergency services and all the people living in a particular region. Here, school children, wearing protective head coverings, dive to safety under their desks.*

1 Why do earthquakes occur?
2 Which parts of the world are most vulnerable to earthquakes?
3 Why are earthquakes more likely in these areas than elsewhere?
4 Explain why scientists use both the Richter and Mercalli scales to measure earthquakes.
5 Why do earthquakes cause widespread death and destruction?
6 Imagine that you are responsible for co-ordinating rescue operations after an earthquake. Describe the sequence of your actions and give reasons for them. Also list long-term priorities; where might you get help for these?
7 Assume you were in Mexico City in 1985 during the quake. Write a report of your experiences.

 # Urban growth and decay

Settlements experience both growth and decay as parts of their life cycle.

Urbanization

For at least the last 4000 years, people have responded to increased prosperity – acquired through trade – by moving from scattered farm communities into cities.
■ Many of Europe's present-day cities were founded as Greek and Roman market centres. But the greatest period of **urbanization** in history began with the Industrial Revolution.
■ During the eighteenth century landowners enclosed common land into large estates. Country people drifted to the cities, where they found work in the new factories. In 1800 less than ten per cent of British people lived in cities. Today over 80 per cent live in urban areas.
■ At the heart of every city is the Central Business District (CBD). This contains the greatest concentration of shops and offices. It is the focus of the transport network and the point of maximum accessibility from the surrounding hinterland.
■ Cities may appear to have grown haphazardly, but by studying the urbanization process it is possible to detect certain models and cycles of growth.

The concentric model

Cities have always grown outwards from the centre. New building takes place on the outskirts where land is cheaper. Better-off people can buy more land and larger houses in suburban areas. The less well-off tend to be trapped in older, smaller houses on more valuable land near the centre. The result is a series of circles, each representing a different use of land. The concentric model explains how settlements have grown historically.

Sector model

Until the beginning of this century the size of settlements was limited by the time/distance between working and residential areas: people generally lived where they worked. But improved transport, such as buses and trains, altered the shape of settlements: people could now live further away from their places of work. Thus urban areas expanded unevenly, growing most along main transport routes. The sector model explains how urban areas have grown for economic reasons.

Multiple nucleii

As urban areas continued to expand they absorbed smaller existing settlements. The patchwork result fitted neither the concentric nor the sector model. Instead there were a number of different-sized centres, including the original CBD, joined together by a transport system. This multiple nucleii model explains the growth of modern conurbations.

Right: *Los Angeles was founded in 1781 as a Spanish missionary post. Today it has expanded to include Long Beach, Hollywood and many other centres, making it a city of multiple nucleii.*

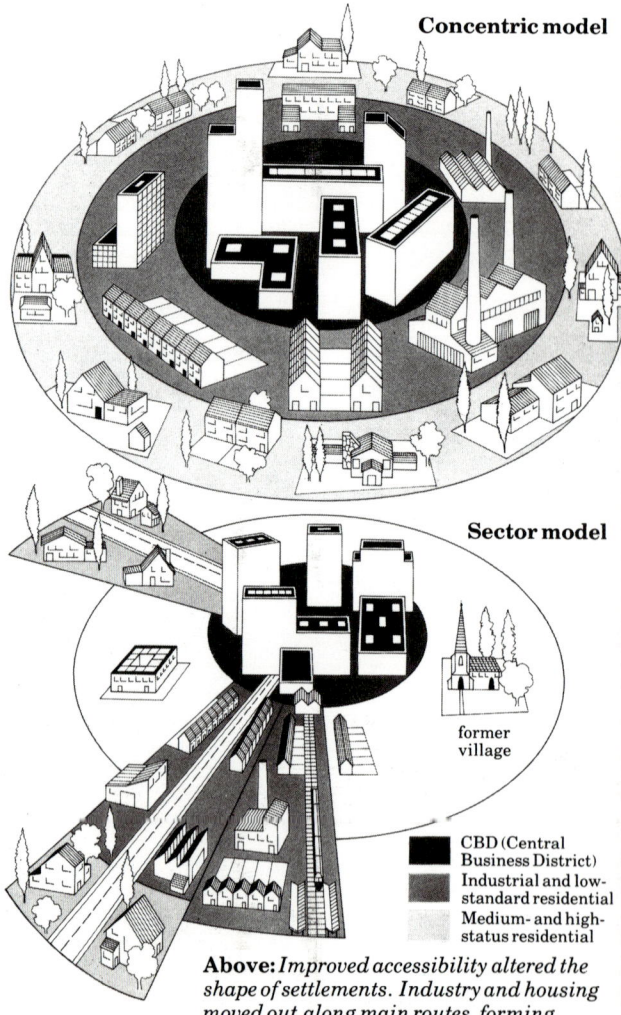

Below: *At the heart of the concentric model is the CBD, the commercial focus of the urban area. Beyond this lies a transitional zone of mixed industrial and poor residential areas.*

Above: *Improved accessibility altered the shape of settlements. Industry and housing moved out along main routes, forming sectors and ribbon developments.*

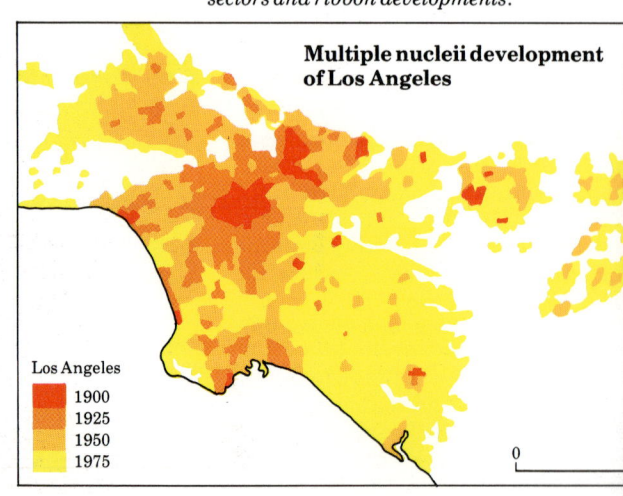

Rise and fall of the 'Pool

Although Liverpool's origins go back to a Royal Charter dated 1207, the great port-city was essentially a product of 18th- and 19th-century industrialization.
■ Liverpool grew outwards concentrically from the pierhead and docks on the Mersey estuary. Its merchants and shippers prospered on the slave trade with America, then on importing cotton for the Lancashire textile industry and exporting the finished goods worldwide.
■ Liverpool's growth and decline mirrored the growth and decline of the British Empire. While Lancashire remained one of the world's top manufacturing areas, the port prospered. But as other industrial countries began to overtake Britain and the colonies became independent, markets were lost to British manufacturers. Once, Liverpool's location facing the Atlantic was ideal for trade with America and the Empire. Today, over 40 per cent of Britain's trade is with the EEC: ports like Dover and Felixstowe now handle more trade than Liverpool.

Effects of inner-city decay

Housing
■ Run-down terraces, over 100 years old, without facilities like indoor lavatories and bathrooms.
■ Houses divided into crowded flats and bedsits.
■ Badly-designed estates where vandalism and crime are normal.

Employment
■ Liverpool has 21% unemployment.
■ Blacks and Asians find it especially hard to get jobs.
■ Very little new investment, although the 1984 Garden Festival provided 4000 jobs. Most new jobs created by development grants have gone to city outskirts.

People
■ Large concentrations of unskilled and unemployed.
■ Many old people who live alone.
■ Many poor, socially disadvantaged people, such as one-parent families, who cannot afford to move out.
■ Large black and Asian populations, often first or second generation British.
■ Low achievement level of children in school.
■ Poor health standards.

Environment
■ Derelict industrial sites and docks.
■ Disused railways.
■ Boarded-up shops and warehouses.
■ Vacant land.

Below: Blacks and Asians in Liverpool face particularly high unemployment. In 1981 only 129 out of 22,000 Liverpool City Council workers were black; (this number has since increased).

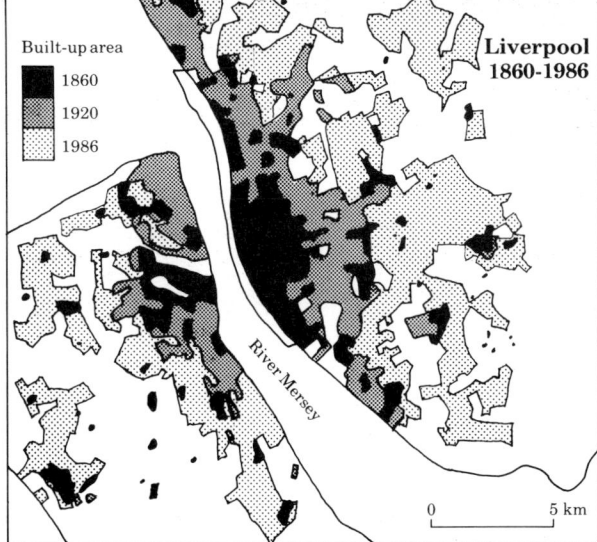

Above: *1860 – Liverpool at the peak of its expansion. As a result of the potato famine, 300,000 Irish came to the city in 1847 alone. Housing conditions were terrible with over 30,000 people crammed into one-room cellars.*
1920 – Liverpool at its largest with a population of 750,000. In the early 1900s, the Council had begun to tackle the housing crisis by building high-density tenement blocks within the city. In the 1930s unemployment reached 25% and there were riots.
1986 – By 1981 Liverpool's population had fallen to 300,000. Over 50,000 jobs have been lost in 20 years as the docks declined and industry moved out. Only three of 12 docks remain, employing 3000 instead of 25,000. Industrial decline has impoverished the City Council which effectively went bankrupt in 1985 owing to its determination to maintain a high level of social services.

Above: *Liverpool's problems came to a head with riots in Toxteth in 1981. Other inner-city areas have since erupted: for example, Brixton and Tottenham in London; St Paul's, Bristol; Handsworth, Birmingham.*

1 This table compares Liverpool neighbourhoods using certain indicators of deprivation. Suggest reasons for differences between neighbourhoods in each of the ten categories.

Indicators of deprivation	High status	Multi-occupation (flats, etc)	Inner-city council estates	Outer-city council estates	Older terraced houses
Long-term unemployment	32	136	250	102	89
Youth unemployment	33	110	199	145	63
Free school meals	29	81	201	147	74
Higher education grants	225	123	32	67	54
Disinfestation orders	58	82	265	84	104
Car ownership	189	105	20	81	77
Shared dwellings	76	508	57	35	75
Ill-equipped dwellings	70	119	74	77	153
Overcrowding	16	170	363	101	55
Single-parent families with 2+ children	27	118	230	117	89

Megalopolis, USA

CYCLES

In developed countries the forces which created large concentrations of population are now leading to population dispersal.

Drawn in, forced out

Large urban settlements in developed countries tend to have multiple nucleii. Since they consist of many urban areas joined together, different parts experience different forces of growth and decay at the same time.

■ The same **centrifugal** forces that encourage some groups to migrate from rural areas to the city (inward migration) simultaneously propel other groups to migrate from the city to rural areas (outward migration).

■ The same **centripetal** forces that attract some people from rural to urban areas (inward), simultaneously attract others away from cities to rural areas (outward).

■ These centrifugal and centripetal forces are similar to the push and pull factors which encourage large-scale migration from one country to another and rural depopulation and urban growth in LDCs.

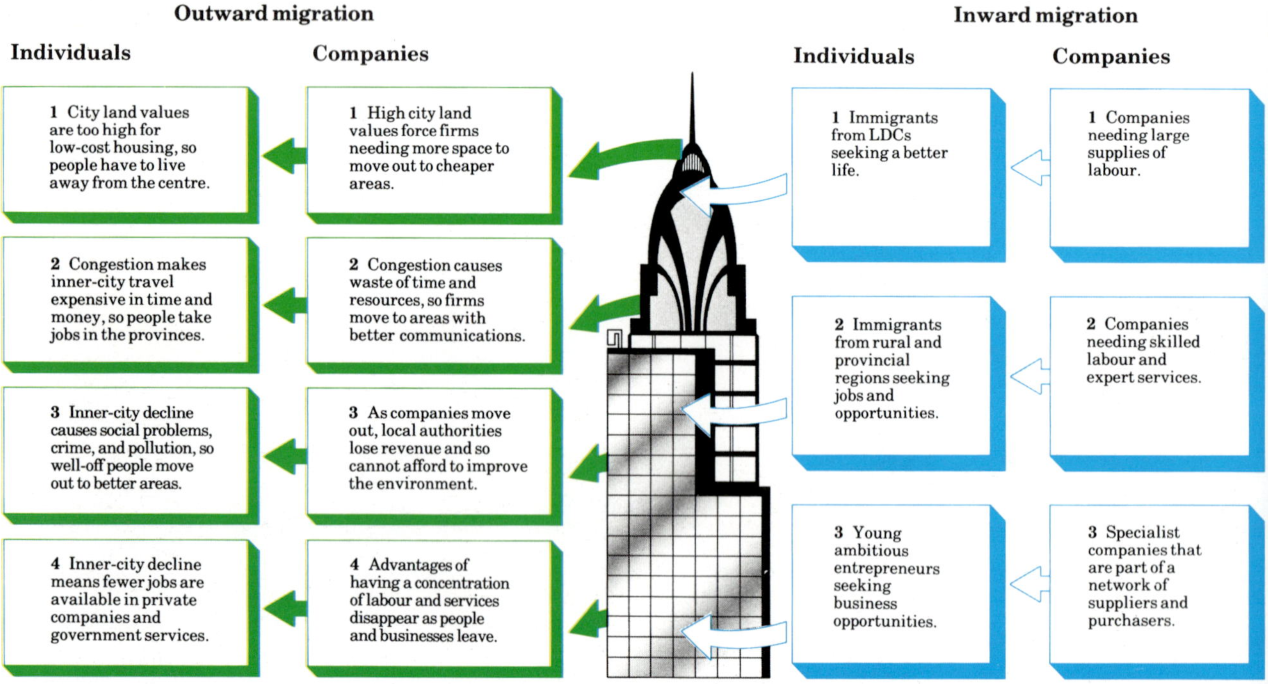

Outward migration
Individuals
Companies
1 City land values are too high for low-cost housing, so people have to live away from the centre.
1 High city land values force firms needing more space to move out to cheaper areas.
2 Congestion makes inner-city travel expensive in time and money, so people take jobs in the provinces.
2 Congestion causes waste of time and resources, so firms move to areas with better communications.
3 Inner-city decline causes social problems, crime, and pollution, so well-off people move out to better areas.
3 As companies move out, local authorities lose revenue and so cannot afford to improve the environment.
4 Inner-city decline means fewer jobs are available in private companies and government services.
4 Advantages of having a concentration of labour and services disappear as people and businesses leave.
Inward migration
Individuals
Companies
1 Immigrants from LDCs seeking a better life.
1 Companies needing large supplies of labour.
2 Immigrants from rural and provincial regions seeking jobs and opportunities.
2 Companies needing skilled labour and expert services.
3 Young ambitious entrepreneurs seeking business opportunities.
3 Specialist companies that are part of a network of suppliers and purchasers.

Bosnywash, San-San and Chipitts

Not a laundrette, a Chinese restaurant and a chip-shop, but the three largest concentrations of population in the world: Boston-New York-Washington, San Francisco-San Diego and Chicago-Pittsburgh.

■ Definitions of an urban area vary from settlements of 250 people in Denmark to Standard Metropolitan Areas (SMAs) of 100,000 each in the USA.

■ In the last 200 years, urban areas all over the world have experienced rapid increases in population. In 1800, four per cent of Americans lived in cities; today it is 80 per cent.

■ As cities have grown, so they have spread out. Some have spread and grown so much that they are classified as **conurbations**. The very largest are **megalopolises**. Originally an ancient Greek word for a super city, the megalopolis idea was revived by French geographer Jean Gottman in 1961. He applied it to the 800 km string of urban areas connecting Washington, D.C., New York and Boston.

US megalopolises
Boston
Philadelphia
New York
San Francisco
Milwaukee
Chicago
Detroit
Pittsburg
Washington
Los Angeles
San Diego
San-San
Chipitts
Bosnywash
0
1000 km

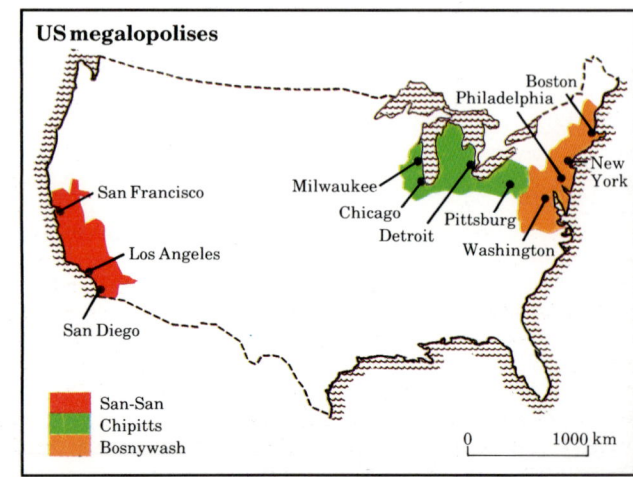

Above: *New York City, financial and art capital of the world. The north-east coast has always been the primate region of the USA: trading with Europe, receiving immigrants and despatching settlers westwards.*

Below: *Chicago, on the shores of Lake Michigan, boasts one of the world's tallest buildings: the Sears tower (centre back), 475 m with mast. Chicago, Detroit, Cleveland/Pittsburgh and Buffalo make up the Chipitts megalopolis. Railways plus water transport on the Great Lakes helped this region to build up its coal and steel industries in the late nineteenth century. It is still a heavy industry area (car production in Detroit).*

Above: *Washington, D.C., capital of the USA since 1790 and, in many ways, political capital of the world today. The Bosnywash megalopolis has 45% of US population, produces 25% of its goods and services and yet covers only 2% of its land area.*

Above right: *A San Francisco tram; on the horizon, Alcatraz island, once notorious for its prison. San Francisco, itself a giant conurbation, is part of the San-San megalopolis. Gold, oil and climate attracted people to the west coast. The entertainment industry (Hollywood), high technology (Silicon Valley and aerospace) and Pacific trade (with Japan) have made this the most prosperous part of the USA.*

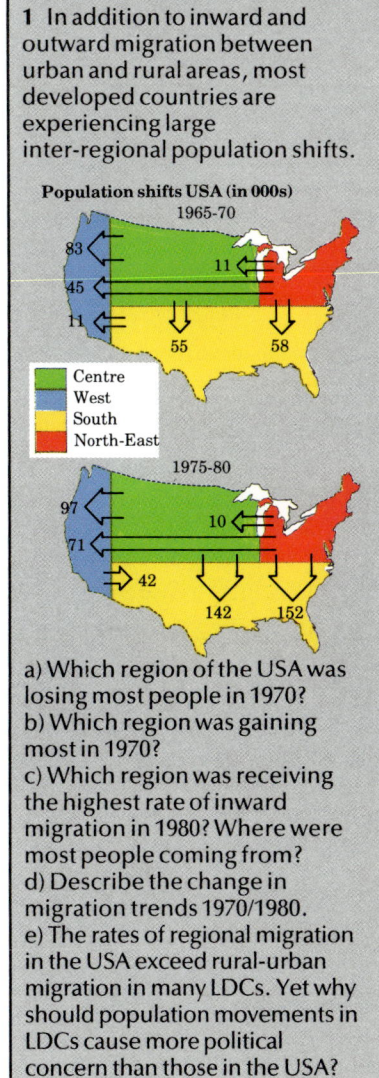

1 In addition to inward and outward migration between urban and rural areas, most developed countries are experiencing large inter-regional population shifts.

Population shifts USA (in 000s)

Centre — green
West — blue
South — yellow
North-East — red

a) Which region of the USA was losing most people in 1970?
b) Which region was gaining most in 1970?
c) Which region was receiving the highest rate of inward migration in 1980? Where were most people coming from?
d) Describe the change in migration trends 1970/1980.
e) The rates of regional migration in the USA exceed rural-urban migration in many LDCs. Yet why should population movements in LDCs cause more political concern than those in the USA?

Moving to the suburbs

As in most developed countries, the core areas of cities like New York and Boston have experienced considerable decay in the last 50 years. Yet the megalopolises continue to grow. A significant redistribution of population is taking place. This process is called **suburbanization**.

■ Bosnywash is not continuously built-up: 19 per cent is urban; 6 per cent is devoted to industry or transport; 75 per cent is woodland or farmland.
■ In suburban and rural counties better-off people can escape the pollution and congestion of inner cities. These people either commute long distances to CBDs (2 million commute daily to Manhattan, the centre of New York) or they work in decentralized offices.
■ New housing in US cities has been concentrated in the suburbs to meet the needs created by population redistribution. In some NY suburbs, for example, the population has risen by 50 per cent in the last ten years while the inner-city population has declined by 13 per cent.
■ The rate of inner-city depopulation is offset by inward migration. People moving into inner cities tend to be under-privileged ethnic minorities.

1 How does a conurbation differ from a megalopolis?
2 Describe how a conurbation develops and how it might become a megalopolis.
3 Why are most megalopolises in the developed world?
4 Explain the redistribution of population taking place in many large conurbations.
5 Use your atlas to identify other large conurbations that might qualify as megalopolises.

19

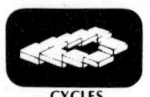 # New and renewed cities

> A cycle of decay can be reversed.

Planned cities

During the Industrial Revolution most cities grew with little or no planning. Then in 1799, Robert Owen built New Lanark, in Scotland, as a model manufacturing town: a century later W.H. Lever built the town of Port Sunlight, in Cheshire, for his soap factory workers. Similar settlements were built by Krupp in the Ruhr, Pullman in Chicago and by other idealists, appalled at the terrible housing conditions of the urban poor.

- The pioneer of New Towns as we know them today was Ebenezer Howard who began Letchworth Garden City in 1903. The success of Letchworth and later Welwyn Garden City led to the New Towns Act of 1946. This concentrated urban development outside existing cities, many of which had suffered war damage.
- The New Towns relieved population pressure in inner cities, rehousing over 2 m people. They pio-

neered pedestrian-only shopping areas and integrated neighbourhoods, with easily accessible shops, community centres and places of work.

- But New Towns have accelerated the decline of existing inner city areas, as people and jobs relocated.

Left: *Early (1907) housing development in Letchworth, the first New Town. The Garden City, a self-contained settlement, was designed with open spaces, gardens and a surrounding green belt.*

Have city, need work

Scotland has five New Towns: Cumbernauld, East Kilbride, Glenrothes, Irvine and Livingston. When East Kilbride was founded in 1947, it had a population of 2400. Overspill from crowded Glasgow raised the population to 70,200 by 1985. But providing jobs for New Town residents has not been easy, with traditional industries in steep decline.

- Government grants, a pool of skilled labour and the need to have a base in Europe, attracted US and Japanese electronics companies to Scottish New Towns in the late 1960s. Small, local companies soon sprang up to supply these transnational giants. Scottish employees of US companies left to set up their own firms. The result is 'Silicon Glen', centred on the Glasgow – Edinburgh axis. The area produces 79 per cent of the UK's electronic circuits and 21 per cent of European output. Over 40,000 Scots now work in electronics – more than in steel, coal and shipbuilding combined.

Above: *The sports institute at Glenrothes. Open spaces and recreation facilities are a major feature of New Town design. All the Scottish New Towns are in Silicon Glen.*

Above: *Livingston is part of Silicon Glen. The Glen's growth was stimulated by the Scottish Development Agency, local finance and expertise from Glasgow and Edinburgh universities.*

20

Left behind in the centre

Between 1780 and 1850 Glasgow grew from 40,000 to 330,000: while smart suburbs were built for the rich, more and more poor people crowded into tenements in the centre. Seventy-nine per cent of families lived in one or two rooms and 23 per cent of them took in lodgers.

- In 1902 the first municipal house building programme began, yet by 1946 little improvement had been made: 700,000 people were still concentrated in an area of 7.7 km^2; 43 per cent of families still lived in one or two rooms, compared to 2.5 per cent on Merseyside.
- The reconstruction of Glasgow began in the 1950s. Many people moved to New Towns. Between 1955–72, 268,000 houses were demolished. By 1970, 17 per cent of accommodation was in council flats and houses.
- As in many inner cities, tower blocks were built in the 1960s, to solve the problems of high population density and lack of space. Today 65,000 Glaswegians live in tower blocks, which include Red Road, at 31 storeys, Britain's highest.

GEARing up

In the 1970s central government policy switched from investment in New Towns to rebuilding inner city areas. The SDA was given the task of improving the East End of Glasgow and founded GEAR (Glasgow Eastern Area Renewal Scheme). It has three priorities:
- the industrial renewal of an area which had lost its largest employers in steel and engineering;
- housing;
- the environment: in 1974, mainly empty factories and disused railways.

The SDA has spent over £25 m a year on GEAR. 15,000 new homes and a new shopping centre have been built. But, so far, few new jobs have been created and unless skilled and trained people are available, industry will not return quickly.

Above: Three-quarters of the SDA's investment in GEAR goes into leisure, sport and environmental projects.

Above: The inner city slums of Glasgow were the worst in the UK. Densities of over 2500 people per ha led to frequent epidemics of typhoid and cholera.

Above: There are over 200 council-owned tower blocks in Glasgow. Recently, architects and planners throughout the UK have realized that tower blocks fail to solve inner city housing problems; many have become modern slums.

Developing Docklands

In 1981 the last of London's upstream docks closed, leaving an area of 22 km^2 available for redevelopment: Europe's largest urban renewal scheme.

- The body responsible for this area is the London Docklands Development Corporation. In its first four years, 1981–85, it invested £200 m in the Docklands, mostly on infrastructure (roads, bus routes and an urban light railway). This has attracted £820 m of private investment in housing, offices and industry.
- In that period over 200 companies moved into the area, helped by the tax concessions available to an Enterprise Zone. Almost 6000 new jobs were created and 5000 new houses were built. Land values tripled.
- Docklands – with satellite receiving station and airport – is now a centre for companies, especially banks and financial services, moving out from the City of London.
- It is proposed that 46 per cent of land will be used for industry; 32 per cent for housing and 22 per cent for environmental and leisure use.

Above: Poster opposing Docklands development. Local people fear that the creation of a totally new environment will destroy existing communities.

Above: Aerial view of the West India Docks with the City of London in the background and an elevated section of the new Docklands Light Railway.

1 Why did early industrial idealists build 'model' settlements?
2 Why have New Towns been built since 1946? Where are they located?
3 What features distinguish them from existing towns?
4 Why are New Towns partly blamed for inner city problems?
5 Why is the Edinburgh–Glasgow axis known as Silicon Glen?
6 Outline Glasgow's problems, how they developed and potential solutions.
7 Imagine you are: a) chairman of a City-based finance company; b) an unemployed docker from Docklands. Justify or oppose the Docklands development.

Agriculture in the EEC

Farming methods go through phases determined by national and supranational policies.

The Common Agricultural Policy

The European Community embraces a wide range of climate, relief and soil conditions. Each of these environments supports a different type of agriculture. Yet the EEC was founded on the principles of:
- a common market for produce;
- a single agricultural policy applicable to all member states;
- a common system of price controls and supports.

When the Community was created in 1957, agriculture employed 20 per cent of the population in France, West Germany and Italy, the three largest of the six founder states. A fifth of these farmers had very small (under 15 ha) inefficient holdings: 85 per cent in Italy, 55 per cent in Germany and 35 per cent in France. A Common Agricultural Policy (CAP), initiated in 1962, aimed to:
- stabilize the market, eliminating fluctuations from year to year and place to place;
- increase productivity to make the Community self-sufficient in food;
- ensure reasonable prices for consumers and a fair standard of living for farmers.

Above: *Strawberries in Somerset. Plastic tunnels, now widely used in horticulture, protect crops and also accelerate growth to benefit from high early-season prices.*

Types of agriculture

Dairy farming (milk and milk products): In warm, wet, western regions. With dairy farmers producing 15% more milk than required, milk price support costs 27% of all EEC spending. Quotas have been set to cut each country's milk production by 10%; farmers must reduce herd sizes and, in some cases, change to other forms of agriculture.

Stock raising (beef): In hilly, wet or remote areas unsuitable for many other farm enterprises. The meat market is subject to strong cyclical tendencies: when prices are high, farmers fatten more stock thereby reducing supply and raising prices even more: when prices are low, producers slaughter animals thus increasing supplies and reducing prices.

Hill farming (sheep): Over 20% of EEC farmland; mainly in peripheral regions, where poor soil, harsh climate and altitude restrict agriculture. CAP and EEC Social Fund combine as problems in these areas are wide-based. Hill farming helps to prevent population drift from the land and to conserve the countryside.

Cereals: In warm, dry lowlands. The CAP, by promoting larger field sizes, a reduced workforce, mechanization and the use of fertilizers, has increased yields so successfully that over-production is now a continuing problem.

Mediterranean (citrus, olives, fruit, vegetables): Hot dry southern regions. Often marginal lands which are too poor to provide a livelihood. CAP and the Social Fund encourage consolidation of holdings as well as investment in irrigation, processing and marketing to increase the value of farm output.

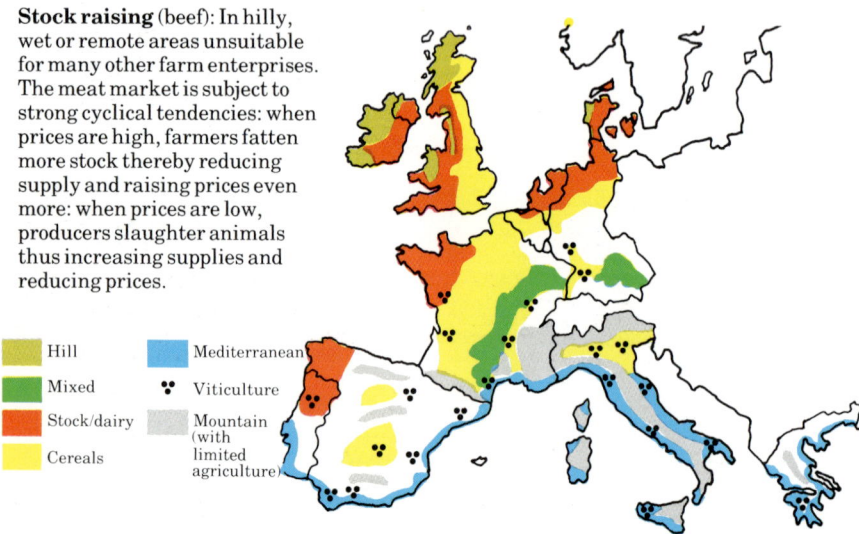

Legend:
- Hill
- Mixed
- Stock/dairy
- Cereals
- Mediterranean
- Viticulture
- Mountain (with limited agriculture)

Above: *Sunflowers in Spain. Since the 1970s sunflowers have become a major crop in Europe and now rank as the world's second source of vegetable oil after soyabean. The oil is used in cooking and to make margarine, paints and plastics; the plant is also good for silage.*

Viticulture (wine): In areas with warm dry sunny summers; now also southern England. In addition to import tariffs and financial controls, the CAP supervises plantings to regulate the area under vines and to maintain disease-free stock. Over-production has increased with Greece, Spain and Portugal in the EEC.

Mixed farming: Persists in peripheral regions. Generally less important now that CAP encourages specialization. Also, guaranteed prices for individual products has removed need to have a variety of crops/animals as an insurance against failure through climatic or market influences.

How the CAP works

The Common Agricultural Policy is a source of great political strain within the Community. Yet, in spite of three EEC enlargements (bringing in farms as widely different as citrus groves in Spain and subsistence crofts in Scotland) the CAP continues to function - within its limitations. Its strategies include:

- **Subsidies and tariffs:** EEC food prices are high by world standards, as farmers are paid high prices. Tariffs are imposed on imports to make them the same price as EEC-produced food. Surplus EEC output is exported at world prices, with the EEC paying producers the difference as a subsidy.
- **Supply management:** An 'intervention price' is set for each commodity annually. If the price falls below that level, the EEC guarantees to buy in the surplus at the intervention price. This policy is responsible for the EEC's intervention stocks (the so-called mountains and lakes). Where production far exceeds supply, as in milk products, the EEC sets quotas.
- **Structural adjustments:** Grants enable farmers to consolidate holdings and improve land.
- **Direct income support:** Subsidies to farmers in marginal areas.

Above: *Italian growers, faced with over-production, throw away their tomato crop; since fruit and vegtables are perishable, surpluses cannot be stored. Other EEC gluts, apart from cereals and milk products, include wine and olive oil.*

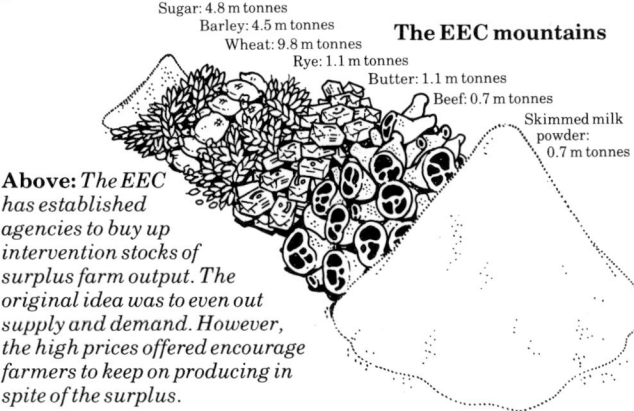

The EEC mountains
Sugar: 4.8 m tonnes
Barley: 4.5 m tonnes
Wheat: 9.8 m tonnes
Rye: 1.1 m tonnes
Butter: 1.1 m tonnes
Beef: 0.7 m tonnes
Skimmed milk powder: 0.7 m tonnes

Above: *The EEC has established agencies to buy up intervention stocks of surplus farm output. The original idea was to even out supply and demand. However, the high prices offered encourage farmers to keep on producing in spite of the surplus.*

Costs of the CAP
– Over 75% of all EEC expenditure, yet agriculture accounts for only 2% of GDP in Britain and up to 8% in less developed member states like Greece and Portugal.
– Surpluses deny LDCs the opportunity to export to the EEC. Subsidized exports are unfair competition for other exporters, many of them LDCs.
– Surpluses and subsidized exports cannnot be justified morally when so much of the world is hungry.
– There are still wide variations in farm income within the EEC. Large-scale producers have benefited more than small-scale farmers.
– The CAP has failed to reduce population drift from rural areas to cities.

Benefits of the CAP
– The EEC is almost self-sufficient, producing over 90% of the food required by its 350 m people.
– Prices are high in world terms but this has improved the living standards of small farmers.
– Agriculture has been modernized. Production is rising by 2-3% p.a. Farm size has increased: Italian farms average 7.42 ha each; French, 25.41 ha; British average 68.7 ha.
– New crops, such as oilseed rape, have been introduced.
– Specialization has been encouraged, replacing old-fashioned mixed farming with intensive farming.

Consumer revolt

It is not only government policy that affects farming trends. Consumer demand for foods that are produced naturally – free from chemical fertilizer and pesticides – is encouraging some farmers to abandon highly-intensive methods. Many supermarkets are now stocking organic produce which is not only grown without artificial treatments but also processed without chemical additives.

Left: *Organically grown rice from Italy, bread from England and wine from France. Organic farming is more expensive because yields are lower, but if consumers are prepared to pay higher prices chemical-free agriculture could help reduce the over-production problem.*

---

1 Describe the aims of the Common Agricultural Policy.
2 What are the main farming types in Europe and where do they predominate?
3 If you were a MEP (Member of the European Parliament), how would you justify to your constituents the amount of money spent on agriculture when so few people are employed in farming?
4 In addition to government strategy and the CAP, what other factors influence farm output?
5 Write a paragraph giving your views on the Community's system of food production.

Building mountains

> The world's major relief features are the result of various cycles of tectonic movement.

Colliding plates

The main cause of mountain building is the enormous pressure exerted by tectonic movement at the boundaries of converging plates. Plate tectonics result in two different types of mountain building processes: subduction and collision.

- **Subduction:** oceanic plate material is heavier than continental plate material. Thus where an oceanic plate collides with a continental plate it is subducted, or forced down into the hot lithosphere beneath the lighter, continental mass. The downward movement of the seabed forms an ocean trench. It triggers off earthquakes and generates enormous heat, which moves upwards as volcanic magma. The continental plate is built up by volcanic eruptions. It is also thrust upwards, folded and faulted as it overrides the lower plate.
- **Collision:** where two continents, such as India and Asia, collide huge mountains are uplifted. The Indian subcontinent is too light to be subducted like an oceanic plate. The result is the massive folding and uplifting of the Himalayas, with frequent earthquakes, but without any volcanic activity.

Left: *The Himalayas are rising by about 1.3 m every 100 years, which is faster than erosion wears them down.*

Rock formation

Above: *High mountains are weathered and eroded. Water transports material to the sea.*

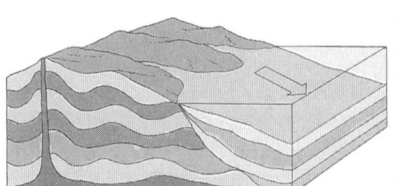

Above: *The products of weathering and erosion are deposited on the seabed in many layers, or strata, of sediment.*

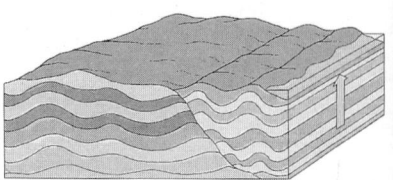

Above: *Tectonic movement uplifts and folds strata. Heat and pressure change sedimentary rock into metamorphic rock.*

The record in the rocks

Geologists can trace the history of tectonic movement.

- Australian scientists discovered the world's oldest rock material. By calculating the rate of radioactive decay of minerals present in certain rocks, they proved that minute grains of some sandstones were formed 4200 million years ago. The oldest existing rocks, dating back 3800 million years, were discovered in Greenland by a New Zealand geologist.
- As the plates moved, different types of rock formed in different places. Today they may be thousands of kilometres from their place of origin: formed under the sea, they may now be on mountain tops, or in the middle of deserts.
- **Igneous** rocks, like basalt and granite, make up about 75 per cent of the Earth's crust. They result either from surface lava flows, or from magma intrusions.
- **Sedimentary** rocks, accounting for just five per cent of the crust, are the most common surface rocks. Some are coarse mixtures called conglomerates; others are fine sandstones; while limestone and chalk are made from deposits of sea creatures' skeletons and shells.
- **Metamorphic** rocks are sedimentary rocks that have been transformed by the intense heat and pressure of tectonic movement. Limestone, for example, becomes marble. Some rocks are heated to melting point, which enables minerals to flow into veins from which they can be mined.
- During certain phases of the Earth's history, plate movement (and thus mountain building) has been more vigorous than at others. The most recent, called the Alpine movement, occurred in three phases in the late Jurassic, Cretaceous and Tertiary Periods, when the Himalayas, Alps and Pyrenees were all folded and uplifted.

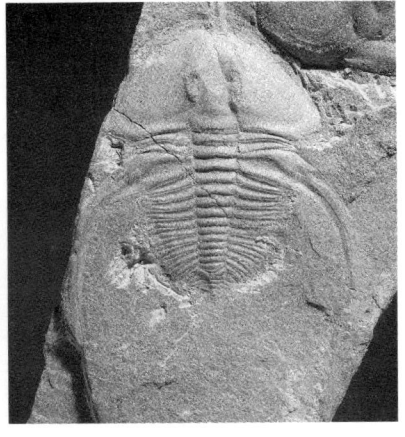

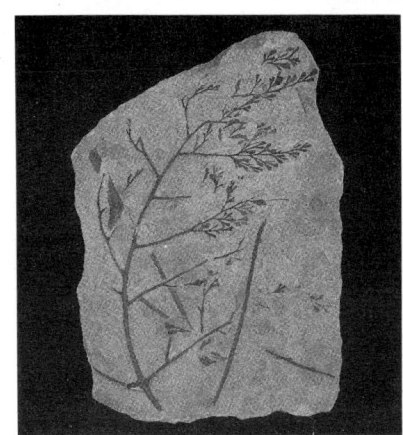

Left: *Trilobites lived under the sea in the Cambrian Period, 570 million years ago. Fossils like these were found in the Appalachians in America. Before the super continent Pangaea broke up 200 million years ago, the Appalachians were part of a single mountain chain that included Scotland and Scandinavia.*

Right: *These fossilized plants grew in the swampy, tropical forests that covered Carboniferous Britain. During this period of vigorous plate movement, mid-ocean ridges formed causing the sea level to rise; inland areas flooded. Rotting vegetation became Britain's coalfields.*

Folds and faults

The results of mountain building and plate movements can be seen in folded and faulted strata of the Earth's crust.

- **Folds** occur where pressure has buckled horizontal strata into arch-shaped structures.
- **Faults** occur where plate movement fractures rock, allowing movement vertically or laterally along the fracture line. Faults can shift rapidly and violently as happens in earthquakes, but more often they occur slowly and gradually.

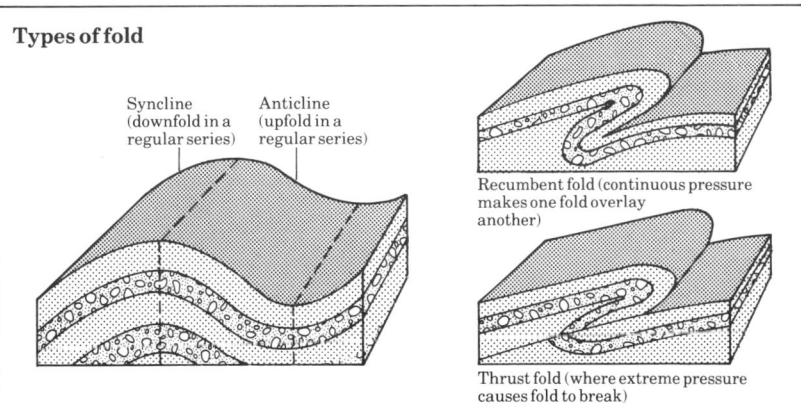

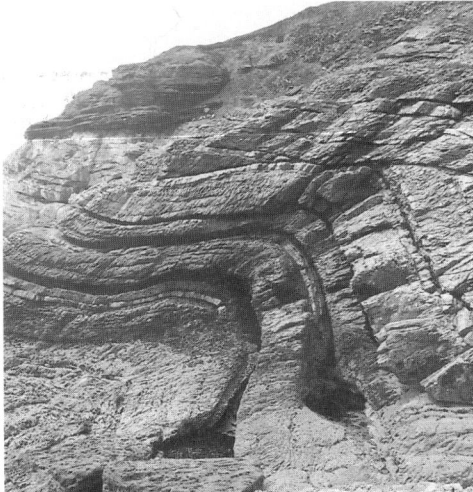

Above: *Limestone laid down in horizontal beds has been folded asymmetrically (leaning over because of greater pressure exerted from one side than from the other).*

1 What age are the oldest rocks? How do we know?
2 Explain the two main mountain-building processes: subduction and collision.
3 Describe the formation of igneous, sedimentary and metamorphic rocks. Give examples of each.
4 Why has mountain building been more active at some periods in the Earth's history than at others?
5 List the differences between faults and folds.
6 What evidence enables us to reconstruct past periods in the geological record?
7 How do we know that mountain building continues today? Describe a major mountain range that is still being formed.

San Francisco Examiner
Monday, March 31, 1986
25c
Streets ★★★

uake rocks Bay Area

Blackouts, minor damage in 5.3 temblor

t crashes in Mexico
Santa Clara
Women taken to the cleaners

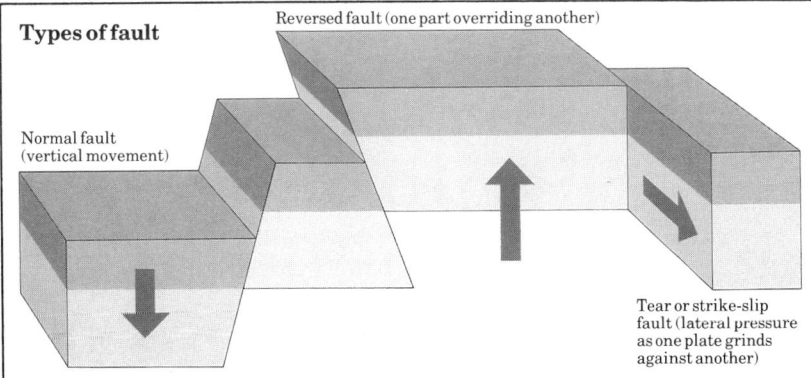

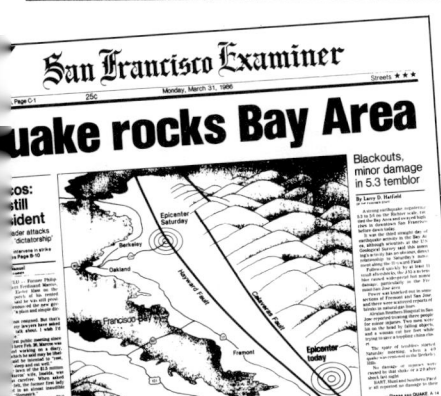

Left: *As the Pacific Plate is subducted beneath the North American Plate, blocks of continental land mass are added to North America. At the same time the edge of the coast is moving north along the San Andreas Fault at about 6 m a century: 50 million years ago parts of Alaska were in California. In the San Francisco earthquake of 1906 (Richter 8.3), the San Andreas Fault moved 5 m at one lurch. Earthquakes on a lesser scale, like the Richter 5.3 reported here, frequently occur in the San Francisco area.*

Restless oceans

Random events can disrupt regular natural cycles.

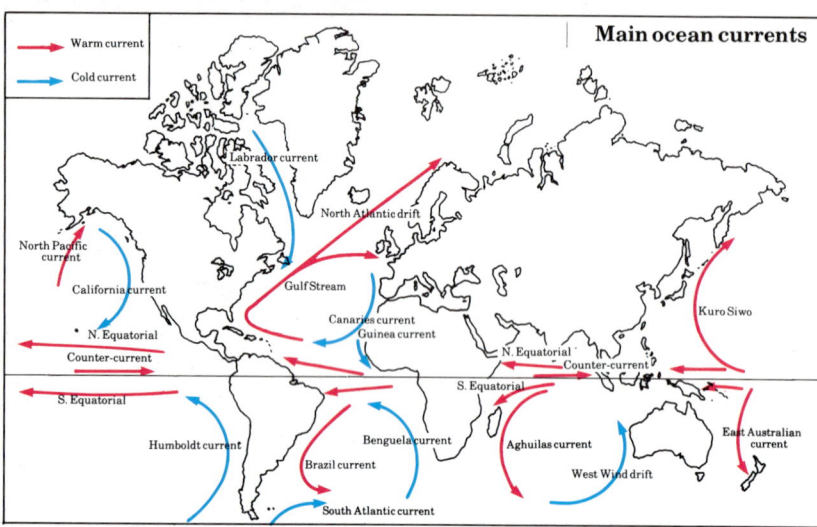

Ocean currents

Seventy-one per cent of the globe is covered by sea. The world's oceans are constantly moving.

- Ocean currents are caused by the rotation of the Earth, by winds and by convection currents in the water.
- In the northern hemisphere most currents flow clockwise; in the southern hemisphere they flow anti-clockwise.
- Cold currents flow north from the Antarctic and south from the Arctic. Onshore winds blowing over cold currents pick up little moisture, resulting in arid coastal areas.
- Warm currents flow north and south from the equator. Onshore winds carry much moisture, resulting in precipitation on coasts such as Britain's, which is warmed by the North Atlantic drift.

The world's richest sea

The complex system of currents off the Pacific coast of Peru has produced a natural food chain which was, until man interfered with it, the most productive in the world.

- The cold Humboldt or Peru current sweeps up from the Antarctic. The coast of Peru is a desert over 2600 km long. Onshore winds are cooled by the Humboldt current and carry little moisture. Also, the S-E trade winds drop their moisture as they rise up over the Andes, leaving the western margin in a rain shadow.
- As the Humboldt waters flow towards the equator, they warm up and flow west across the Pacific.
- Deep, cold, counter-currents flow back towards South America.
- These combine with upwellings from the 6000 m-deep Peruvian Trench to bring rich nutrients from the seabed to feed plankton on the surface.

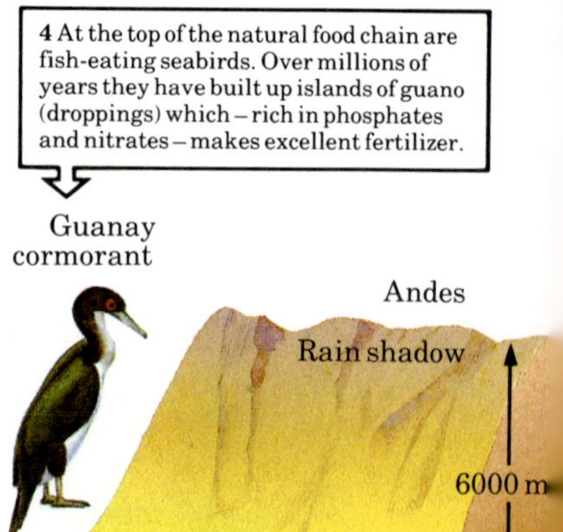

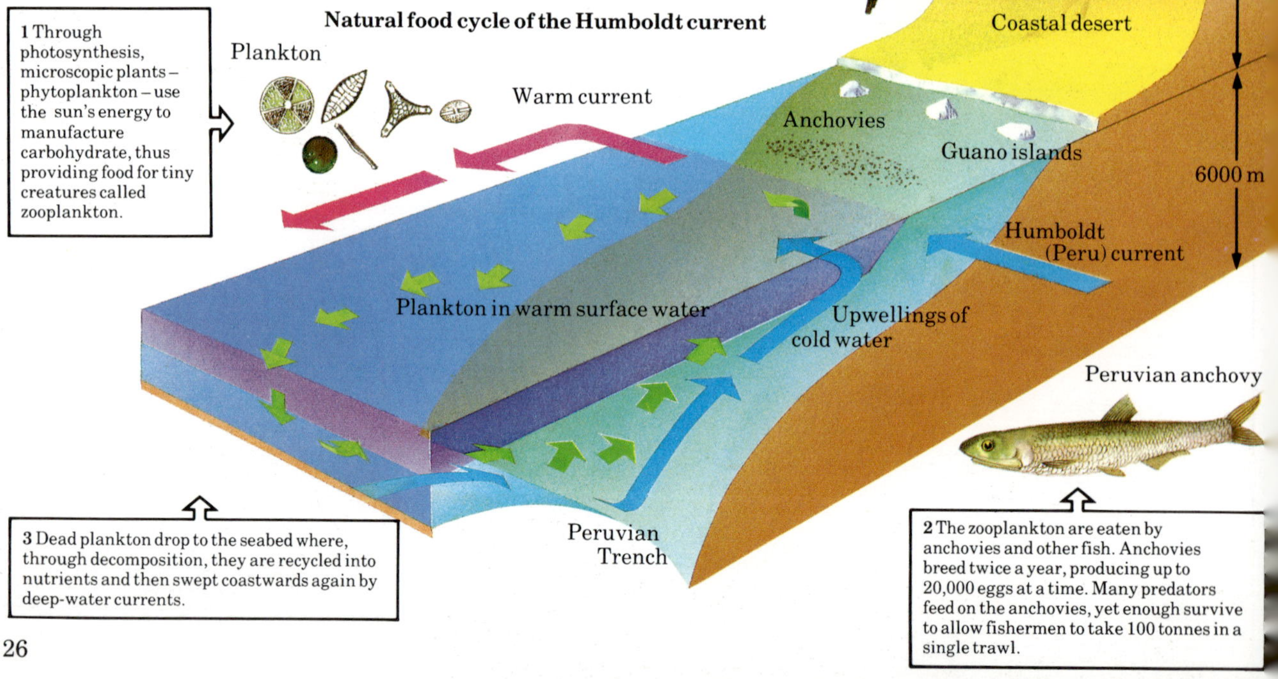

Natural food cycle of the Humboldt current

1 Through photosynthesis, microscopic plants – phytoplankton – use the sun's energy to manufacture carbohydrate, thus providing food for tiny creatures called zooplankton.

2 The zooplankton are eaten by anchovies and other fish. Anchovies breed twice a year, producing up to 20,000 eggs at a time. Many predators feed on the anchovies, yet enough survive to allow fishermen to take 100 tonnes in a single trawl.

3 Dead plankton drop to the seabed where, through decomposition, they are recycled into nutrients and then swept coastwards again by deep-water currents.

4 At the top of the natural food chain are fish-eating seabirds. Over millions of years they have built up islands of guano (droppings) which – rich in phosphates and nitrates – makes excellent fertilizer.

Breaking the cycle

The natural productivity of the Humboldt current cycle has been broken by overfishing the anchovies and by cutting out the seabirds as manufacturers of fertilizer.

■ In the 1960s Peru became the world's leading fishing nation. Fish-meal factories were built to provide cattle feed and fertilizer; new industries canned, dried and froze the fish, earning 33 per cent of Peru's foreign exchange. By 1970, Peru was hauling in 14,000 million tonnes of fish – one fifth of the world's catch.

■ Within a decade the catch was less than a quarter of that amount. Overfishing was one reason for the decline; another was that the cycle had also been broken by a natural phenomenon.

■ In 1982-83 El Niño struck. Named after the Christ child, this is a warm current that – for some unknown reason – flows south, replacing the cold current. It occurs at Christmas time about once in every five to ten years.

■ Normally El Niño's effects are limited, but in 1982-83 it had a catastrophic impact as far afield as Australia, Africa and North America. Off Peru, the warm current, lacking nutrients and plankton, caused the anchovies to migrate.

■ Overfishing and El Niño between them decimated the Peruvian fishing industry: anchovies are now almost an endangered species. Also, the seabird population – deprived of its food – fell from 25 million to under one million, causing a drastic decline in guano fertilizer stocks.

Above: *In February 1983, a duststorm engulfed Melbourne, smothering the city in tonnes of topsoil. For Australia, drought – killing millions of stock – duststorms and bushfires were all part of the El Niño disaster.*

Above: *A flooded car-park in Long Beach, California. El Niño brought unprecedented havoc to the US west coast: freak tides smashed seaside homes, devoured beaches and demolished piers while record rains swamped crops and ravaged landscapes. The damage bill totalled billions of dollars.*

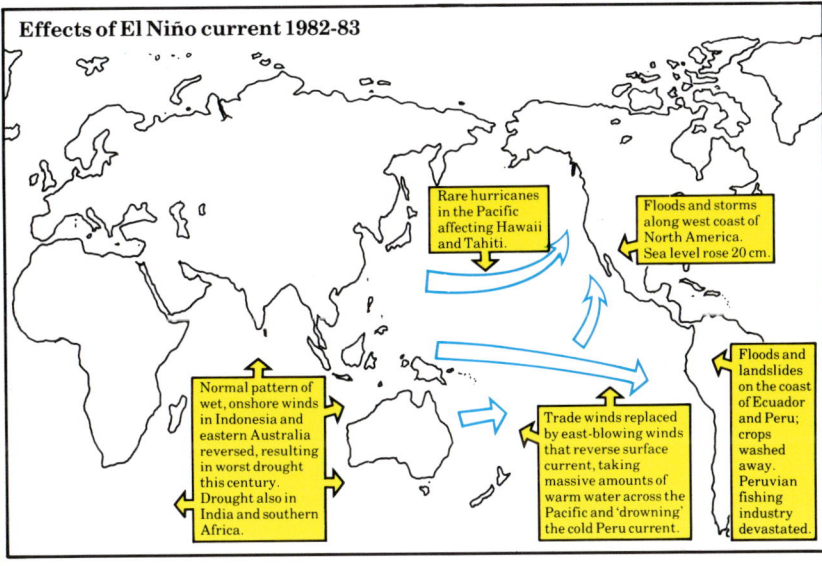
Effects of El Niño current 1982-83

- Rare hurricanes in the Pacific affecting Hawaii and Tahiti.
- Floods and storms along west coast of North America. Sea level rose 20 cm.
- Normal pattern of wet, onshore winds in Indonesia and eastern Australia reversed, resulting in worst drought this century. Drought also in India and southern Africa.
- Trade winds replaced by east-blowing winds that reverse surface current, taking massive amounts of warm water across the Pacific and 'drowning' the cold Peru current.
- Floods and landslides on the coast of Ecuador and Peru; crops washed away. Peruvian fishing industry devastated.

Below: *Redundant fishing boats anchored off Chimbote in northern Peru. In the early 1970s, the Peruvian fishing industry – based on anchovy – employed 40,000 people in 1500 boats and 150 processing plants. Chimbote was the leading port.*

Right: *Some of Peru's fishermen are still working but today their catch primarily consists of sardines, not anchovies, and is mostly for local consumption rather than export. The food processing industry takes an increasing share of the catch for canning and freezing.*

1 What is an ocean current?
2 How is it formed?
3 In which directions do ocean currents flow?
4 Describe the natural food cycle generated by the Humboldt current.
5 Explain how this cycle was broken and the consequences.
6 Why are ocean currents generally predictable?
7 How do currents affect the climate of bordering land masses?

On the outskirts

A commercial site must be easily and rapidly accessible.

Market to city

British towns often carry their history in their names – Newmarket, Stowmarket, Market Drayton. In many cases the market was the original reason for the existence of the town. Improved transport links enlarged the sphere of influence of the most successful markets. Market stalls became permanent shops and, eventually, groups of shops grew into the CBDs of towns and cities.

- By the 1960s, the CBDs of major cities had fallen victim to their own success. They became heavily congested with traffic, largely because the number of privately-owned cars had greatly increased. As a result, the inner city environment deteriorated badly. Heavy traffic caused pollution, damage to old buildings and costly delays.

Moving out of town

High property costs and congested conditions in the CBD caused many businesses to move out to the suburbs, where they are more accessible to the increasing numbers of people living there. In the USA in the 1950s, in continental Europe and Australia in the 1960s, and in the UK from the 1970s, retailers began to build out-of-town shopping centres.

- As car-ownership increased, it became more convenient to drive out of town, rather than into town, to go shopping.
- Retailers can sell goods cheaper, because of cheaper premises, the economies of scale of large operations, and improved productivity. Supermarkets keep down shopping costs, but they lack the personal service of small traders.

Germany's largest

Ruhrpark shopping centre is the largest in Germany. It was built in 1965 by a Canadian company along the lines of North American one-stop shopping centres.

Below: *This car, parked in a restricted area, is being clamped by the police. Although control measures, such as clamping, plus better public transport ease city-centre congestion, they are not sufficient to halt CBD decline.*

Above: *Ruhrpark is centrally located in Germany's most heavily industrialized region. It is at the interchange of the east-west Ruhrschnellweg (Ruhr Expressway) and the north-south Autobahn, between Recklinghausen and Wuppertal.*

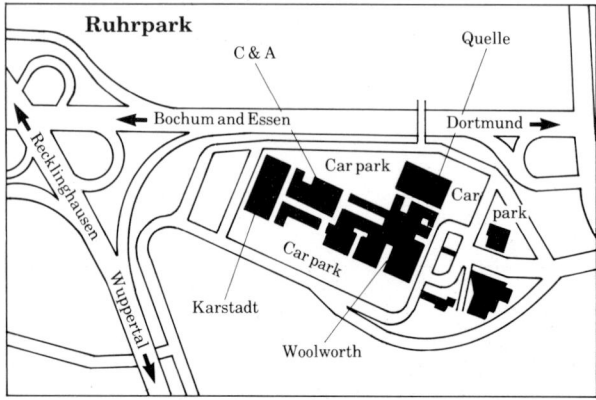

Above: *Ruhrpark has over 85 shops and services, including C & A, Karstadt, Woolworth and Quelle department stores; its 90,000 m² of retail space also features restaurants, garden centres and even an art gallery.*

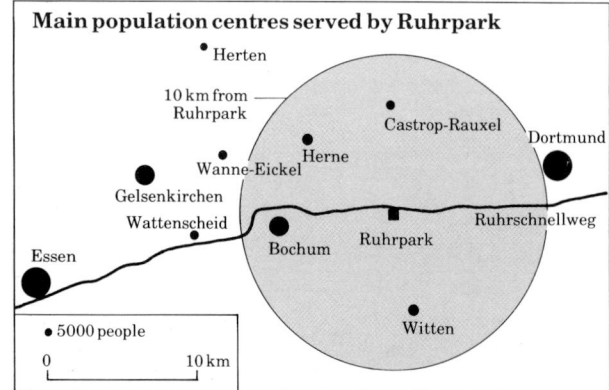

Above: *Three million people live within 20 km of Ruhrpark. For most of them it is quicker to shop at Ruhrpark than in the CBDs of Bochum and Dortmund. But CBD shopping has not died altogether.*

International trade fairs

It is not only shopping centres that have to be easily and rapidly accessible. Today, markets for many products are international. Buyers and sellers meet at trade fairs. These are not a new idea: in the Middle Ages merchants from all Europe met at Champagne Fairs in France.
■ The National Exhibition Centre in Birmingham is Britain's largest trade fair location. It advertises itself as being in the heart of England, with rapid local, national and international links.
■ The NEC holds 45 exhibitions a year, ranging from furniture to computers.
■ But to be a success a trade fair must attract large numbers from the widest sphere of influence possible. For specialized fairs this means a worldwide market.

Europe's largest trade fair centres

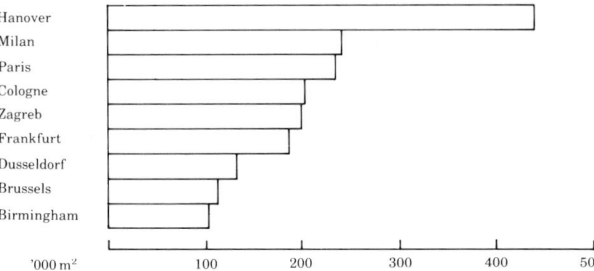

Above: *Many of Europe's top trade fair locations are in West Germany; apart from those listed, Hamburg, Munich and Berlin are also important. Within Europe, West Germany's central position and industrial strength make it an ideal international market-place. Although Hanover has the largest facilities, Frankfurt ranks as Europe's busiest trade fair centre.*

Right: *Exhibitions are big business. Visitors spend an average of £50 each. The Motor Show attracts 750,000 people.*
Below: *The M42 motorway, linked to the M1, M5 and M6, gives easy access to the NEC. There are also rail and air services.*

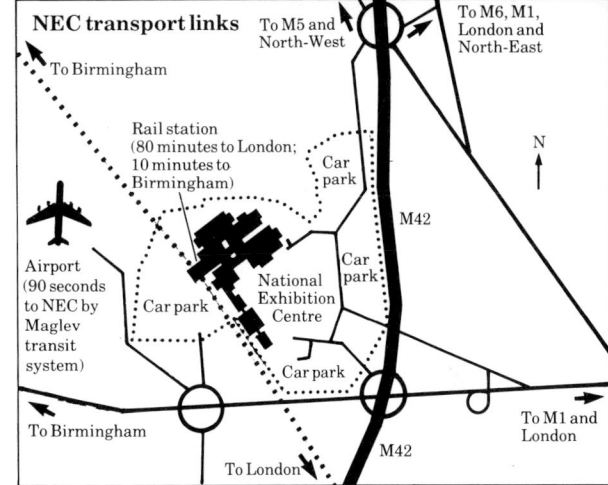

Accessibility and the environment

New commercial sites, built for maximum accessibility on the outskirts of cities, often meet opposition from environmentalists wishing to preserve green space close to urban areas.
■ The London greenbelt was established in the 1950s. It is 20-25 km wide, covers 430,000 ha and, by virtually stopping all development within that area, provides open space for the recreation of Londoners.
■ In the 1980s several threats to the greenbelt have emerged. The M25 London orbital motorway has brought with it many new commercial/industrial developments. Sites along the M25 are easily accessible to the Channel ports, London, the airports and to the rest of Britain through motorway connections. As a result the greenbelt is under great development pressure.

For greenbelt development	Against greenbelt development
– greenbelt increases land prices by restricting the supply of land for sale. – greenbelt increases commuter costs by making journeys to and from London longer. – greenbelt constricts size of properties and open space within London. – many parts of the greenbelt are not open countryside, but derelict land that would be improved by development.	– new houses are not needed as neither the population nor the number of households in the S-E is increasing. – developers' interest is in profit, not in the needs of existing residents. – investment would be better used in the inner city, where people can live without commuting. – greenbelt is a local and national amenity and prevents urban sprawl.

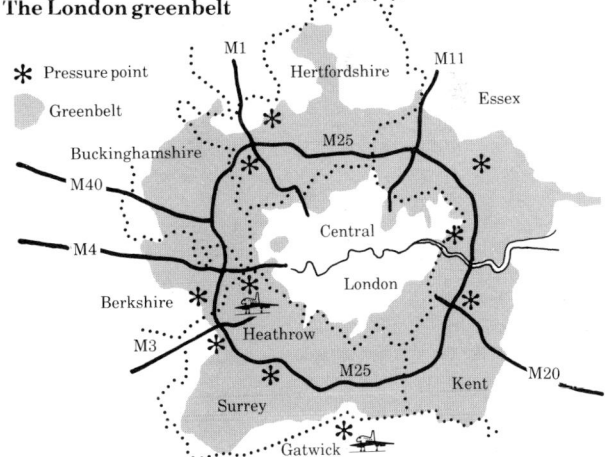

Above: *One of the first advocates for a London greenbelt was Queen Elizabeth I who wished to halt 'the city of great multitudes'. Today, the protected area is threatened by development plans, including a scheme to build 15 new towns around the capital.*

1 What factors influence the siting of a new shopping centre away from the CBD?
2 Why has the NEC been built at its present location just outside Birmingham?
3 A building consortium is planning a large-scale development (housing with associated commercial facilities) in a greenbelt area. Write a letter – either in support or protest – to the local newspaper.

The tourist industry

Leisure activities occupy more time and involve greater distances than ever before.

Holiday boom

Long ago the only days people had off were religious festivals: Holy Days. Today people are taking more and longer holidays every year. And every year more people spend more time further away from home.
■ In 1951 about 500,000 British people spent a holiday abroad. By 1985, 21.6 million Britons went abroad; just over 2.5 million of them holidayed outside western Europe.
■ In 1951 less than 750,000 foreigners visited Britain. In 1985, 14.6 million came, 3.8 million of them from the USA.

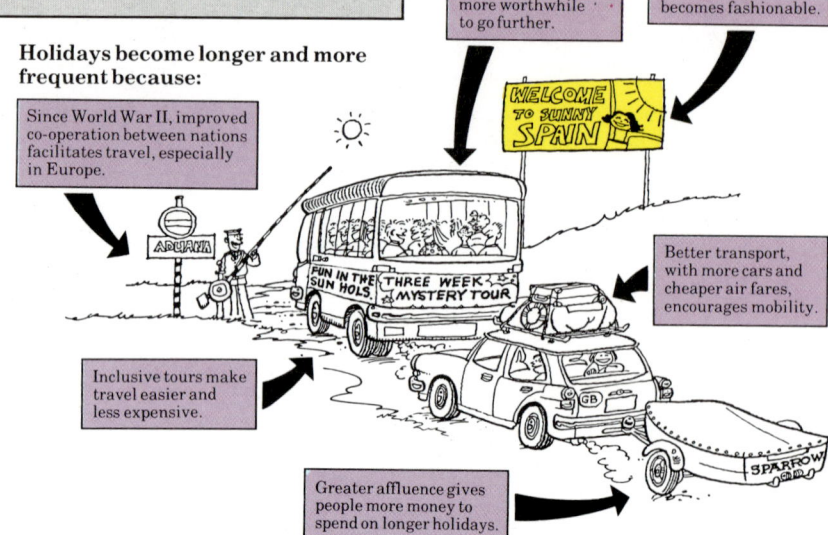

Holidays become longer and more frequent because:

- Since World War II, improved co-operation between nations facilitates travel, especially in Europe.
- Inclusive tours make travel easier and less expensive.
- Greater affluence gives people more money to spend on longer holidays.
- Longer holiday allowances from employment make it more worthwhile to go further.
- Growing travel industry advertises heavily; travel becomes fashionable.
- Better transport, with more cars and cheaper air fares, encourages mobility.

Destination: Spain

Europe's first mass package-tour destination was Spain, in particular the Costa Brava.
■ As air travel became faster and cheaper, countries like Spain became more easily accessible to tourists from northern Europe.
■ The Mediterranean coast of Spain had the right mix of good beaches and hot, dry summers.
■ In the 1950s the Spanish government, realizing the potential of tourism, promoted the building of hotels and tourist facilities.
■ Today Spain attracts almost 50 million tourists a year: 11 million of them from France, 6 million from Germany and 5 million from Britain.
■ Tourism has become a major industry in Spain. But developments have not always been well planned environmentally: ugly high-rise hotels and apartment blocks often spoil the coastline.

Right: *Air transport, bringing holiday destinations nearer, was crucial to the growth of world tourism.*

How Spain and Barbados have come closer to London

- London
- Barcelona today: 1h 55 min by air — 2 hours
- Barbados today: 8h 35 min by air (direct) — 4 hours
- Barcelona 1952: 3h 20 min by air — 8 hours
- Barbados 1952: 3 days 13h by air (7 stopovers) — 16 hours
- 32 hours
- Barbados 1930: 16 days by sea — 64 hours
- Barcelona 1930: 36 hours by sea/rail
- 16 days

Travelling in style

Since the eighteenth century there have been three consistent trends in the growth of tourism.
■ The rich have always set the fashion. Others have followed, as travel becomes cheaper and quicker. Two hundred years ago English aristocrats would spend up to two years on the Grand Tour: visiting classical sites on the Continent by horse-drawn coach. In the nineteenth century the wealthy visited the Continent, especially spa towns like Vichy and Baden Baden, by train. From 1889, travelling to the French Riviera in the Blue Train from Paris became the fashion. The Côte d'Azur remained an exclusive destination until after World War II. But today it is popular with millions of ordinary people, who travel by air, rail or by road.
■ The search for new destinations has taken tourists further and further afield. In the 1960s, wealthy tourists discovered the West Indies; in the 1970s, the Pacific Islands and South-East Asia; in the 1980s, the cultural attractions of China.
■ The tourist industry brings major changes to the destinations. Spain was an LDC when mass tourism began in the 1950s and 1960s. It made a big contribution to the country's economic growth and now represents five per cent of GDP (Gross Domestic Product) and employs four per cent of the population directly. In today's LDC holiday destinations, such as Tanzania and Mexico, tourist revenue is an important aid to development.

Above: *The attractions sought by tourists have changed little with time. The Grand Tourists were cultural visitors; so too are those who go to the Great Wall of China. George IV went swimming at Brighton using a bathing machine (top left), just as people today go for a beach holiday in Majorca (left).*

Tourism and development

Barbados is a small independent island in the Caribbean. In 1955 it received 15,000 tourists; in 1985 there were 400,000, plus 150,000 day-visitors from cruise ships. Tourism contributes 12 per cent to the island's GDP, more than any other industry including manufacturing (11 per cent) and sugar (5.4 per cent). Tourism has stimulated the economy of Barbados and brought improvements to its infrastructure: the deep-water harbour was built in 1961 and an international airport in 1980. But there are costs as well as benefits.

Below: *Selling handicraft products at a souvenir shop in Barbados. Since tourism only provides seasonal work, it has little effect on long-term unemployment, currently 18%.*

The costs of tourism in Barbados

Land use: Although the areas developed for tourism are restricted, and the rugged east coast has been preserved as a National Park, hotels and apartments take up land that local people require for agriculture.

Finance: Developments have been paid for by foreign investors so profits are not kept in Barbados. The government has now built its own developments to avoid this. Food must be imported, so reducing the balance of payments benefits from tourist income.

Labour: Tourism takes labour away from agriculture, but not throughout the year since tourism is seasonal (winter peak).

Society: The contrast between the wealth of the tourists and the poverty of the islanders causes resentment and crime. Many islanders regard tourism as a modern version of the slavery which originally brought them from Africa to the West Indies.

1 Describe and explain the expansion of mass tourism since World War II.
2 How do less well-off tourists manage to follow the trends set by wealthier travellers?
3 What makes tourism seasonal and why does the travel industry try to even out fluctuations through the year?
Class activity: Imagine that you live on an Indian Ocean island. An election is imminent. The Progressive Party supports the development of tourism as a means of improving the island's economy. The rival National Party advocates gradual development of agriculture, fishing and industry. Take the part of the following people: a) the leader of the Progressive Party; b) the leader of the National Party; c) a fishing-boat owner; d) a shop owner; e) an agricultural worker; f) an hotel owner; g) an unemployed person with a driving licence; h) a sugar-plantation manager. Present each case saying how would you vote, and why.

The information industry

In advanced economies the majority of employment is in the tertiary sector where rapid communications are essential.

Information is wealth

The first person in London to know about Wellington's victory at the battle of Waterloo was Nathan Rothschild, the banker. He informed the British government, but only after he had bought up shares in French companies that would have been worthless if Napoleon had won. Having information ahead of others made him a fortune.

- Since the Lombards of the fourteenth century, bankers have lived by knowing where to borrow money, where to lend it, where and when to buy and sell. But even in Nathan Rothschild's time there were very few people in this early form of **tertiary** industry – that is, working with information, skill and capital, rather than with crops to grow, or products to make and trade. The Treasury, which handles the finances of the British government, employed only 37 people at the beginning of the Napoleonic wars. Today it employs 4000, with another 70,000 in the Inland Revenue!
- Today many LDCs are in a similar position to Britain 150 years ago. They are just beginning to industrialize. Most of their population still works on the land, in **primary** industry.
- NICs have more developed economies with about 40 per cent of people working in **secondary**, manufacturing industry.
- Most developed countries have more mature economies, with up to 70 per cent of the workforce in **tertiary** and **quarternary**, service industries.

Right: As a country's economy matures, the proportion of people employed in each sector of industry changes.

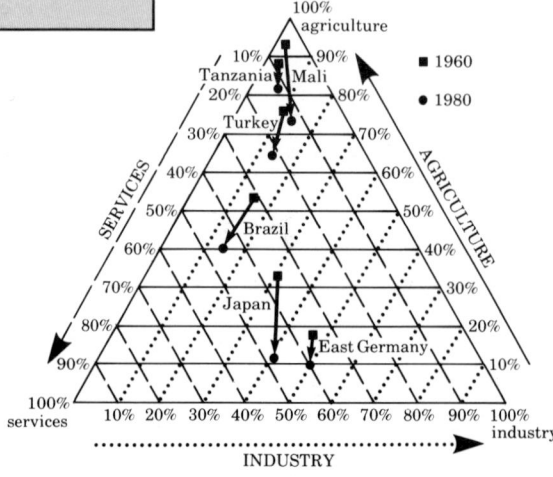

Changes in sectoral distribution of labour force, 1960–80

	Year	Primary	Secondary	Tertiary
Developed				
Japan	1960	32%	31%	37%
	1980	11%	40%	49%
East Germany	1960	18%	47%	35%
	1980	10%	50%	40%
NIC				
Turkey	1960	77%	12%	11%
	1980	65%	13%	22%
Brazil	1960	53%	15%	32%
	1980	40%	14%	46%
LDC				
Tanzania	1960	89%	4%	7%
	1980	82%	8%	10%
Mali	1960	94%	3%	3%
	1980	73%	12%	15%

Offices – more work and faster

Date	Invention	Effects
1876	Bell telephone	Telephone and telegraph enabled companies to open branch offices worldwide. Previously, business relied on mail and messengers.
1879	Remington typewriters	Only 400 sold in the first year, but soon became essential office equipment: 65,000 sold in 1890.
1881	Gestetner copier	First duplicating machine to use a wax stencil which greatly simplified the copying process.
1883	Burroughs calculating machine	First labour-saving device. Fewer, less-skilled people could handle machine accounts more quickly.
1913	Punched-card storage system	One operator could now do the work of two clerks; yet office employment continued to increase.
1946	Electronic computer	Initially, only for use by government and armed forces. Employed very few, highly skilled people.
1957	Xerox copier	First means of copying a document any number of times: revolutionized office paperwork.
1971	Commodore pocket calculator	Compact, electronic calculator; made book-keeping quicker.
1977	Commodore PET	First personal computer. By the 1980s, home and office computers in general use.

The office industry

Until the Industrial Revolution, world volume of trade was very small and most commercial transactions were carried out face-to-face. There were few offices as such. But as the scale of commerce grew, so did the need for offices – separate rooms for people who simply recorded sales and purchases. Clerical jobs occupied only two per cent of the UK population in 1871. Today that figure is 17 per cent.

Now offices are far more than counting houses, detailing sales and purchases. They themselves are a major industry. They make products, such as insurance policies and advertisments. They process information, such as news and financial advice, which can be sold worldwide.

The sale of services abroad, called **invisible exports**, is extremely important to the economy. Britain imports more manufactured goods than it exports, so it has a deficit on its balance of trade in goods of about £2 bn a year. But invisible exports, such as banking, transport services, and tourism, more than make up much of the difference. Britain frequently has a balance of payments deficit, although in 1985 there was a surplus of £5 bn. The balance of payments is the difference between total payments made by Britain for all goods and services bought abroad, and total income from all goods and services Britain sells abroad.

Global marketplace

The City of London is the world's third largest financial centre, after New York and Tokyo. It has more foreign banks (over 500) than any other city in the world. Banking alone employs over 500,000 people. Together, banking, insurance and finance firms generate an annual surplus of £4.6 bn in invisible earnings. The City is part of a global network, trading 24 hours a day: London markets close when it is lunchtime in New York; New York closes as Tokyo opens; Tokyo closes as London gets up.

Like similar financial organizations in the USA, Japan, Hong Kong, Sydney, Paris and Frankfurt, City of London companies trade in:

- **Shares** in the world's major companies: Share prices move up and down by the minute as people buy and sell all over the world. Computerized information services, communicating via satellite, bring the latest prices to dealers.
- **Foreign currencies:** Companies may need to buy dollars to purchase oil, or sell pounds they have accumulated from selling exports to Britain. Currencies change value by the moment, according to the political and economic situation of each country.
- **Government bonds:** All governments (local and national) borrow money, for periods of a few days or many years. These debts are bought and sold by investors.
- **Commodities:** Industrial raw materials, such as copper and cotton, are traded for immediate and future sale. On Futures markets investors can buy beef not yet born!
- **Insurance:** Lloyd's of London, operating worldwide, insure anything: a satellite, a pop singer's voice, the life of a racing driver, a million-tonne oil tanker or a child's bicycle.

All these markets depend on accurate, fast information transmitted by high-technology communications. Like Nathan Rothschild, the stockbroker who hears of a major company sale before anyone else does, can make a fortune.

Above: *Until recently shares in companies could only be bought and sold on the trading floor of the Stock Exchange. Today financial service companies can arrange deals through computer-telephone links.*

Above: *Reuters, once simply a world news service, now offers electronic information services to business. Foreign exchange dealers in 64 countries can get instant quotes on currency exchange rates and interest rates.*

Above: *The Lutine bell in Lloyd's Underwriting Room was traditionally rung twice to announce good news, once for bad. But today, news travels electronically and the bell is mainly used for ceremonies. It came from HMS Lutine, which sank in 1799 with the loss of its crew and a cargo of gold and silver insured by Lloyd's.*

Above: *Lloyd's new building in the City. Originally a 17th century coffee house where traders met to insure ships and their cargoes, Lloyd's is now the centre of a worldwide insurance market with invisible earnings of almost £1 bn a year.*

> **1** Why and how has technology revolutionized information?
> **2** What is the impact of information technology on: a) office jobs? b) office appearance? c) the City of London?
> **3** What are invisible exports?
> **4** Explain balance of payments.
> **5** From the triangular graph, explain the shift (1960-80) in the percentage employed in primary, secondary and tertiary sectors. Why are fewer people employed in the tertiary sector in Mali than in Japan? What is happening to the proportion of people employed in the tertiary sector in all countries? Refer to page 89 and use this progression as an indicator to place each country on the Rostow model.

 **TIME/DISTANCE**

Moving with the seasons

> The more scattered and scarce resources are, the longer it takes to exploit them.

Right: *On the move. Fulani families with herds of cattle near the end of their month-long migration to the Jos plateau. Every year the journey becomes more difficult as land-management schemes destroy natural vegetation and block traditional routes.*

Nomadism in Nigeria

Nomadism is the traditional response of rural communities to scarce resources. If they cannot produce enough food locally – because of poor soil or arid grazing – they shift camp and move on in search of better conditions. The Fulani, from the savanna lands of northern Nigeria, have been nomads for over 600 years.

■ This part of west Africa has an alternating wet and dry season. During the dry months, pastures are too parched for raising livestock.

■ The Fulani solve this problem by following the rain. In winter, the dry season, they take their sheep, goats and cattle south to the Jos plateau which is wetter and more fertile. They return north to their homelands with the summer rains. In the past, the entire community took part in this seasonal migration.

■ Today, many Fulani have become semi-nomadic. Resources are now less scarce. Improved farming methods and new irrigation schemes make semi-nomadism possible. While nearby urban populations provide an expanding market for agricultural produce there are now permanent Fulani settlements in the north where they grow crops. Many Fulani stay there all year.

■ Only young herdsmen still make the annual trek to the Jos. But even this limited form of nomadism is dying out. Many traditional grazing and waterhole zones near towns have been taken over for intensive cultivation, displacing the Fulani and their herds. Large-scale irrigation projects have altered the local **eco-system**; as a result trees, which provide shade and fodder for migrating animals, are disappearing.

■ Faced with these pressures some Fulani have abandoned their nomadic existence altogether to lead a new settled life as cultivators. Others will follow their example.

The Fulani year, adapted to semi-nomadism

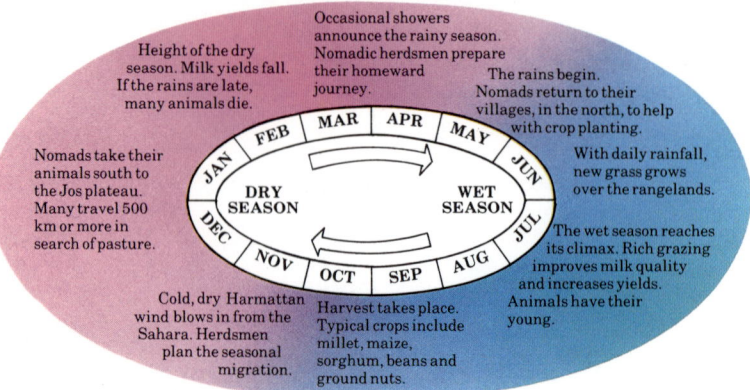

Height of the dry season. Milk yields fall. If the rains are late, many animals die.

Occasional showers announce the rainy season. Nomadic herdsmen prepare their homeward journey.

The rains begin. Nomads return to their villages, in the north, to help with crop planting.

Nomads take their animals south to the Jos plateau. Many travel 500 km or more in search of pasture.

With daily rainfall, new grass grows over the rangelands.

The wet season reaches its climax. Rich grazing improves milk quality and increases yields. Animals have their young.

Cold, dry Harmattan wind blows in from the Sahara. Herdsmen plan the seasonal migration.

Harvest takes place. Typical crops include millet, maize, sorghum, beans and ground nuts.

Above: *Fulani women taking milk to market. The population explosion in Nigerian cities has increased demand for agricultural produce. Many settled Fulani, even though they have abandoned nomadism, still raise livestock for milk and meat by growing fodder crops.*

Left: *A Fulani herdsman watches over cows at a waterhole. Many watering places are being developed into irrigated market gardens and are therefore no longer available for animal use.*

Transhumance in the Swiss Alps

The seasonal migration of people and animals in search of pasture is not limited to the LDCs. It also occurs, in a more modernized form, in a number of developed countries.

■ For centuries, transhumance – moving livestock up to high alpine pastures (*alpage* or *mayen*) in summer – was an integral part of life in the mountain valleys of Canton Valais, Switzerland.

■ In summer, up on the *alpages*, the cows' milk was turned into butter and cheese for the coming winter; down in the valleys, hay was grown for winter feed.

■ Since the 1930s, strawberries and raspberries have been grown in the Valais as a cash crop. Transhumance continues – but modified to give farmers the necessary time for soft fruit cultivation.

These two diagrams summarize the old and new ways of life.

The old ...
1 When did cattle remain indoors?
2 Why did they have to stay under cover at this time of the year?
3 When did families, with animals, begin their annual migration to summer pastures?
4 How did they get to the summer pastures and how long did their journey take?
5 Where did people and animals stop on their way up to the *alpages*?
6 How long did animals graze at the upper limit of pasture?
7 How long did the return journey take and when did they arrive back at the village?
8 What happened to milk on the summer pastures?
9 What was growing on the village fields during the summer?
10 Why was transhumance such an important part of life?

The new...
1 When do cattle stay indoors? Is it the same period as before? Why does it still happen?
2 When does migration to summer pastures begin?
3 How are animals transported to summer pastures?
4 For how long do animals graze on the highest pastures? Is it the same length of time as before?
5 What happens to milk from the summer pastures? How do people in the village get fresh milk?
6 What is grown in fields around the village?
7 Who looks after these crops and what are they used for?
8 Where does winter feed for animals now come from?
9 Explain why and how the people in Canton Valais have adjusted their way of life and modernized the ancient tradition of transhumance to meet present-day circumstances.
10 Imagine you are a long-standing resident of the Valais; express your feelings and opinions about the changes.

 TIME/DISTANCE

Natural disasters

The impact of a natural disaster decreases with the distance from its centre.

Black Sunday

At breakfast time on Sunday 18 May 1980, Mount St Helens in Washington State – dormant for 123 years – exploded. A geologist, David Johnston, had been on the spot monitoring the mountain for seven weeks. At 08.32 he shouted over his radio link to base, 'This is it!' He died almost immediately.

- A Richter scale 5 earthquake caused the north side of the mountain to collapse. The world's largest recorded mud flow plunged through Spirit Lake (leaving it boiling hot), climbed 400 m up the opposite mountainside and then raced down the Toutle river valley, burying parts of it 60 m deep.

- The eruption had a devastating effect on Mount St Helens itself. It blew out a new crater 650 m deep and lowered the summit by 400 m.

- Ash 7.5 cm deep covered the ground 35 km away. Although most people were evacuated, 72 died.

- Within an hour the city of Yakima 145 km away was brought to a halt by 600,000 tonnes of super-fine ash that blocked drains, clogged engines and brought total darkness.

- An ash cloud 21,000 m high crossed continental USA within three days of the eruption and circled the earth within 17 days.

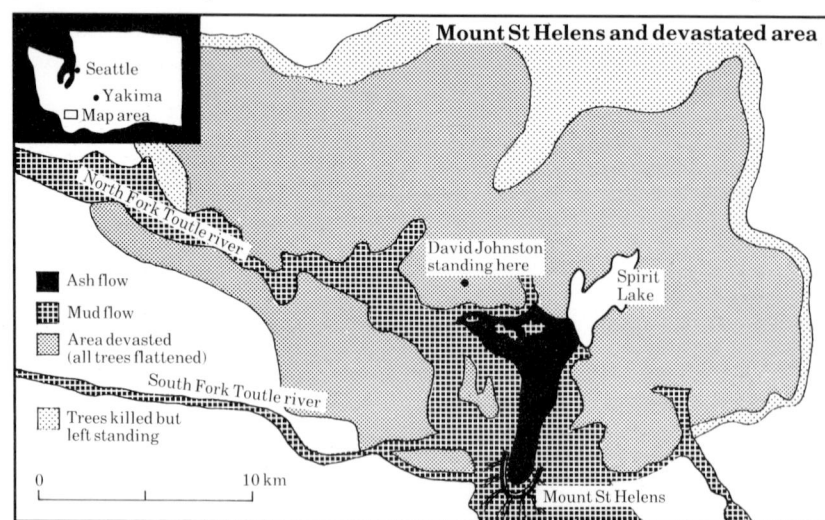

Left: *A year before the eruption a bulge appeared in the side of Mount St Helens caused by thick heavy magma welling up from the vent below the crater.*

Below: *The eruption; Mount St Helens lies within the Ring of Fire volcanic belt.*

Above: *The devastated area extended in a wide arc to the north of Mount St Helens.*

Below: *Mature trees, 30 m tall, fell like matchsticks. In all, the blast cleared 250 km² of forest and exterminated all wildlife in the area.*

Ash Wednesday

On Ash Wednesday, 16 February 1983, bushfires raged out of control in the hills around Melbourne. By the time they had been quelled four days later, 72 people and 300,000 head of livestock had died; 1700 houses were destroyed; 250,000 ha of forest and 500,000 ha of farmland were devastated.

■ The Ash Wednesday fires broke out during a serious drought, when rainfall had only been 28 per cent of normal for three months. On more than half the days in the previous month, the temperature had exceeded 30°C, frequently rising to 40°C.

■ The eucalyptus trees of the Australian bush provide particularly hazardous fuels. They have dry bark that falls to the ground, making a tinderbox of woody litter. They exude inflammable oils and, under extreme heat, will ignite spontaneously. On this occasion winds of up to 80 km/h fanned the fires.

■ The size of the disaster meant that it affected the whole country. Help was brought in from all over Australia: 588 fire-fighting units, 21,000 people, 15 aircraft and 13 helicopters fought the blaze. Afterwards, the Federal government allocated $16 m for disaster relief and a further $6 m was raised by public subscription.

Above: *Flames tear through a property at Belgrave, Victoria. The devastation caused by the Ash Wednesday fires resulted in insurance claims of over $200 m.*

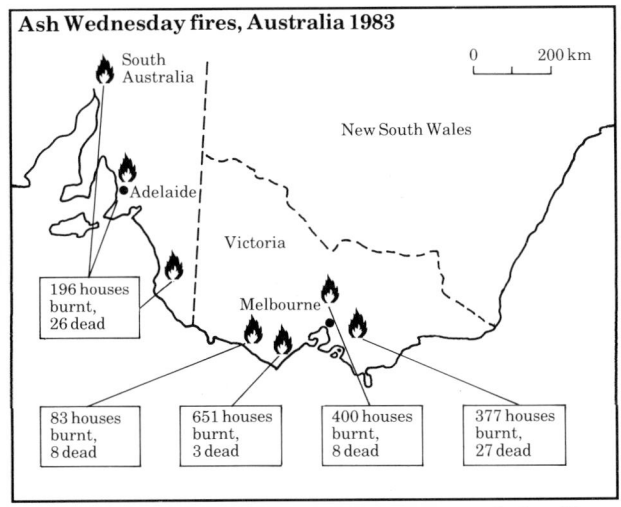

Ash Wednesday fires, Australia 1983

- 196 houses burnt, 26 dead
- 83 houses burnt, 8 dead
- 651 houses burnt, 3 dead
- 400 houses burnt, 8 dead
- 377 houses burnt, 27 dead

Above: *As the fires raged, states of emergency were declared in South Australia and Victoria. In addition to those killed, 111 people were hospitalized and 1260 treated for injuries.*

Above: *A dead koala, one of the many bushfire victims on Mt Macedon, Victoria. The impact of the disaster on animals and their habitats was immeasurable.*

1 Describe the effects of the Mount St Helens eruption:
a) on the mountain summit;
b) at Spirit Lake; c) at Yakima.
2 What effects of the eruption would the area immediately round Mount St Helens still be suffering today?
3 As a Forest Ranger in Victoria, Australia, draft a notice for bush-walkers, describing a state of extreme fire danger.
4 Write a paragraph describing each of the following: a) the economic effects of a natural disaster; b) the ecological effects; c) the psychological effects on survivors.

Class activity: Imagine that four of you are directors of an insurance company faced with huge claims from a natural disaster. In turn, argue in favour of each of the following solutions: a) suggest your clients move to a safer area, or you will not reinsure them; b) ask the government to take on the responsibility of insuring people who live in dangerous areas; c) retain the insurance cover, but increase greatly premiums of those living in high-risk areas; d) charge higher premiums to all your clients to make up for the increased risk.

The politics of oil

> The level of production in one place is dictated by the level of consumption in another.

The oil crisis

World production and consumption of oil (millions of tonnes per year)

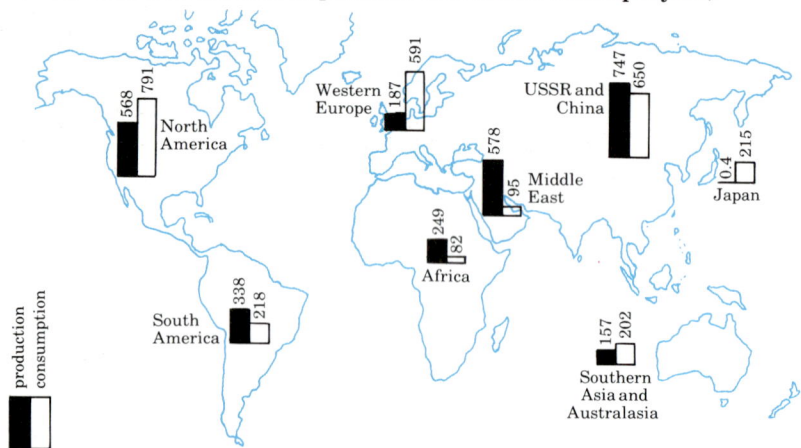

North America: production 568, consumption 791
Western Europe: production 187, consumption 591
USSR and China: production 747, consumption 650
Japan: production 0.4, consumption 215
Middle East: production 578, consumption 95
Africa: production 249, consumption 82
South America: production 338, consumption 218
Southern Asia and Australasia: production 157, consumption 202

Rate of oil extraction (worldwide)

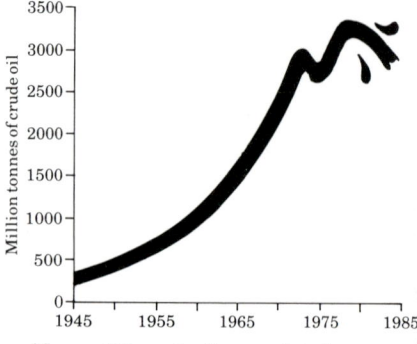

Above: *Oil production escalated following World War II and, in the 1960s-70s, it kept pace with rising energy needs. But today, oil's share in world energy is decreasing.*

1973-74 was the year of the oil crisis. It proved to be a turning point in modern industrial geography.

■ Until about 1950 most industrialized countries were almost self-sufficient in energy, using locally produced coal. But since the 1920s (when naval and merchant fleets converted vessels from coal to oil) oil had been gradually supplanting coal as the main source of primary energy. As a result, oil production – centred on the Middle East – increased dramatically. From 1945-73 oil was cheap and easily available. Consumption was largely in North America, Europe and Japan. Middle East supplies were mostly extracted and refined by the 'Seven Sisters', the world's greatest oil companies. Five of them are American, one British (BP), and one Anglo-Dutch (Shell). They market petroleum products worldwide.

■ In 1973 the effects of the Arab-Israeli war spilled over into the world oil market. The Arab countries decided to use their domination of oil as a weapon against Western countries, which they felt favoured Israel. They withheld supplies and quadrupled prices. Initially, consumer countries had no option but to pay the inflated prices demanded by OPEC (Organization of Petroleum Exporting Countries).

■ The short-term effect was severe and caused a chain reaction: higher costs; a slump in world trade; a slowdown in industry; a rise in unemployment (from 3.5 m in the EEC in 1974 to 13 m in 1984); inflation of up to 20 per cent in many countries.

■ The longer-term effects resulted in different energy policies. The 1979 revolution in Iran (a major oil exporter) and the subsequent Iran-Iraq war caused more oil price rises. In 1973 oil had been $6 a barrel; by 1981 it was $36. Western countries decided to limit their dependence on such unreliable and expensive supplies. They increased efforts to: find non-OPEC sources of oil; reduce their dependence on oil by increasing output from other sources such as nuclear power; conserve energy; speed up research into alternative energy sources. These policies have reduced demand for oil, so that both prices and Middle East production have fallen.

Left: *Maintenance work on a production platform in the North Sea. Extracting oil and gas from the North Sea requires very advanced technology to cope with natural hazards such as deep water (up to 200 m), gale force winds reaching 222 km/h and storm waves towering 30 m high.*

Right: *Natural gas was discovered in the southern North Sea in 1965, oil further north in 1970. Norway is the other major North Sea producer, although the Dutch sector produces gas and the Danish, oil. North Sea oil is mostly high grade, light crude; heavier grades are still imported from the Middle East.*

Above: *Increasingly, the world's search for oil has extended to hostile environments such as the Amazonian jungle, the North Sea and the Arctic Circle. This snow-swept rig is on the Prudhoe Field, in Alaska. Prudhoe, the largest field in the US, produces 74 m tonnes of oil a year.*

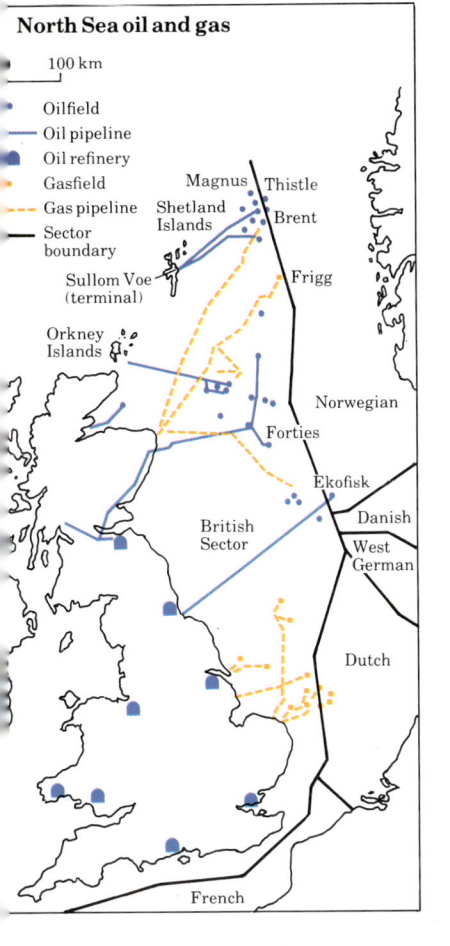

Above: *The control room of a production platform in the Frigg field. Frigg, lying half-way between the Shetlands and Norway, produces both oil and gas. The sophisticated electronic and pneumatic equipment controls output and detects faults.*

Hooked on oil

Like the developed nations, some newly industrializing countries (NICs) have become heavily dependent on oil.

- Over the last 30 years Brazil has been 'developing from above' – attracting large amounts of foreign capital to expand energy-consuming industries. Volkswagen in Brazil now produces more cars than Volkswagen, Germany. With a large domestic market (130 m) and cheap labour, Brazil is an excellent base for manufacturing and exporting.

- The oil Brazil needs for this rapid development of western-style industry has to be imported. Oil imports and development projects have been financed by international loans. Brazil is now the world's biggest debtor nation, owing $99 bn. These debts can only be supported by reducing the amount of money available for wages. Salary rises are limited to 80 per cent of inflation.

- Each year the Brazilian government calculates a 'basic ration': the minimum wage required to support an average family of six. The number of working hours needed to earn this wage has increased so much that 65 per cent of workers at Volkswagen – considered well paid – earn less than the basic ration.

Right: *To reduce oil imports, Brazil developed an alcohol-driven car. The alcohol, obtained from sugar cane, is more efficient than petrol but is costly in land use. Today, all cars run on either 100% alcohol or a 20% alcohol-petrol mix.*

North Sea oil and gas

1 Describe and explain the rapid growth in world oil production and consumption since 1945.
2 Which countries produce most oil and which consume most?
3 How did OPEC gain control of world oil markets and what has happened to OPEC since 1973-74?
4 Why has oil come to dominate the world energy market?
5 What has been the effect of rising oil prices on LDCs?
6 Why was it so important for Britain to develop its own oil supplies from the North Sea?
7 Look at the map of the North Sea. Why does Britain have refineries at Fawley and Milford Haven?
8 There will be a surplus of North Sea oil available for export until about 1990. Should Britain profit from those exports now, or conserve oil and put off the day when oil must be imported again?

39

Trans-national companies

> The presence of a trans-national company can bring both advantages and disadvantages to the host nation.

Business everywhere

From the moment we get up in the morning to the time we go to bed, our lives are conditioned by major, international businesses. Companies that operate in many different countries are called **trans-nationals**, or multi-nationals. They have their headquarters in one place, but subsidiary offices and factories in many other parts of the world.

The trans-national day

In the bathroom...
Soap: Unilever (Anglo-Dutch)
Toothpaste: Colgate-Palmolive (US)
Medicines: Ciba-Geigy (Swiss)

In the kitchen...
Coffee: Nestle (Swiss)
Cereal: Kelloggs (US)
Refrigerator: Electrolux (Swedish)

In the car...
Car: Nissan (Japanese)
Petrol: Exxon (US)
Tyres: Michelin (France)

At the office...
Computer: IBM (US)
Telephone: Ericsson (Swedish)
Photocopier: Canon (Japan)

Back home...
Television: Philips (Dutch)
Audio: Sony (Japanese)
Soft drink: Coca Cola (US)

Anatomy of a trans-national

Many of the largest trans-nationals began as **resource companies**, especially in oil. John D. Rockefeller began his first oil-refining business in 1863. Sixteen years later his Standard Oil Company controlled 90 per cent of the US oil industry. Standard Oil used its dominant position to undercut rivals and put them out of business. Rockefeller's methods were so questionable that, in 1897, his company was broken up into 30 parts by law. Today Exxon, one of those parts, is the largest company in the world: two others (Mobil and Texaco) are among the world's top six oil companies.

- The top 500 trans-nationals operate on a huge scale. Their combined annual sales rival the GNP of the USA (approx. $3000 bn).
- They are geographically very widespread. Unilever, for example, operates in 75 countries and Ciba-Geigy in 82.
- Most originate in the USA, but each of the developed nations has one or two major trans-nationals; a few, smaller ones originate in NICs.
- They develop and produce brand-name goods.
- They are efficient at large-scale production.
- They employ many people: the top 250 trans-nationals have over 40 m employees worldwide.
- The top 100 account for one-third of all world trade.

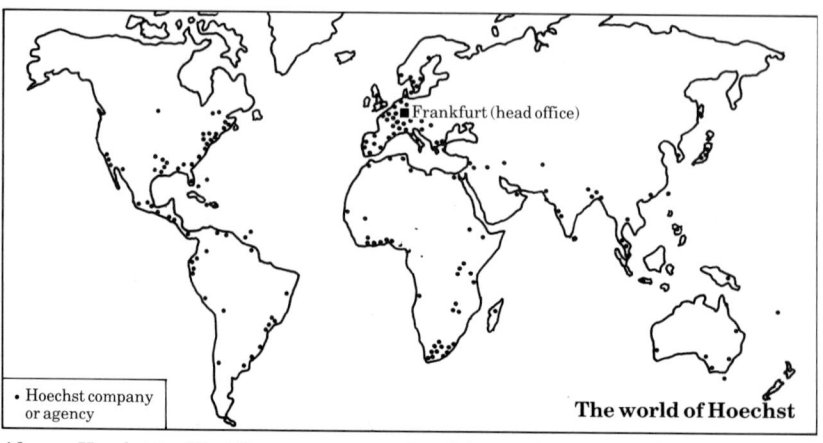

Above: Hoechst is a West German trans-national. Among its many products are fertilizers, textiles, building materials, medicines, electronic components, printing machinery, plastics and paints, researched, produced and marketed in over 120 countries.

Advantages of trans-nationals

	In developed country	In LDC
Investment	Large sums and high level of expertise	Capital not available from other sources
Development	Brings new industries and new products	New industries and raw material sources
Employment	Jobs created directly and also in supplier companies	People trained for types of employment new to country
Production	Large scale makes products cheap	Surplus production sold as exports
Profit	Some may be retained in host country	Some may be retained for reinvestment

Disadvantages of trans-nationals

	In developed country	In LDC
Investment	Can go elsewhere if profits better	Can leave if political conditions adverse
Development	Manufacturing products developed elsewhere	Resource extraction with no value added
Employment	Maximum mechanization means as few people employed as possible	Using low wages in LDCs to make worldwide products cheaply
Production	High efficiency can mean control of market	Making products which LDC does not need
Profit	Usually returned to international HQ	Usually returned to international HQ

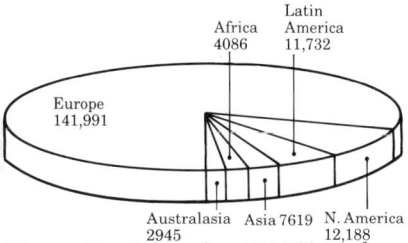

Above: *Hoechst employs 180,561 people worldwide.*

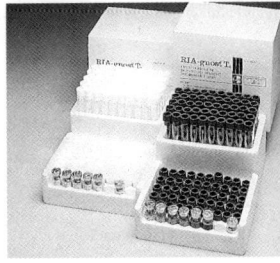

Right: *Paints, plastics, cosmetics, animal vaccines and pharmaceuticals are among the thousands of products manufactured by Hoechst.*

Taming trans-nationals

Trans-national companies have entered many different overseas markets in order to expand and make larger profits than they could in their original home market alone. They need to diversify abroad to:
- obtain raw materials they do not have at home;
- obtain cost advantages from cheaper labour or materials;
- reach markets protected by import tariffs;
- reach markets too difficult, or too big, to penetrate by exports alone.

The operations of trans-nationals can be particularly damaging to LDCs.
- After **decolonization** in the 1960s, some countries were dependent on large foreign companies for investment, expertise and employment. This was a form of economic colonialism, in which the country's resources were exploited for very small returns.
- Often LDCs do not need the products of trans-nationals. For example, they are capable of making their own soft drinks. Yet part of American culture is forced upon them by Coca Cola.
- A trans-national is unlikely to want a host LDC to change from a capitalist to a communist system; it may therefore use its wealth to influence political affairs.

The fact that trans-nationals need host markets gives the latter some bargaining power. But this is limited by the ability of a trans-national to move elsewhere if conditions become unfavourable. Today many LDCs have found ways of dealing with trans-nationals which ensure benefits for both.
- **Joint enterprises:** a firm or government in the host country sets up a joint company with the trans-national; profits are shared. China has set up joint companies in oil development and telephones.
- **Licences:** a host country firm acquires rights to make a brand product, paying a proportion of the profits to the trans-national. Austin Rover produces Honda cars under licence from the Japanese company.

Right: *Trans-national companies develop products to penetrate markets at all economic levels. The development of cool-wash detergents, for example, has opened up outlets in LDCs. Here, a Unilever product is demonstrated in Zimbabwe.*

NICs strike back

Small, but very successful trans-nationals have grown up in various NICs. The Argentinian Bunge y Born Group is typical.
- It is based on resources and simple technology. It handles grain exports, flour, textiles and paint.
- Its main markets are in other NICs (especially Brazil).
- It grew by small-scale innovation, not by massive investment.
- It has licence agreements with trans-nationals such as ICI.

Another example is Brazil's arms industry, which has grown into the world's fifth largest.
- It began under a military dictatorship, which wanted local supplies of weapons.
- Its main markets are LDCs and NICs, who prefer not to buy arms from the world powers.
- It produces weapons, such as French missiles, under licence.

Left: *This Embraer-111 Bandierante patrol plane was built in Brazil for the Gabonese air force.*

---

1 What is a trans-national?
2 How have trans-nationals become so large and powerful?
3 How do LDCs benefit from the presence of trans-nationals?
4 How do LDCs suffer from the presence of trans-nationals?
5 The American business magazine, Fortune, wrote: 'The hard financial core of capitalism is composed of not more than 60 firms... Recent forecasts claim that in 25 years 200 multi-national firms will completely dominate world production and trade and account for over 75% of the corporate assets of the capitalist world'. If this forecast proves to be correct, do you think that people in developed and less developed countries will benefit or suffer?

Nuclear power

National policy decisions can affect local, national and global environments.

Why nuclear power?

Most developed countries now have an energy gap. They consume more energy than they produce.
- For political reasons they prefer not to be too dependent on oil supplies from unstable areas of the world like the Middle East.
- For economic reasons they do not wish to import more fuel than necessary, especially when prices could soar as in the 1973-4 oil crisis.
- Fossil fuels, such as coal and oil, are limited and non-renewable. North Sea oil and gas, for example, will begin to run out early next century.
- Dependence on too few energy sources is dangerous. Strikes can halt coal production or oil deliveries.
- Almost all suitable hydro-electricity sites are already in use.
- Alternative energy sources, such as wind and solar power, are not yet able to meet large-scale requirements.

For these reasons many countries, including Britain, are diversifying their energy sources and pursuing a co-co-nuke policy – conservation, coal and nuclear power.
- Energy demand is rising, but not as fast as predicted. Industry and transport are using energy more efficiently since the 1973-4 oil crisis.
- Britain has large coal reserves, but these are expensive to mine. West Germany has lignite, but opencast mines cause environmental problems.
- Nuclear power produces cheaper electricity than coal or oil. Uranium, the fuel for nuclear reactors, comes from several countries including France, Namibia and Australia.

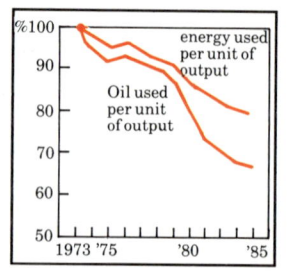

Above: *The OECD (Organization for Economic Co-operation and Development, including the USA, Japan, West Germany, France, Britain, Italy and Canada) is achieving total industrial output with 20% less energy and 35% less oil than in 1973.*

Electronuclear Europe

In 1956, the world's first nuclear power station opened at Calder Hall (now part of the Sellafield complex) in Cumbria. Over the next twenty years, other European countries followed Britain's lead and developed nuclear-energy programmes.
- Today Britain ranks as Europe's third electronuclear state behind France and West Germany. Nuclear power accounts for 10-12 per cent of British electricity production.
- France, using its own uranium, produces more nuclear power than any country in the world except the USA. In 1985 over 60 per cent of French electricity was nuclear generated – rising to 70 per cent by 1990. A cable under the Channel enables France to export electricity to Britain at half the cost of UK coal-fired power.
- Sweden currently generates 35 per cent of its electricity by nuclear power. But in 1980, via a national referendum, the people voted to halt nuclear production by 2010 because of environmental dangers.
- Eastern European countries have few energy sources and must rely on costly Soviet oil and gas. Both they and the USSR, which needs to export its oil to the West, have turned to nuclear power. Hungary's first plant opened in 1982 while Czechoslovakia aims to be 50 per cent nuclear by 2000. Until the Chernobyl disaster, 11 per cent of Soviet electricity was nuclear-generated, with a planned increase to 20 per cent by 1990.

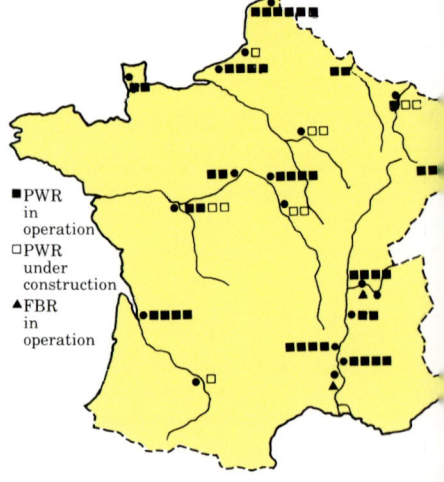

■ PWR in operation
□ PWR under construction
▲ FBR in operation

Above: *French nuclear power plants. France has limited energy sources and must import 97% of its oil, 75% of gas and 54% of coal. The 1973-4 oil crisis caused a major review of the country's energy policy and resulted in an intensive nuclear programme. By 1986, 43 PWR (pressurized water reactor) units and 2 fast-breeders were in operation; a further 10 PWR are under construction. France is Europe's top electronuclear state.*

Left: *A French PWR plant at Paluel, on the Channel coast. Nuclear power stations must be sited away from large towns and cities, but near a source of cooling water – a river or sea – and, because of their weight, in a geologically stable area.*

Russia admits worst atom plant disaster ever

NUCLEAR NIGHTMARE IS HERE

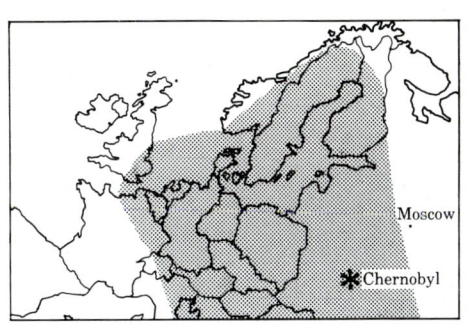

Right: *Extent of airborne radiation from Chernobyl a week after the explosion. Within nine days, the nuclear cloud had affected 20 countries and reached N America and Africa.*

Above: *Headline reporting the world's worst-ever nuclear accident at Chernobyl, in the USSR, on 26 April 1986.*

Right: *A 'nuclear power –no thanks' badge from Sweden.*

Nuclear power - no thanks!

In most developed Western countries nuclear power stations are now unpopular. People fear possible accidents, like the Chernobyl disaster, or even terrorist attacks. Environmental groups oppose nuclear power because of the disposal problems for radioactive waste and because of radiation in the atmosphere.

- British opposition centred on the Sizewell B station, approved in 1987.
- In Switzerland there were violent demonstrations against a nuclear plant close to the city of Basel.
- In Australia there has been great controversy over the mining of uranium, especially in Aboriginal reserves. Every 1000 tonnes of uranium mined produces 100,000 tonnes of solid radioactive waste and 3.5 m litres of liquid waste.

For Sizewell

Is it needed?

Sizewell B is expensive (£1200 million) but over 35 years of operation it will more than cover its cost by saving fossil fuels and by replacing old, less efficient nuclear stations.

Future demand is mainly in the south of England. Heavy industry in the north is shrinking. The north also has many coal-fired power stations.

For reasons of national security Britain should be as self-sufficient as possible in electricity.

Is it safe?

Although it is a PWR reactor, it will be built and operated to far stricter safety standards than at Three Mile Island – where the reactor almost reached meltdown point.

Like most British nuclear power stations it is on a fairly remote coastline. Fewer than 500 people live within 2.4 km; less than 10,000 live within 8 km.

Large investments have been made to ensure safe storage of spent fuel.

Geological conditions are good.

What about the landscape?

There is already one nuclear station at Sizewell. The infrastructure of power lines and maintenance facilities exists already. There is ample cooling water. Being isolated, it is as unobtrusive as any large building could be.

Against Sizewell

Is it needed?

The CEGB already has 30–40% more generating capacity than it needs. Past predictions of future demand have been proved wrong. Even if they were right, coal-fired or alternative energy power stations would be cheaper.

Alternative sources – such as solar, wind and wave – might produce large-scale power if £1200 million were spent on them. £1200 million would insulate half Britain's lofts, so conserving vast amounts of power.

Is it safe?

Even if modified, it is still a PWR. CEGB reports indicate that PWRs are more economic but less safe than the current British design of Advanced Gas-cooled Reactor (AGR).

Disposal of nuclear waste is an unsolved problem. At present, Britain's nuclear waste is stored in concrete ponds at Sellafield, Cumbria. It will remain active for thousands of years. Dumping underground and at sea are both hazardous.

What about the landscape?

Sizewell is surrounded by an area of outstanding natural beauty, all along the Suffolk coast. The flora and fauna, especially birdlife, are of particular significance. The area is valued by naturalists, ramblers and fishermen.

Below: *An anti-nuclear demonstrator, in a skull mask, peers into the Sizewell Inquiry. The sticker recalls America's worst nuclear accident at Three Mile Island, Harrisburg, in 1979.*

1 What is the 'energy gap'?
2 Why are countries diversifying their energy sources?
3 What reasons influence the siting of nuclear power stations?
4 Describe your reactions to the Paluel nuclear power station on the coast of Normandy.
5 Imagine you are the government inspector chairing an enquiry into an application for the construction of a new nuclear power station. Summarize the arguments for and against and announce your decision, giving reasons.
6 Why have some countries, such as France and Sweden, invested more heavily in nuclear power than others?

43

Aid for development

Developed countries provide aid to the developing world for many different reasons and with many different results.

Why give aid?

Rich countries aid poorer ones through both generosity and self-interest.
- Main donors are the developed nations of the North: the USA, Europe, Japan and some OPEC countries, especially Saudi Arabia.
- Principal recipients are LDCs in the South, many of which suffer human as well as natural disasters.
- Aid comes from three main sources: governments, companies and private individuals (through charities).
- It is distributed in several different forms: as gifts of food, equipment or services; as cash grants or cheap loans arranged directly between donor and recipient governments; as grants or loans arranged through international agencies, such as the United Nations; as loans or direct investment by trans-national companies and banks.
- Donor nations have different priorities in allocating aid. Many European countries favour former colonies (France, for example, aids North African states like Morocco, Algeria and Tunisia). Normally donors choose LDCs which are political allies: the USSR channels most of its aid to communist countries; the USA helps anti-communist governments; OPEC donors favour Muslim countries.

Top ten donor countries 1982

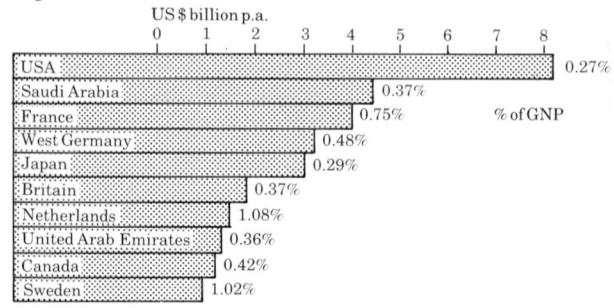

US $ billion p.a.

Country	% of GNP
USA	0.27%
Saudi Arabia	0.37%
France	0.75%
West Germany	0.48%
Japan	0.29%
Britain	0.37%
Netherlands	1.08%
United Arab Emirates	0.36%
Canada	0.42%
Sweden	1.02%

Right idea, wrong reason

The relationship between donor and recipient is extremely complicated.
- Many donors give with good intentions, if only to ease their consciences.
- Organizations, especially governments and companies, expect a return on their investment – either in political goodwill or in profits.
- Recipients may accept aid, not for the good of the country, but to benefit individuals or keep a particular government in power.

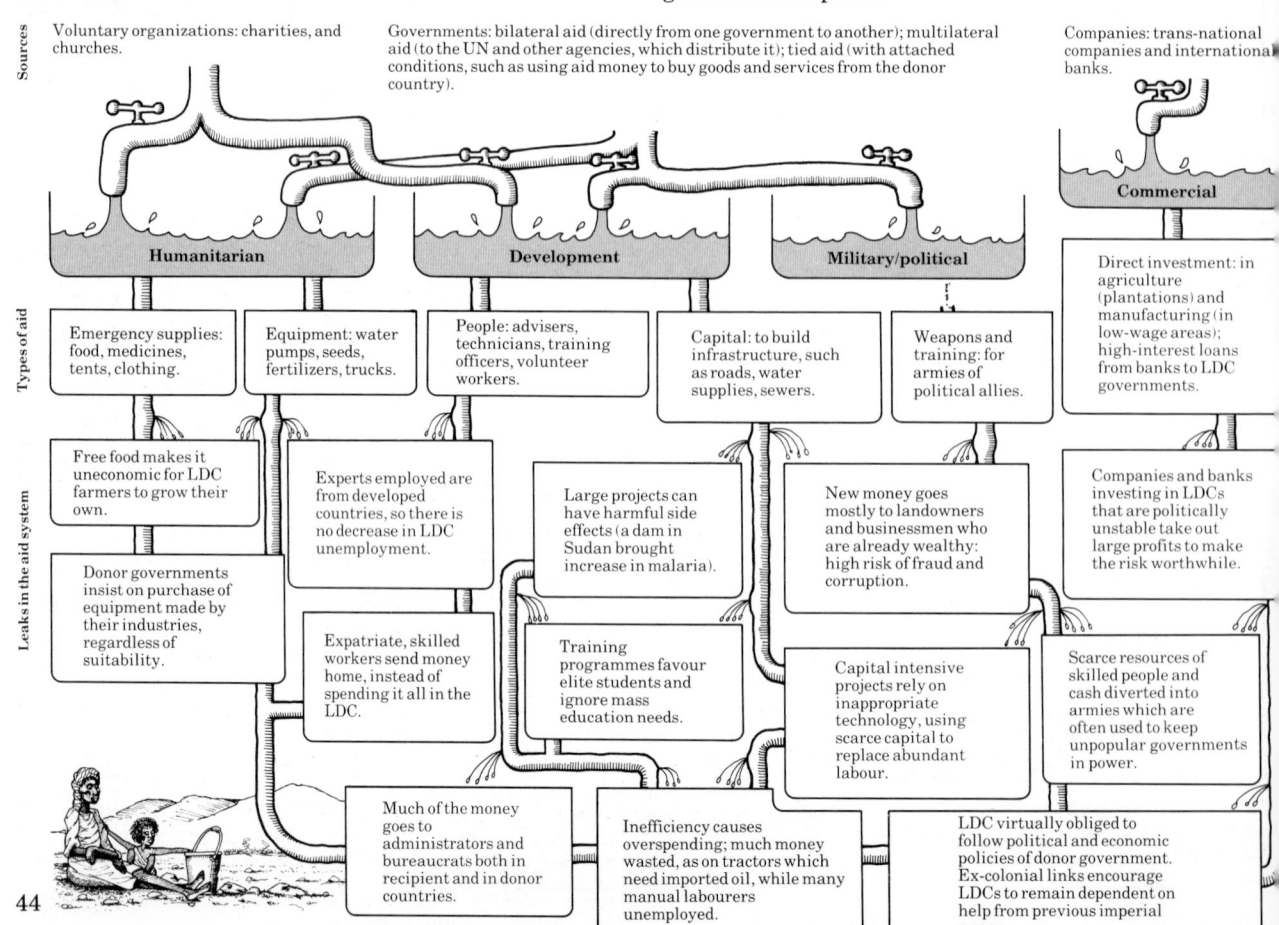

Sources

Voluntary organizations: charities, and churches.

Governments: bilateral aid (directly from one government to another); multilateral aid (to the UN and other agencies, which distribute it); tied aid (with attached conditions, such as using aid money to buy goods and services from the donor country).

Companies: trans-national companies and international banks.

Humanitarian | Development | Military/political | Commercial

Types of aid

- Emergency supplies: food, medicines, tents, clothing.
- Equipment: water pumps, seeds, fertilizers, trucks.
- People: advisers, technicians, training officers, volunteer workers.
- Capital: to build infrastructure, such as roads, water supplies, sewers.
- Weapons and training: for armies of political allies.
- Direct investment: in agriculture (plantations) and manufacturing (in low-wage areas); high-interest loans from banks to LDC governments.

Leaks in the aid system

- Free food makes it uneconomic for LDC farmers to grow their own.
- Donor governments insist on purchase of equipment made by their industries, regardless of suitability.
- Experts employed are from developed countries, so there is no decrease in LDC unemployment.
- Expatriate, skilled workers send money home, instead of spending it all in the LDC.
- Large projects can have harmful side effects (a dam in Sudan brought increase in malaria).
- Training programmes favour elite students and ignore mass education needs.
- New money goes mostly to landowners and businessmen who are already wealthy; high risk of fraud and corruption.
- Capital intensive projects rely on inappropriate technology, using scarce capital to replace abundant labour.
- Companies and banks investing in LDCs that are politically unstable take out large profits to make the risk worthwhile.
- Scarce resources of skilled people and cash diverted into armies which are often used to keep unpopular governments in power.
- Much of the money goes to administrators and bureaucrats both in recipient and in donor countries.
- Inefficiency causes overspending; much money wasted, as on tractors which need imported oil, while many manual labourers unemployed.
- LDC virtually obliged to follow political and economic policies of donor government. Ex-colonial links encourage LDCs to remain dependent on help from previous imperial power.

Future hopes and problems

There have been major successes in aid programes to the Third World: for example, the Green Revolution transformed India from a famine area to a surplus producer of food. But plenty of problems remain.

- The World Bank was set up in 1946. It has lent money to 137 countries, most of them very poor: 90 per cent of loans go to countries with a GDP per person of under US $400. It charges virtually no interest, yet makes a profit and has no bad debts. Originally World Bank policy was to invest in industry, but today most money goes into agriculture and energy projects.
- Charities and even individuals have also made an important contribution. Oxfam, for example, continues to provide emergency relief but also operates as a development agency. While in 1985, Bob Geldof's Band Aid raised £56.5 m in the UK alone for the starving people of the sub-Sahara.
- Both private and government agencies have realized that policies adopted in developed countries are not necessarily effective in LDCs. Technology should be appropriate to the place: small windmills for power generation and simple well systems to provide clean water.

- Many experts think that self-help is the only way for LDCs to improve their standard of living. Some of the poorest nations are investing 15 per cent of GDP in their own development – more than today's rich countries invested when they were developing a century ago.
- Today the biggest problem facing LDCs is their indebtedness. Many developing countries have borrowed heavily from developed world banks. As a result, money earned from exports – instead of being channelled into development – goes on interest payments.

Top ten borrowers
US$ billion

Country	US$ billion	interest as a % of exports
Brazil	~100	37%
Mexico	~95	35%
Argentina	~50	52%
South Korea	~48	10%
Indonesia	~30	13%
Venezuela	~32	23%
Poland	~27	41%
Philippines	~25	27%
South Africa	~20	9%
Chile	~20	43%

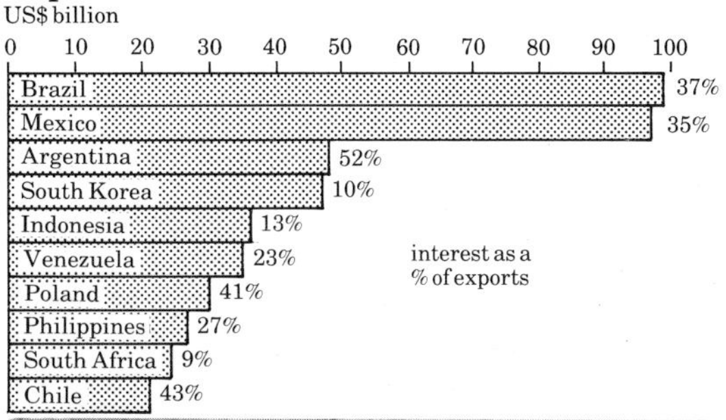

Above: *Following the Live Aid rock concert, which was staged in the UK and US and televised worldwide, Bob Geldof receives Japan's contribution towards famine relief.*

Right: *Indian farmers bring milk to a village collection centre, funded by the World Bank; the centre also gives advice and technical assistance.*

Above: *A metal workshop in Zaire, supported by Oxfam, makes watering cans for use on local farms. Self-help schemes like this aim to prevent famine and poverty at source.*

Above: *Another World Bank project involved setting up a ropeway in Nepal for carrying food and farm supplies.*

1 What is aid?
2 Why do the richer, developed countries give aid to the LDCs?
3 Why do LDCs accept aid?
4 Why is aid given in different ways?
5 What circumstances prevent all aid given from reaching its destination?
6 If governments allocate a proportion of their budget to providing aid, why do charities such as Oxfam and Save the Children need to exist? And why was Bob Geldof's Live Aid necessary?
Class activity: Debate the motion 'Charity begins at home'.

Manufacturers to the world

> Economic achievement can depend on human resources even more than on natural resources.

At a disadvantage

From an economic point of view, Japan has many disadvantages but one major asset – its people.

- Japan's natural disadvantages include: being a chain of volcanic islands in an earthquake belt; coasts prone to tsunami (tidal wave) and typhoon damage; a shortage of flat terrain for agriculture and industry (only 14 per cent of land area can be farmed); difficult communications because of mountains and forests (covering 68 per cent of land area).
- Japan's human disadvantages include: isolation from the outside world until Commodore Perry's US naval expedition arrived in 1853; a feudal society until 1871, and an Emperor-god up to 1947; total defeat in 1945 following atomic bomb destruction of Hiroshima and Nagasaki.

Above: *A 200-year isolationist policy, forbidding all foreign contact, came to an end when Commodore Perry arrived with a fleet of US warships to demand trade agreements. Defenceless Japan could not refuse. To impress the Japanese, Perry brought industrial products – like this model locomotive – as gifts.*

Left: *Two Japanese walking through the ruins of Hiroshima – target, in August 1945, of the world's first atomic bomb. Over 130,000 people were killed or injured.*

Human achievements

Left: *A road viaduct under construction – one of many engineering projects helping to improve communications. In the foreground, flooded rice fields: 100 years ago, agriculture employed 80% of the 35 m population; today, only 9% of 120 m.*

Right: *Japan has become a rich and virtually classless society. In 1940 national income per person was about £40 p.a. Today it is £5843 (the UK's is £4719). It is westernized in many ways. Businessmen wear suits. Occasionally, women (unliberated by western standards) still wear kimonos.*

Left: *Like many industrial sites the Mitsui shipyard at Chiba, south-east of Tokyo, uses land reclaimed from the sea. Shipbuilding and other heavy industries were developed after World War II; today, Japan ranks as the world's second largest economy (after the US) and its largest manufacturer. Industrial giants, such as the Mitsui company, dominate much of Japanese business.*

Anatomy of success

There are many theories to explain Japan's economic success.

Traditions dating from the feudal society mean that people are disciplined and loyal to their companies.

Education is highly competitive from kindergarten onwards: 90 per cent of 15 year-olds stay on at school while Japan's universities produce ten times more engineers than Britain's.

Large firms offer employment for life, company housing and hospitals.

Many small, entrepreneurial firms supply larger manufacturers.

There is a team spirit that may have its origins in the communal efforts necessary to grow paddy-field rice. Businesses operate by consensus.

Above: *The whole world is one market for Japanese companies like Canon. These ads are for cameras in China, copiers in the USA and typewriters in Spain.*

Above: *Japan's highly-educated workforce allows companies to take on increasingly complex projects. New industrial frontiers include space communications, seabed-mining, robots, aircraft, and electronics. This is a meteorological satellite built by NEC.*

Japanese companies are expert at:
- Development: As yet Japan has not produced many original inventions. But Japanese engineers are constantly improving products. Video tape recorders (VTRs) were first produced in America; they were expensive and so for professionals only. Japanese companies turned VTRs into consumer products and now have 90 per cent of the world market (£8 bn p.a.).
- Investment: Factories are constantly overhauled. Over 60 per cent of Japan's plant machinery is under five years old, while 60 per cent of America's is over ten years old.
- Marketing: Japan treats the globe as its market, selling the same cars, cameras, hi-fi systems, photocopiers and other high-value products worldwide.

Trading upmarket

Japanese manufacturers are constantly developing new products and markets. They leave older technologies to subsidiaries in other countries (Sony TVs in Wales) or less-developed competitors (South Korean shipyards). To develop products and markets requires research, capital, management and marketing skills – all available from Japan's human resources.
- VTRs are now old technology, made at low cost in many parts of the world. So Japan is reducing its own output and concentrating on more sophisticated products. This is called trading upmarket.
- This process happens throughout Japanese industry. Computer manufacturers are racing the Americans to produce fifth-generation machines with artificial intelligence.

Japan and the world

Japan's economic success has had a profound effect on the rest of the world. It has also made Japan re-examine its role in international politics. Japan is a democracy and an ally of the US but, so far, has maintained a low-profile foreign policy.

In spite of economic progress, many problems remain. Japan is still heavily dependent on old technology: steel, cars, electrical goods and machine tools make up 74 per cent of exports.

Japanese trade surpluses with the US and Europe are causing anger in countries which Japan needs as markets. To assure future markets, Japanese companies are investing in overseas factories. Investment and aid projects are not enough to prevent criticism of Japan's trade surplus with LDCs.

- Japan's importance is shifting the economic centre of world trade from the Atlantic (Europe and US East Coast) to the Pacific. The Pacific Basin is the world's fastest-growing region. It has technological leadership from Japan and California; raw materials from Australia, Canada and Siberia; NICs in Taiwan, Hong Kong, South Korea; and vast markets in China and South America.

---

1 List Japan's disadvantages.
2 How has Japan overcome its:
a) topographical barriers to transport and communications?
b) lack of flat land for industry?
3 'Let's put our strength and minds together, Doing our best to promote production, Sending our goods to the people of the world...' How does this extract from the Matsushita Electric Company song illustrate: a) the discipline of the workforce? b) the Japanese group ethic? c) worldwide marketing outlook?
4 Explain 'trading upmarket'.

Migration of labour

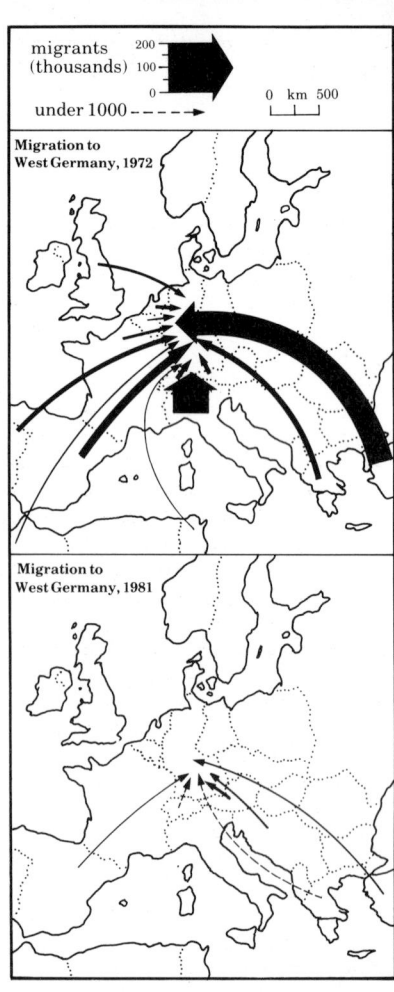

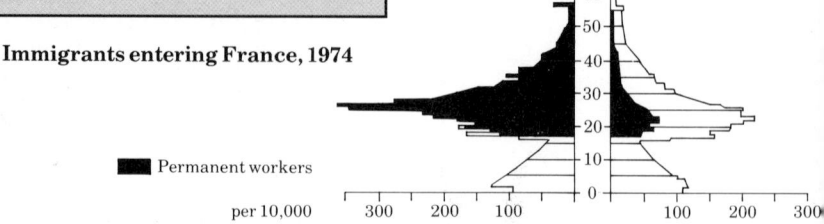

Uneven levels of economic development generate migration flows between poorer and richer areas of the world.

Immigrants entering France, 1974

Permanent workers per 10,000

Migration to West Germany, 1972

Migration to West Germany, 1981

Guest workers of Europe

Mass migrations of peoples form an important part of European history. This century has seen ethnic groups such as the Jews flee Nazism and other oppressive regimes; some 25 million people were made homeless by World War II.

Since then, the pattern of migration has involved the less well-off populations – from Mediterranean countries and former colonies of European countries – seeking their fortunes in the industrial economies of northern Europe. The pattern has several obvious characteristics:

- Large numbers of people were involved: 12.6 m into the EEC. Almost 2 m came from Turkey; over 2 m from North Africa; around 3 m from India, Pakistan and Bangladesh.
- Migration took place over large distances (Turks and Yugoslavs went to West Germany; North Africans and Portuguese to France).
- Initially, most migrants were men. Later their families came. Of the 12.6 million, about half are workers.
- The majority of immigrants were unskilled and filled employment gaps left by the native population, unwilling to take dirty, low paid or low status jobs. Their arrival was encouraged in the boom years of the 1950s and 1960s, when there was a shortage of labour in Europe.
- The authorities expected migrants to be short-term visitors, but many have chosen to remain in their adopted countries – or cannot afford to return home.

Immigrants in western Europe		
	Immigrants (millions)	% of population
West Germany	5.0	8
France	4.5	8
Britain	2.8	5
Switzerland	1.0	15
Belgium	0.85	8.5

Since the oil crisis

By 1973 France and Germany were recruiting fewer foreign workers.

Above: *Demonstration by immigrant workers in Paris against compulsory repatriation. Lacking skills, immigrants are often the first to become unemployed in a recession. They frequently do jobs which are dirty or dangerous. Scandals have revealed exploitation of immigrants in Germany.*

Above: *These shanty huts are near Nice, on the south coast of France. Bad housing can lead to poor health. Immigrants' language and religion (many North Africans in France are Muslims) often cut them off from host communities. Their situation is made worse by racist attitudes amongst the majority.*

Immigrant occupations

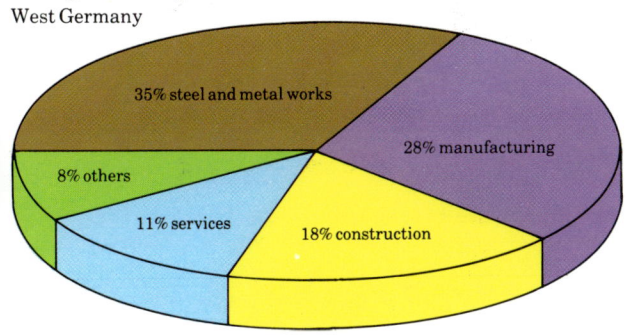

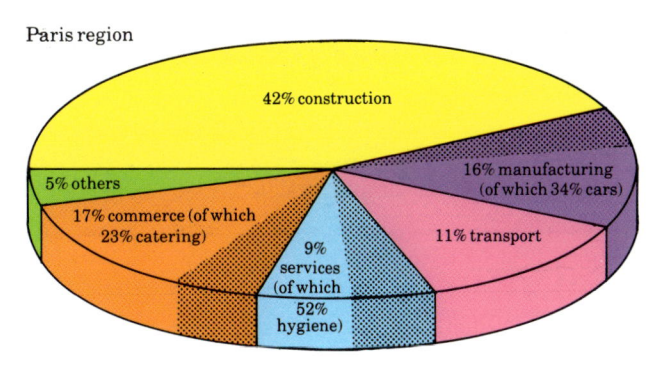

West Germany:
- 35% steel and metal works
- 28% manufacturing
- 18% construction
- 11% services
- 8% others

Paris region:
- 42% construction
- 16% manufacturing (of which 34% cars)
- 11% transport
- 9% services (of which 52% hygiene)
- 17% commerce (of which 23% catering)
- 5% others

Above: *There is a distinct pattern to the type of jobs done by immigrants, which segregates them from the rest of society.*

Then OPEC doubled oil prices and this caused a recession in industry.
- The immigrant (or guest worker, *Gastarbeiter*, in German) began to compete with the native population for increasingly scarce jobs. Youth unemployment among immigrants in Germany is now at 60 per cent.
- This has raised tension between the host and immigrant communities. In places this developed into outbreaks of racial violence, especially in France. A poll in 1982 found that 65 per cent of Germans thought all immigrant workers ought to be sent home.
- But the immigrants form an important part of the labour force. If they leave, certain sectors of host economies would have problems.
- There has been some return migration, but many workers going home find there are no jobs for them in their own countries.
- Today all host countries have reduced immigration to almost nil. However, an immigrant's close relatives can still gain entry. So can people claiming political asylum.

Immigrants become residents

Most immigrants to France and West Germany have been segregated from the rest of society by their work and where they live.
- Particular sectors of French and German industry are heavily dependent on foreign labour. At the Ford plant near Cologne almost half the workforce of 33,000 is non-German and 11,500 are Turkish. In the Renault factories near Paris 40 per cent of the workforce are immigrants.
- Most immigrants live in large towns and within certain districts of those towns. For example, 40 per cent of all foreigners in France live in the Ile de France region surrounding Paris.
- This segregation is unlikely to last in its present form. In 1973 only 20 per cent of immigrants spoke German. But now, the children of immigrants have been educated in the host countries and speak their languages perfectly. Thus they do not face exactly the same employment problems as their parents. In West Germany there are 1.2 million children of immigrants under the age of 16; half are of Turkish origin.

The 12 m immigrant workers in western Europe have now become a permanent part of the population, even if many still live under great social and economic disadvantages.

Improving relations

A number of policies have been put forward to improve relations between immigrant and host communities. Here are some of them:
- **Repatriation:** Extremists have suggested compulsory repatriation. In 1980, France introduced a measure – since repealed – to repatriate those without papers. Both France and Germany have offered immigrants financial incentives to leave.
- **Rotation:** Short-term labour contracts, with migrant workers taking turns at jobs in host countries.
- **Integration:** Immigrants accept the host country's way of life and are assimilated into the host society.
- **Multi-culturalism:** Migrant and host communities keep their own cultures, respect each others' and extend tolerance to everyone in a multi-ethnic society.

Above: *Many immigrants experience outright hostility from host populations, especially in times of unemployment. These immigrants are clearing up their dormitory area at Vitry-sur-Seine, near Paris, after 50 men vandalized and bulldozed it on Christmas Eve. The dormitory housed 300 men from Mali.*

1 Why do workers migrate?
2 What are the origins of recent migrants to France and Germany?
3 Why do most migrants congregate in ethnic groups in or near the central areas of the larger cities forming ghettos? Describe the conditions found in these districts. How are these likely to affect the attitudes of the migrants who mainly come from rural areas in their home countries? What factors might eventually reverse ethnic segregation?
4 Why are Western European governments reluctant to repatriate immigrants?
5 Why do tensions arise between host and immigrant communities?
6 Imagine you were a migrant worker faced with the choice of staying in France or Germany or going home. Explain what you would choose to do and why.
7 What are the advantages of a multi-cultural, multi-ethnic society? How can it be achieved?

Holiday economics

PATTERNS

Most countries attempt to balance their tourist budgets.

Balancing the books

Tourism, bringing in over £10 bn a year, accounts for a large part of Britain's invisible trade. Like most countries the UK tries to ensure that tourist income (money spent by foreign travellers in the UK) is at least as great as expenditure (money spent by Britons abroad). If overseas visitors spend more in Britain than British holidaymakers spend abroad, there is a **surplus** on the tourist budget. But if the British spend more abroad than visitors spend in the UK, there is a **deficit**. A tourist budget surplus or deficit has an important effect on the balance of payments.

Right: *This graph, using 1983 statistics, shows a deficit on Britain's tourist budget. But tourism in the UK is now a growth industry. In 1985, spending by 14.6 m overseas visitors was up 19% over the previous year to give Britain its first tourist budget surplus: £617 m.*

Below: *Sightseeing outside Buckingham Palace. There is a heavy imbalance in the UK's internal tourist budget: 90% of foreign visitors come to England (rather than Scotland, Wales or Ulster) and spend half their time and two-thirds of their money in London.*

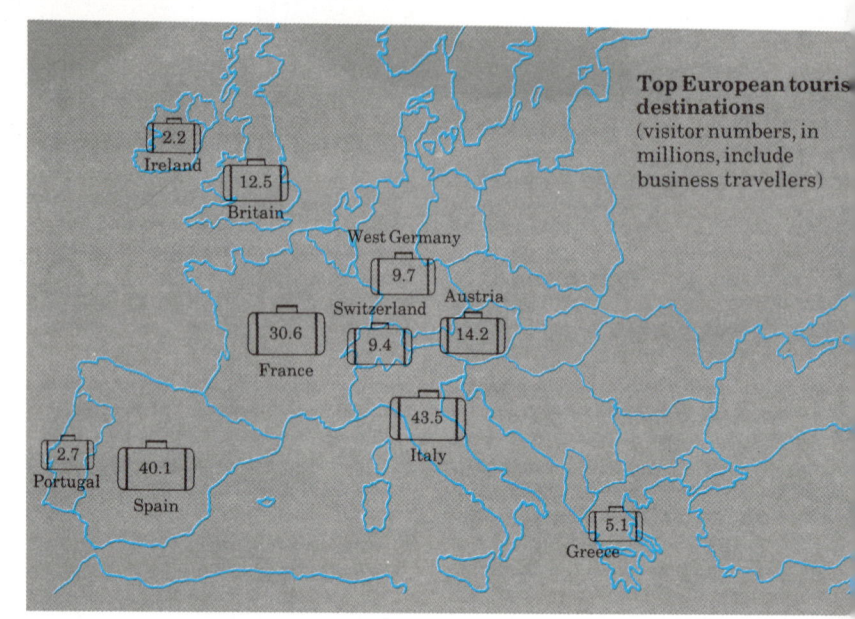

Top European tourist destinations (visitor numbers, in millions, include business travellers)

- Ireland 2.2
- Britain 12.5
- West Germany 9.7
- Switzerland 9.4
- Austria 14.2
- France 30.6
- Italy 43.5
- Portugal 2.7
- Spain 40.1
- Greece 5.1

Britain's tourist budget

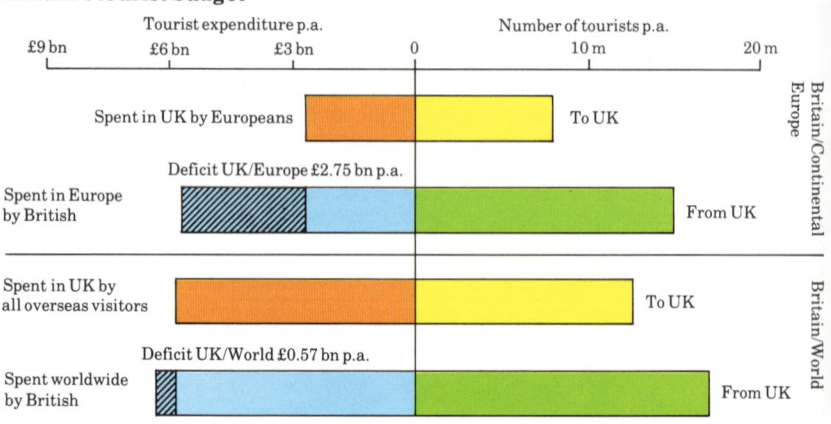

Britain/Continental Europe
- Spent in UK by Europeans — To UK
- Deficit UK/Europe £2.75 bn p.a.
- Spent in Europe by British — From UK

Britain/World
- Spent in UK by all overseas visitors — To UK
- Deficit UK/World £0.57 bn p.a.
- Spent worldwide by British — From UK

Factors affecting the tourist budget

Transport: British airlines and travel companies help to balance the tourist budget by selling over £1 bn worth of services abroad each year. Heathrow is the world's busiest international airport.

Exchange rate: When the value of the £ falls against other currencies, more overseas visitors come to Britain because it is cheaper than other destinations. But Britons find other countries more expensive so fewer go abroad. This boosts the budget towards a surplus. When the value of the £ rises, the reverse happens.

Publicity: The British Tourist Authority spends £4.5 m p.a. promoting Britain as a tourist destination. But reputation counts as much as advertising. Poor service, bad food, street crime and terrorism deter tourists, in spite of other attractions.

Weather: The UK's cool, wet climate encourages Britons to take holidays in warmer places, so normally creating a budget deficit. Britain cannot compete with Mediterranean lands for beach holidays; it must rely on attractions like historic buildings, art collections and London theatres.

The Hajj

Just as the Christian Church requires religious observance on Holy Days, the Islamic religion demands that all able-bodied Muslims should make the Hajj, the pilgrimage to Mecca, at least once in their lifetime, if they can afford to do so.

■ As a result, during the last month of the Islamic year, the population of Mecca, Mohammed's birthplace, trebles. Over a million pilgrims come from all parts of the Muslim world. This influx gives Mecca (and Saudi Arabia) a vast surplus on its tourist budget.

■ A great deal of money has been invested in Mecca's transport, accommodation, health, food and water services. Yet almost the entire tourist income is generated during one month of the year.

Above: *Mecca (population 500,000) is located in the arid Sirat Mountains, where rainfall is less than 30 mm p.a. Temperatures reach 45° C in summer. In a normal month Mecca uses 785 m litres of water; during the Hajj it uses 2500 m litres. Water comes from 100 km away.*

Above: *The great mosque has been enlarged to allow 300,000 pilgrims to walk round the Kaaba, built by Abraham and Ishmael and venerated as Islam's holiest shrine. The seasonality of the Hajj means that all facilities, from mosques to hospitals, must be able to deal with large numbers of people; yet, they are only fully used for one month a year.*

Below: *In spite of modern rebuilding, Mecca has a population density of 12,000 per km², so most pilgrims are housed in tent cities. Buses are provided to take pilgrims to the great mosque in the city centre and to other holy sites outside Mecca. New roads and pedestrian walkways have been built to ease congestion.*

Above: *Pilgrims once came to Mecca by camel caravan. Today they fly. But as the terrain around Mecca is too mountainous for an international airport, pilgrim flights come to Jedda, 70 km away; passengers transfer to Mecca by bus. Increasing affluence in Arab countries and modern transport methods have increased pilgrim traffic to 1 m, from only 60,000 in 1946.*

1 What is a tourist budget?
2 How does a surplus or deficit on a country's tourist budget affect its balance of payments?
3 Why is tourism an invisible export?
4 Explain how imbalances arise in tourist budgets and why certain countries and places within those countries may have a surplus or a deficit.
5 Why does a country like West Germany have a larger total of visitors than a holiday destination like Greece?

Catching votes

Political patterns should reflect changing population distributions.

One person, one vote

Parliamentary democracy is based on the principle of equal voting rights for all adults, regardless of race, sex, income, or religion. The government is then elected by a majority of votes. But this ideal is difficult to achieve. British parliamentary democracy has been developing for over 700 years, yet it is still far from perfect.

■ The territory which one Member of Parliament represents is called a **constituency**. Constituency boundaries are drawn to make the number of voters in each constituency as equal as possible. For constituencies to have equal numbers of voters, they must have very unequal areas. In the countryside voters are more widely dispersed than in cities.

■ The way in which constituency boundaries are set is crucial to fair elections, because the winner is the party with the most seats, not necessarily with the most votes. In Britain this often means that a government is elected by a minority of votes over the whole country.

■ In most other European countries there is a form of **proportional representation** (PR). This is a voting system by which seats in parliament are allocated in proportion to the number of votes cast for each party.

Changing the pattern

Constituency boundaries have to be changed frequently, because of population movements. If changes are not made, one party may gain an unfair political advantage.

The map and tables show the electoral boundaries of the London Borough of Redbridge, and describe how the people of each ward have tended to vote in recent elections.

Redbridge: 1981 Census

Tenure of houses

	Loxford	Monkhams	Hainault	Valentines
Owner-occupied	71%	86%	43%	59%
Local authority	15%	7%	56%	5%
Private-rented	14%	7%	1%	36%

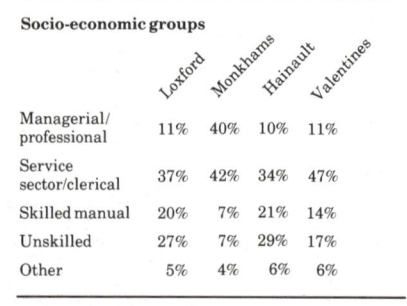

Socio-economic groups

	Loxford	Monkhams	Hainault	Valentines
Managerial/professional	11%	40%	10%	11%
Service sector/clerical	37%	42%	34%	47%
Skilled manual	20%	7%	21%	14%
Unskilled	27%	7%	29%	17%
Other	5%	4%	6%	6%

Above: *Wards are the basic unit of the British electoral system for both local and parliamentary elections. Redbridge, an outer London borough with a population of 225,000, has 21 wards. Each ward returns three councillors and has between 9000 and 12,000 voters.*

Redbridge ward by ward – housing and voting trends

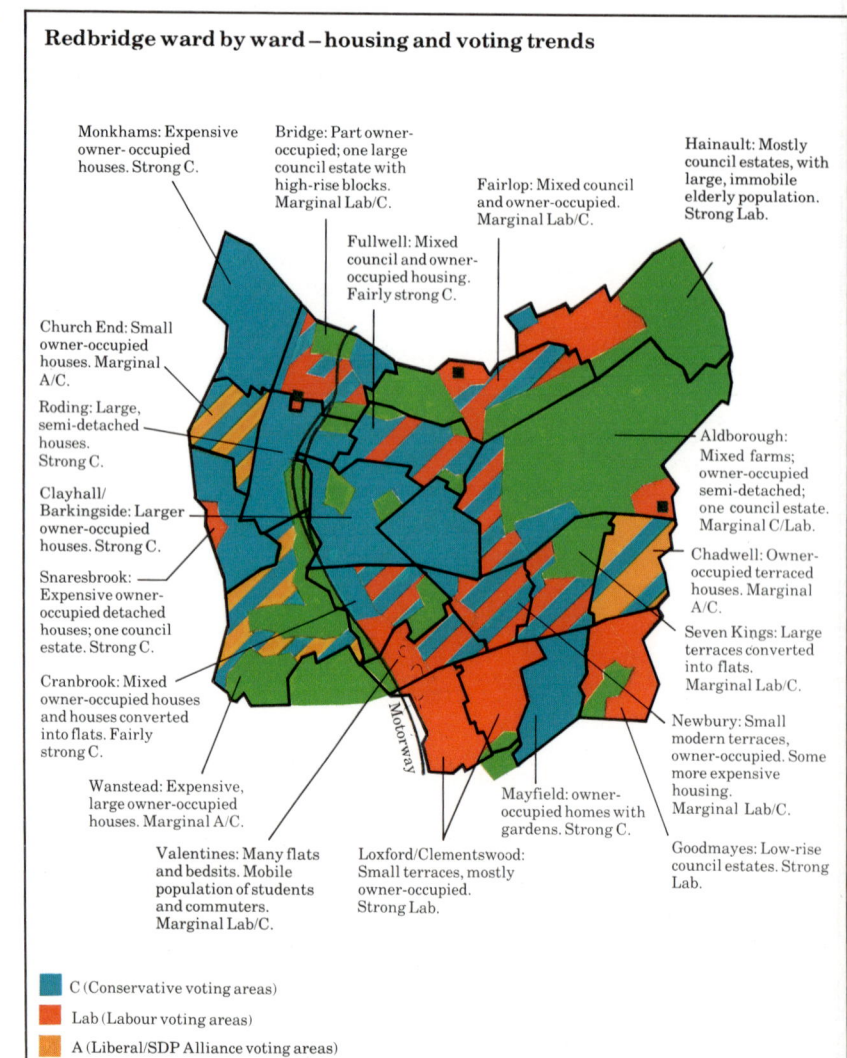

Monkhams: Expensive owner-occupied houses. Strong C.

Bridge: Part owner-occupied; one large council estate with high-rise blocks. Marginal Lab/C.

Fairlop: Mixed council and owner-occupied. Marginal Lab/C.

Hainault: Mostly council estates, with large, immobile elderly population. Strong Lab.

Fullwell: Mixed council and owner-occupied housing. Fairly strong C.

Church End: Small owner-occupied houses. Marginal A/C.

Roding: Large, semi-detached houses. Strong C.

Clayhall/Barkingside: Larger owner-occupied houses. Strong C.

Snaresbrook: Expensive owner-occupied detached houses; one council estate. Strong C.

Cranbrook: Mixed owner-occupied houses and houses converted into flats. Fairly strong C.

Wanstead: Expensive, large owner-occupied houses. Marginal A/C.

Valentines: Many flats and bedsits. Mobile population of students and commuters. Marginal Lab/C.

Loxford/Clementswood: Small terraces, mostly owner-occupied. Strong Lab.

Mayfield: owner-occupied homes with gardens. Strong C.

Aldborough: Mixed farms; owner-occupied semi-detached; one council estate. Marginal C/Lab.

Chadwell: Owner-occupied terraced houses. Marginal A/C.

Seven Kings: Large terraces converted into flats. Marginal Lab/C.

Newbury: Small modern terraces, owner-occupied. Some more expensive housing. Marginal Lab/C.

Goodmayes: Low-rise council estates. Strong Lab.

■ C (Conservative voting areas)
■ Lab (Labour voting areas)
■ A (Liberal/SDP Alliance voting areas)
■ Open space
■ Council estate

Distorting the pattern

In most countries the initiative for boundary changes lies with the government. As a result, it is possible to abuse the system and manipulate boundary changes to favour one party.

■ In a marginal constituency, where there is no clear majority, it is possible to change the boundaries so as to include areas where people favour the government, and exclude areas opposing it. This manipulation of boundaries to influence an election result is called gerrymandering.

Left: *These diagrams represent the voting intentions of people living in two local authority areas with five and four wards respectively. If each party altered the ward boundaries as it wished, it could influence the election result in its favour.*

Constituency A: 64R; 28L; 8C

Ward 5
18V;12R

Ward 1
22V;14R

```
L R R R L R R L L
L L R R L C C C R L
L L C R R L L R C R
R C R R R R R L L L
R R L L R R R R R L
L L R R L R R R R R
R R R C R L R R R R
R L R L R L R R R R
R R R L R R R R L R
R R L R C R R R R R
```

Ward 2
18V;12C

Ward 3
19V;12R

Ward 4
22V;14C

Constituency B: 38L; 26R; 16C

Ward 1
20V

```
L C L L R R L L R C
L L R L R R L R C L
C L C R R L L L C L
C C L L R R R R C R
R R L C L L R C R C
C C R R L L L L L L
R R L L L L L C C
L R L L L L L L L R
```

Ward 3
20V

Ward 2
20V

Ward 4
20V

L = Left wing party
R = Right wing party
C = Centre party
V = 1 voter

Rules: 1 There are five wards. 2 Each ward must have at least ten voters. 3 Wards cannot be broken up into fragments. 4 The winning party must have a simple majority – that is, 50 per cent + 1 (no coalitions). Result shown: All five wards have a Right wing majority.

Rules: 1 There are four wards. 2 Each ward must have exactly 20 voters. 3 Wards cannot be broken up into fragments. 4 No voter can have a boundary on more than two sides. 5 All ward boundaries must be vertical or horizontal. 6 No coalitions.

1 Look at Constituency A. How would you change the boundaries to give the Left wing party four out of five seats?
2 Look at Constituency A. By changing boundaries, how many seats is it possible for the Centre party to win?
3 Look at Constituency B. Arrange the boundaries so that the Left wing party wins all seats.
4 Look at Constituency B. How would you arrange the boundaries so that the Right wing party wins three seats?
5 Look at Constituency B. Arrange the boundaries so that the Centre party wins two seats.

---

1 Look at Bridge Ward. The Boundary Commission drew a straight line division between Bridge and Roding Wards. Why did the Labour Party want to include Broadmead Estate – which includes tower blocks – in Bridge Ward and not Roding?
2 Why might the Conservative Party want the council estate in Aldborough Ward transferred to become part of the borough next door?
3 If the Council had housing land for sale in Newbury Ward how could it be developed:
a) to help the Conservative Party?
b) to help the Labour Party?
4 Many council houses have been sold in Fairlop Ward. How might this help the Conservative Party?
5 There is usually a very low turnout of voters at elections in Valentines Ward. Why do you think this would be?
6 Chadwell Ward has the highest owner-occupancy rate (89%) in the Borough. Why is it a marginal ward?

Joh's gerrymander

In Queensland, Australia, the National/Country Party, led by Sir Johannes Bjelke-Petersen, has never held more than 28 per cent of the vote. Its support has been as low as 19.3 per cent. Yet, in coalition with the Liberal Party, the National/Country Party has been in power since 1957.

■ The National/Country Party has achieved this by arranging the boundaries to its advantage. Instead of the state being divided into 82 constituencies of about 14,000 voters each, the rural constituencies have as few as 8000 voters while urban constituencies have up to 26,500. In rural areas, the National/Country Party is dominant; urban areas are Labor Party strongholds. This means it takes three times as many city voters to elect one Labor member, as rural voters to elect one National/Country Party member.

■ Boundaries are set by the ruling party. No objections are allowed. In this way opposition voters are locked up in densely-populated city constituencies that are small in area, while National/Country Party voters are distributed in small numbers over large areas of the outback.

Right: *Australian Labor Party publicity opposing the Queensland gerrymander, organized by the National/Country Party. The ALP successfully opposed similar gerrymanders in the States of Victoria and South Australia.*

53

River patterns

> Natural processes tend to create predictable patterns.

Rocks and rivers

The shape of a river system, its **drainage pattern**, is dictated by the type of rock over which the water flows. There are two main types of drainage pattern.

- **Dendritic:** This is shaped like a tree. The main stream is joined by large tributaries, which in turn are joined by small tributaries. This pattern occurs where the underlying rocks are of equal resistance to water throughout the drainage basin.
- **Trellis:** This occurs where the rocks are of unequal resistance. The river follows the line of weakest rock. It cuts its bed deeply, capturing other streams flowing off harder rock bands. The result is a shape similar to that of a garden trellis.
- Most river courses, since they flow through different geological areas, contain examples of both patterns.
- All drainage patterns have been modified over long periods by natural events such as mountain building.

Dendritic drainage pattern

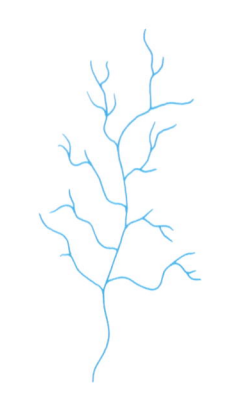

Trellis drainage pattern

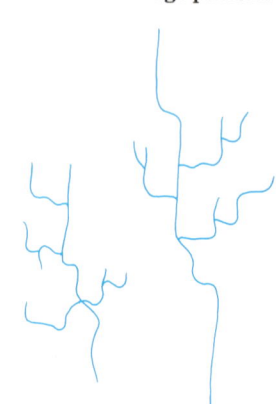

Swinging rivers

Mark Twain wrote in 1883: 'In the space of 170 years the lower Mississippi has shortened itself by 242 miles. This is an average of over 1½ miles a year. Therefore any calm person, who is not blind or idiotic, can see that in the old Oolitic Silurian Period, just a million years ago next November, the lower Mississippi was 1,300,000 miles long and stuck out over half the Gulf of Mexico like a fishing rod. And by the same token any person can see that 742 years from now the lower Mississippi will be only 1¾ miles long.' (Life on the Mississippi).

- Rivers follow predictable patterns, not simply in their shape, but also in their behaviour – although we cannot foretell exactly when they will do what. Mark Twain's statistics were a little eccentric but, as a river-boat pilot, he knew that river beds are never stable.

- As a river slows down in its lower course, it drops its load of suspended material. Gradually this **deposition** builds up the level of the river bed. So, when the water run-off increases, there is a flood.
- Every time the river overflows the flood is momentarily checked at the edge of the channel. As a result the coarsest material is dropped and forms a low bank or **levee**.
- During floods, layers of fertile alluvium are deposited over the river's flood plain.
- When a river reaches the sea, its flow stops and its load is deposited in a **delta**, which is usually fan-shaped. The deposited material silts up the mouth, unless removed by strong tides. The obstruction promotes the division of the river into many **distributaries**.

Man against the Mississippi

In 1717 a company run by John Law, a Scottish banker in Paris, was given control of Louisiana by the French Crown. One of its first actions was to build New Orleans on swamps of unstable alluvium near the mouth of the Mississippi. Unfortunately eighteenth century engineers did not understand the behavioural patterns of rivers. No one realized that the Mississippi had:

- a minor flood every year;
- a major flood every few years;
- an extraordinary flood about every ten years;
- and a disastrous flood once a century.

Today, costly engineering works are necessary to control the river. If left to its natural pattern the Mississippi would flow to the sea via the shorter Atchafalaya river, leaving New Orleans – people and industry – without fresh water.

Left: *A Mississippi steamer loading cotton in the 1870s. Plantations, set behind the river's natural levees, flourished on the rich alluvial soil but were constantly menaced by floods.*

Lower Mississippi and delta, 1986

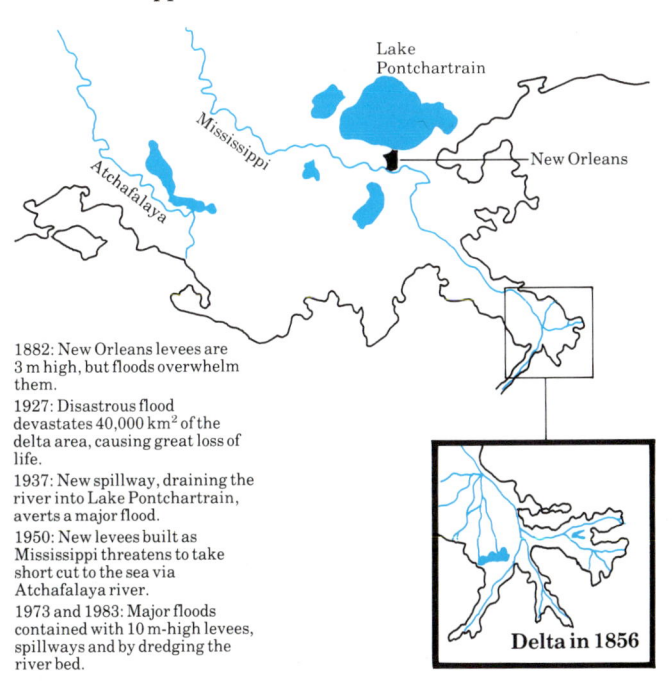

1882: New Orleans levees are 3 m high, but floods overwhelm them.
1927: Disastrous flood devastates 40,000 km² of the delta area, causing great loss of life.
1937: New spillway, draining the river into Lake Pontchartrain, averts a major flood.
1950: New levees built as Mississippi threatens to take short cut to the sea via Atchafalaya river.
1973 and 1983: Major floods contained with 10 m-high levees, spillways and by dredging the river bed.

Delta in 1856

Left: *The Mississippi has a bird's foot delta, not a fan-shaped one. The river extends out into the sea in lobes (1856). Later, the space between the lobes is filled in. Today, the delta covers an area as large as Great Britain.*

Below: *During the 1937 floods, chain gangs of convicts were drafted in to work on the levees.*

China's sorrow

The Hwang Ho or Yellow river is known as 'China's sorrow' because it carries away vast amounts of valuable soil and causes terrible floods.

■ The river is so powerful that, at any moment, it is carrying some 1600 million tonnes of sediment in suspension – more than any other river in the world. It accounts for 60 per cent of all sediment stripped from the land of China and 10 per cent of all sediment removed from the Earth's surface.

■ Most of the sediment comes from unconsolidated **loess** deposits in the middle Yellow river basin. In this region there is not enough rain (300-500 mm p.a.) to support dense vegetation that could stabilize the hills.

■ Half the river's load is deposited in the delta. The progressive extension of the delta reduces the river's gradient, so that more deposition takes place upstream. This raises the level of the river bed, causing it to flood. During floods in 1958 over one million people worked to raise the banks by one metre along 600 km of river.

■ Silt deposition in the lower course of a river causes the stream to split up into a **braided pattern** of interlaced distributaries. The main river can change course very suddenly with disastrous results. Once, the Hwang Ho shifted its main channel by 120 m in one day. The 1887 flood caused by a change of channel drowned over a million people.

■ Further upstream deposition has choked reservoirs built to control floods (up to 40 per cent of the volume of water is silt): one reservoir lost 20 per cent capacity in three years through silting. Terracing, afforestation and check dams in gullies have helped, but the power of the Hwang Ho is still largely uncontrolled.

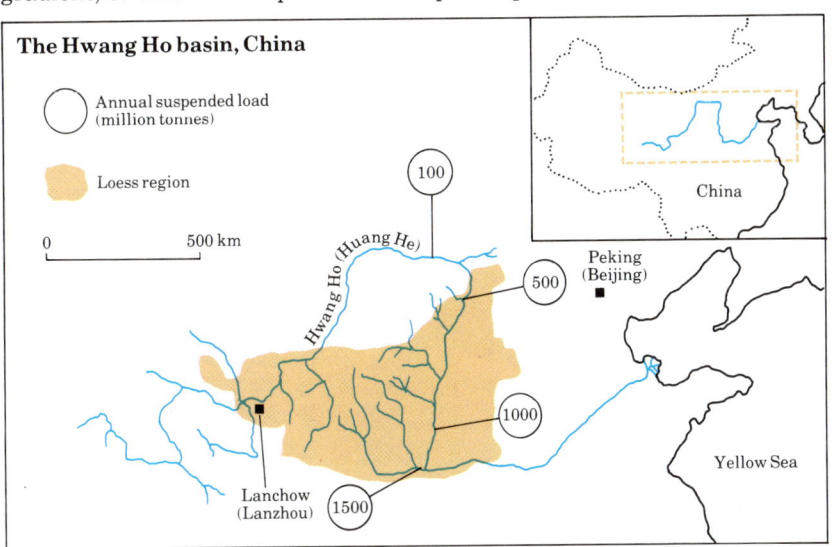

The Hwang Ho basin, China

○ Annual suspended load (million tonnes)

Loess region

0 — 500 km

1 Why would a boat pilot like Mark Twain need to understand the behaviour of rivers?
2 How could each of these events influence a river's flow: a) a heavy thunderstorm? b) a mud flow following a volcanic eruption? c) a severe drought? d) a large dam on the main channel? e) a new housing estate on land formerly used for agriculture?
3 Write paragraphs to explain the connections between the climate region in which the river is located; the type of rock over which the river flows; the course adopted by the river; the river as a potential hazard.

Microclimates

Variations in terrain and human activities can modify climate.

Climate and landscape

The world has various climate zones; within each one all places have similar overall climatic conditions, although large variations can occur inside a zone. These local variations are called **microclimates**. They are often caused by factors present in the natural landscape.

- **Soil type:** Soils affect local climates by their different reactions to the sun's heat: their capacity to store, reflect and conduct it.
- **Aspect and exposure:** Some places are more sheltered than others from the wind; some places are higher and therefore more exposed to cold.
- **Topography:** Deep valleys can help or hinder air flows and thus have a marked effect on temperature.

Right: *A stable layer of cloud, seen here in the Val de Bagnes, Switzerland, characteristically marks the upper limit of temperature inversion.*

Local factors affecting climate

1a Light, sandy soils have lots of air in them. Air is a poor conductor of heat, a good insulator. Sand on a beach can be very hot on the surface, but cool just below.

1b The air above light sandy soils tends to be hot by day and cool at night, as the soil does not release heat to warm it. This makes sandy soils susceptible to frosts and can shorten the growing season by 6-8 weeks.

1c A light-coloured soil reflects the sun's radiation and warms up less rapidly than a dark one. But it magnifies the radiant heat of bright sunshine.

2a Heavy, clay soils hold lots of water. Water is a good conductor of heat and a poor insulator.

2b The air above clay soils is less likely to reach extremes of heat or cold, as the soil cools and warms the air above it slowly.

2c Dark soils, such as clay, get less hot on the surface, but the heat is absorbed deep down. Wet clay soils only dry out by evaporation: at the end of winter, they remain cold and damp longer than light soils like sand and chalk.

3 Vegetation can also modify local climate. Long grass traps air, which is warmer by day and cooler by night than the soil beneath it. This is why on clear, cold nights shallow mists develop over grasslands.

4a Hilltops are more exposed then valley floors. A hilltop may have sunshine, but altitude makes it colder. On average, temperatures decrease by 1°C for every 150 m of height. It is also likely to be windier and wetter than the valley floor.

4b Exposure to wind can alter the local climate dramatically. A temperature of 0°C in still air becomes the equivalent of -15°C in a wind of 75 km/h. This is called the chill factor. Wind can also cause great damage. At 105 km/h it exerts a force of 6 kg per m².

5 A sunny aspect, facing south in the northern hemisphere, or north in the southern hemisphere, makes a place warmer.

6 Snow affects local climate like a light-coloured soil. It reflects up to 80% of the sun's rays. It absorbs little heat, so melts slowly, keeping the land cold. In exposed places drifts form, lasting even longer.

7a The microclimates of valleys depend on how the topography helps or hinders the flow of air.

7b In clear, calm weather air near the ground, affected by the soil surface, cools in the evening and radiates heat into the atmosphere. Cold air, denser than warm air, drains down valley sides, gathering in the bottom to form frost hollows.

7c Moisture in the cool air collects into a cloud which hangs between the valley sides, obscuring the valley floor. During the day, as the air warms up, the cloud lifts. The process can repeat itself with cold air draining into the valley bottom each evening and cloud rising each morning. This is called temperature inversion.

8a In mountain regions the aspect of a valley is an important climatic factor. In the Alps, a north-facing valley side (called **ubac**) receives relatively little sun. It is thus less suitable for farming and habitation, and is often devoted to forestry.

8b The south-facing slope (called **adret**) is warmer as it receives more sun. Villages and fields can be sited higher on an adret slope than on the colder, ubac side of the valley.

Make your own climate

Human activity can also have an effect on local conditions, creating artificial microclimates.
- In flat regions farmers often plant belts of trees to shelter crops from prevailing winds. Wind blows more or less parallel to the ground surface. Its velocity increases with height since air close to the ground is held back by friction. The effectiveness of a shelter belt of trees at right angles to wind direction depends on how impenetrable it is. In places such as the Rhone valley, where the Mistral can reach 130 km/h, shelter belts are used to protect fruit crops and vines.
- Urban areas today are so extensive that they have a significant influence on local climate. Tall buildings create an uneven surface, which increases frictional drag on the wind at lower levels. At the same time the location of tall buildings can create wind funnels and turbulence. As a result, gale force gusts may occur, blowing vertically as well as horizontally.
- City buildings, warmed by heating inside and by sunshine outside, act like radiators, giving out heat at night when the air temperature falls. This process produces urban heat islands. In calm, clear conditions at night the temperature difference between the rural and urban areas can be up to 5°C.

Above: *Double protection for market-garden crops growing in a commune near Peking. The bamboo fence shelters young plants from cold winds while rush matting, rolled across at night, prevents frost damage.*

Land and sea breezes

Land and water, when exposed to the sun's warmth, heat up and cool down at different rates. The resultant temperature differences generate breezes which blow either from sea to land, or from land to sea.
- On hot summer days an onshore breeze (from sea to land) often develops during the day. At night an offshore breeze blows in the opposite direction. In Indonesia local fishermen, in their sailing boats, rely on this pattern: they go out at night with the offshore breeze and return by day with the onshore breeze.
- Just as daily temperature differences cause microclimatic variations, so annual temperature differences create macroclimatic variations. Large land masses, like India, build up such high temperatures in summer that strong winds are drawn inland from the cooler, surrounding ocean. This is called the monsoon. So powerful are the forces creating monsoons, that they overcome the normal planetary circulation in certain parts of the world. In winter the ocean is warmer than the land so winds blow seawards. Thus winters are generally dry and summers wet.
- Climate in monsoon regions varies from desert to tropical forest. The greatest amount of rain falls on mountainous west coasts. Summer heat and high rainfall makes many monsoon regions suitable for rice. However, monsoon rains can be as unreliable as they are torrential. Cherrapunji, in the monsoon area of Bangladesh, is the world's wettest place with 1270 mm in one month. Yet half the year it is dry.

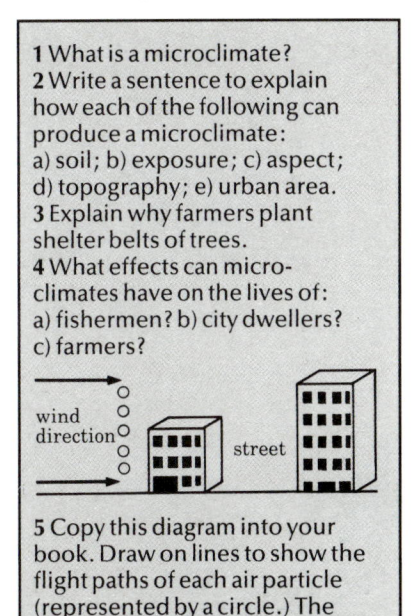

Below: *On average, severe cyclonic storms strike every fifth year in the tropics, causing widespread chaos. Warning systems, including posters like this one from India, aim to reduce the damage.*

---

1 What is a microclimate?
2 Write a sentence to explain how each of the following can produce a microclimate:
a) soil; b) exposure; c) aspect; d) topography; e) urban area.
3 Explain why farmers plant shelter belts of trees.
4 What effects can microclimates have on the lives of:
a) fishermen? b) city dwellers? c) farmers?

5 Copy this diagram into your book. Draw on lines to show the flight paths of each air particle (represented by a circle.) The flight paths should demonstrate the turbulence of wind in cities.

Conservation matters

LANDSCAPES

> The decision to exploit a landscape can raise environmental issues.

All-electric island

A major hydro-electric scheme, planned for a wilderness area in south-west Tasmania, caused great public concern, divided local communities and haunted Australian politics for almost four years.

■ Unlike mainland Australia, Tasmania has limited energy resources: no natural gas, no oil and only small quantities of coal. But its mountain rivers do have enormous water-power potential.

■ Hydro-power first came to Tasmania in 1895. Today, 25 generating hydro-stations with a total capacity of 1931 MW, give Tasmania the largest hydro-electric scheme in Australia.

■ In 1979, the Tasmanian Hydro-Electric Commission outlined plans for further development: a dam and generating station, with 296 MW capacity, on the Lower Gordon river below its junction with the Franklin. The 105-metre high dam would create a lake of 12,000 ha, flooding 35 km of the Franklin river.

Dam under debate

The Commission's proposal brought immediate reaction from conservation groups. Determined to halt the flooding, they campaigned vigorously against the scheme. The arguments covered more than just conservation versus development.

Below: *Map showing the proposed Gordon-below-Franklin (GBF) scheme, designed to re-use water from the large storage areas of lakes Gordon and Pedder which are already harnessed for hydro-power.*

For		Against
At peak construction stage, the scheme will provide 2500 jobs: a bonus for Tasmania's 16,000 unemployed – 12 per cent of the workforce.	**JOBS**	Employment opportunities are for the construction period only; once in operation, the new scheme will require only 30 personnel.
Less than one per cent of the S-W conservation area will be flooded; in particular, none of the region's top beauty spots will be affected.	**ENVIRONMENT**	The new lake and the dam's access road will destroy a unique wildlife area, famed for its rare Huon pines – up to 2000 years old – and limestone gorges.
Archaeologists have nine years to investigate the site before the new lake is created. Any artefacts will be removed and displayed in museums, where they will be more accessible to more people.	**CULTURE**	The lake will flood recently-discovered caves, inhabited by Aborigines around 2000 years ago. Of world significance, they contain 100,000 artefacts covering 5000 years of prehistory.
Although the capital cost of the scheme is high, the end product – electricity – will be cheap. And, Tasmania has no viable alternative to HEP.	**COST**	Hydro-power is no longer cheap. Hydro schemes now use up 52% of the state's capital works expenditure while housing and education have just 7% each.
Launch cruises on the new lake will be a major attraction; a campsite is planned for the dam area, and possibly a motel.	**TOURISM**	The scheme will reduce adventure activities like rafting and bushwalking and remove the wilderness experience for tourists.
Even allowing for an annual increase in demand for electricity of only 2.7 per cent (much lower than on the mainland), current output will not be able to meet requirements by 1990.	**POWER**	Tasmania does not need more electricity especially as major consumers like aluminium smelters and pulp mills have left the island. The state already has too much electricity.

Campaign countdown

- In May 1980 an opinion poll showed that 58 per cent of Tasmanians favoured saving the Franklin and 10,000 people attended a protest march in Hobart.
- In July 1980 the Tasmanian government decided to adopt an alternative dam scheme which would flood a smaller area - but met opposition from within parliament. The situation became deadlocked.
- Meanwhile the 'No dams' campaign gathered momentum. The government finally announced a referendum for December 1981.
- At the referendum, 45 per cent of voters ignored the two official options and wrote 'No dams' across their papers. The government interpreted this as a sign of approval and the Gordon-below-Franklin scheme was given the go-ahead.
- On 14 December 1982, conservation groups set up a blockade of dam construction work.
- That same day, two of the national parks affected were accepted on to the World Heritage list.
- In March 1983, the Labor Party won the federal election and immediately promised to stop the dam. The new government claimed that the Commission was violating an international treaty by building in a World Heritage area.
- In July 1983 the Australian High Court ruled in favour of the Federal government: the dam was abandoned.

Above: *The Irenabyss, a spectacular length of the Franklin, lies upstream of the projected lake and was not threatened by GBF. But other scenic gorges further downstream would have been flooded.*

Above: *Protesters during the blockade in January 1983. A total of 3000 people took part, almost half were arrested. Although the blockade did not succeed in stopping construction work, it made GBF headline news throughout Australia.*

Below: *For the more adventurous, rafting is an exciting way of exploring the Franklin. Conservationists claimed that activities, such as rafting and bushwalking, were threatened by the GBF scheme.*

Above: *There are five kinds of cushion plant in the world, three grow only in Tasmania; flooding by the GBF dam would make them even rarer.*

'The escalating needs of soaring numbers have often driven people to take a short-sighted approach when exploiting natural resources. The toll of this approach has now become glaringly apparent: a long list of hazards and disasters, including soil erosion, desertification, loss of cropland, pollution, deforestation, eco-system degradation and destruction, and extinction of species and varieties. This situation underlines the need for conservation.' (World Conservation Strategy, 1980)

1 There are many 'development' case-histories in this book.
a) Find an example for each 'hazard and disaster' listed above.
b) What was the development motive in each case? c) What were the conservation interests?
2 Take a specific activity, such as forestry or mining, and explain why conservation should be an integral part of exploitation.

Desert takeover

LANDSCAPES

> Marginal human and natural influences can destroy fragile environments.

Global threat

Desertification – the deterioration of productive land into desert-like waste – affects over 100 countries: it threatens 35 per cent of the Earth's land surface and 19 per cent of its population. One of the worst-hit areas is sub-Saharan Africa, from Mauritania in the west to Ethiopia in the east: here the Sahara is spreading southwards at a rate of 150 km a year.

Right: *Although the problem does occur in developed nations, desertification is worse in LDCs which depend on subsistence farming.*

Risk of desertification
- Very high
- High
- Moderate
- Existing deserts

Desertification around the world

The human factor

The main cause of desertification is the misuse of land: overcultivation, overgrazing, deforestation and poor irrigation. The main cause of land misuse is overpopulation.

- Africa has the highest population growth in the world: in four out of five countries, populations will double in 20 years.
- More mouths to feed means growing more crops; so cultivation extends into low-rainfall 'marginal' zones previously reserved for grazing animals.
- Traditionally, long fallow periods allowed dry croplands to regain their fertility. Now, continuous cultivation exhausts the soil and accelerates erosion: each year, Ethiopia's cultivated areas lose more than 1000 million tonnes of topsoil.
- Worn-out soil cannot support intensive cultivation and crop yields fall: Sudan produces 50 per cent less grain per hectare than it did ten years ago.
- More mouths to feed also means raising more livestock like cows, sheep and goats. But with the loss of grazing lands to arable farming, there is not enough pasture. Overgrazing – too many animals on too little land – destroys natural vegetation and encourages erosion.
- Deforestation is a key problem. Where trees and shrubs are destroyed, wind and water tear away the exposed topsoil to make new deserts.
- Most trees are cut down for fuel: over 90 per cent of people in Africa's developing countries depend on wood for cooking and heating.
- Bad irrigation turns farmland into waterlogged, salty wastes where nothing will grow; (if irrigation raises the water table, sub-soil salts come to the surface and cause salinization). In the Sahel, as much land is being devastated through irrigation as is being improved.

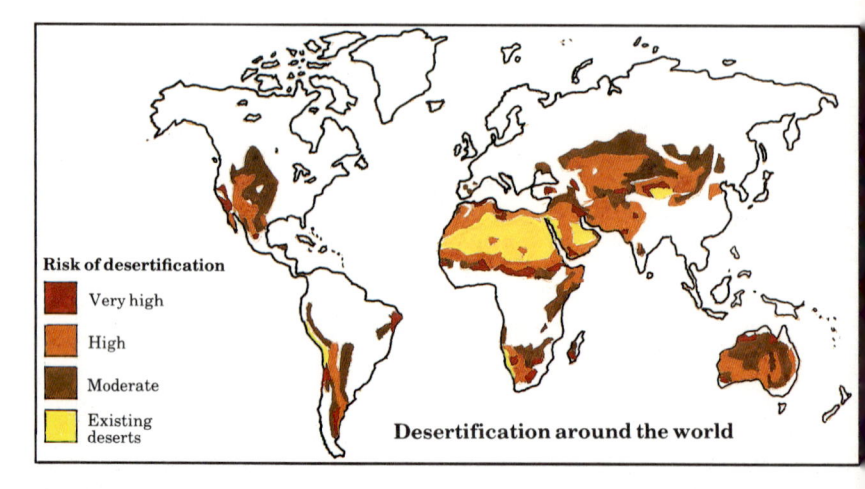

Nature's role

In the desertification story, drought is a trigger rather than a cause. It speeds up the process of land destruction. The worldwide drought of 1970-1985 is the worst in the past 150 years. Its effects have been disastrous, particularly in Ethiopia and Sudan: millions of people and animals have died; millions more are at risk.

- Rainfall levels in 1984 were the lowest in 20 years.
- Without rain, natural vegetation dies off leaving soil prone to erosion.
- Many waterholes and wells dry up, increasing the pressure on others: the surrounding land is overgrazed and its topsoil loosened by trampling hooves.
- Inadequate rainfall impoverishes soil and increases its salinity; as a result crops fail and famine follows.

Survival strategies

The world has already lost 40 per cent of its productive land through desertification. If the trend is not halted, desertification will become a global catastrophe by the year 2000. Solutions include:

- Restrictions of settlement in arid areas with controls over nomadism.
- Soil-conservation measures such as terracing, contour-ploughing and windbreaks.
- Improved farming techniques to include crop rotation and the use of fertilizers.
- Cultivation of new crops: drought-resistant strains to increase yields; and leguminous vegetables, like peas and beans, which enrich the soil by fixing nitrogen in it.
- Development of local industries, such as canning, to provide alternative work to agriculture.
- Stock improvement, through disease-control and breeding.
- Pasture conservation through re-seeding and controlled grazing.
- Construction of new wells, waterholes and irrigation schemes.
- Development of new energy sources like solar power and biomass, which uses agricultural waste; introduction of wood-burning stoves – more efficient than open fires.
- Afforestation on a massive scale: in sub-Saharan Africa, an estimated 20.4 million hectares of trees must be planted to halt the advancing desert and meet fuel requirements.

1 As more land comes under the plough, livestock is pushed out into barren zones. Once these goats, in Sudan, have eaten all they can reach peasants will break up the rest of the bush for fuel. When all vegetation has gone, rain – instead of sinking down – runs off quickly, stripping away the topsoil. If there is no rain, the sun-baked earth dries into a powder and is blown away by the wind.

2 A Sudanese camel train brings in firewood from distant forests. Throughout Africa's drylands, there is an acute shortage of fuel: local wood supplies are exhausted and villagers must either trek miles to find a few meagre sticks or pay high prices in the market. At present, dry Africa has only enough wood left for 60% of its population.

3 In the absence of wood, cow-dung is a replacement fuel. This Ethiopian woman is patting dung into cakes which will then be left to dry in the sun. But dung could be better used as manure for crop-growing.

4 A well under construction in Niger. When finished, it will be covered over with concrete to prevent contamination: dirty water is responsible for 80% of Africa's disease. From the new well, water will be piped to nearby villages for domestic use and for channelling into vegetable plots.

5 Dune control in Somalia: women bring in brushwood to build protective barriers around their village. The brushwood takes root, catches the wind-blown sand and so prevents dunes from moving in and smothering the village. Deforestation is a prime cause of shifting dunes.

6 In the early 1900s, trees covered 40% of Ethiopia. Deforestation has since reduced that figure to 4%, exposing much of the land to erosion. In the fight against erosion 700,000 km of terraces have been built to check shifting soils and 500 m tree seedlings planted.

---

1 What is desertification?
2 Describe its extent and causes.
3 What is being done to combat desertification?
4 'Ten years ago my harvest was good; now all I have is a harvest of dust.' Explain what this Ethiopian peasant means. What do you think has happened during the last ten years?
5 What are the consequences of desertification and what could happen if control measures fail?
6 Construct a flow diagram to chart the progressive stages of desertification starting with overpopulation. At what stage(s) do you think intervention is most likely to succeed?

The use of land

LANDSCAPES

> Making the best use of land requires a thorough understanding of it.

Above: Aerial view of the Isle of Purbeck taken off Durlston Head (Handfast Point). To the left is the chalk ridge of the Purbeck Hills, with clay and sand valleys on either side. Beyond lies the limestone plateau that makes up the cliffs of the southern shore.

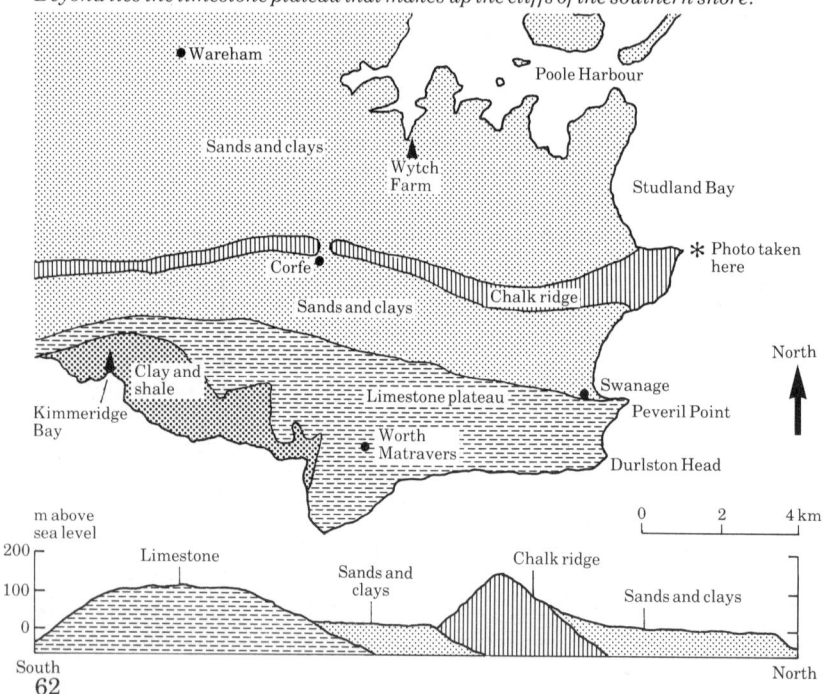

Popular Purbeck

The Isle of Purbeck, a promontory of 100 km^2, juts out between the English Channel and Poole Harbour. It contains geologically important coastal landscapes; popular tourist resorts; rare fauna and flora; valuable deposits of stone, clay and oil; farmland; and military training grounds. Half a million people live within 50 km of Purbeck. In any place with so many potential uses, there is a danger that competing interests in the land could destroy it. Therefore, to make the best use of an area, it is first necessary to make a thorough study of it.

Geology

The unusual relief of the Isle of Purbeck is the result of its unique geological make-up. This has also provided the area with valuable minerals.

■ The Isle consists of four parallel bands of rock, running east-west. To the north, lies a sand and clay lowland behind Studland Bay and Poole Harbour. Then comes a narrow chalk escarpment, called the Purbeck Hills, which gives way southwards to another band of sand and clay: the Corfe river and Swanage valleys. On the south coast there is a limestone plateau in the east (Durlston Head to Worth Matravers) with a clay and shale enclave to the west, round Kimmeridge Bay.

■ Quarrying on Purbeck is at least 2000 years old. From Roman times to the late 1600s, it centred on marble, from the limestone near Peveril Point; Purbeck marble, a mottled grey-green, adorns many of England's cathedrals. During the 18th and 19th centuries, Purbeck stone was in demand for building.

■ The clay and shale lowlands round Kimmeridge Bay have been a source of coal and oil for centuries and there is an oil pumping station there today. To the north, on Poole Harbour, BP Oil are developing Europe's largest onshore oilfield, Wytch Farm, which will produce as much as a medium-sized North Sea field. In the central sand and clay valley, English China Clays are proposing to extract ball clay. This is only found in three locations in Britain and is used to make ceramic tiles and sanitary ware.

Landscape

The Isle of Purbeck has some of Britain's rarest scenery. Tall limestone cliffs, lush valleys and woodlands, heathlands, and a magnificent chalk ridge, which ends at the sea in the chalk pillars of Handfast Point. As a result Purbeck is a popular tourist destination – a 'honeypot', attracting thousands of visitors a year. It is also a rich agricultural area; in addition, large sections are reserved for military use.

- For many years Purbeck has been officially recognized as an Area of Outstanding Natural Beauty. In 1973 Durlston Head was designated a Country Park. In 1974 the 113 km Dorset Coast Path was opened; much of its route is classified as Heritage Coast. Purbeck has five National Nature Reserves (NNR) and 17 Sites of Special Scientific Interest (SSSI). There is an immense variety of wildlife: the Studland Heath Nature Reserve is the only place in Britain where all six native reptiles still live; Furzey Island, where new oil-wells are proposed, has a colony of red squirrels. There are rare plants, such as spider orchids and marsh gentians, as well as various butterflies and dragonflies.

- The area's popularity with tourists has caused much damage to the local environment. Until Durlston Head became a Country Park, cars wore away the turf and campers left litter in hedgerows. Now the 65 ha Park has carparks, campsites, picnic areas and toilets. Tourists may object to being organized, but Durlston Head is now protected.

- Throughout the region livestock (sheep, dairy and beef) predominate, with some arable farming (cereals) in the clay zones. Farmers have been clearing heathland in the north for grazing. The Nature Conservancy Council is anxious to prevent this and preserve the habitat of endangered species, particularly the Dartford Warbler.

- The army uses a large area between Lulworth Cove, Worbarrow Tout and Povington Heath, as gunnery ranges. Much of this land is inaccessible to the public.

Settlement

The Isle of Purbeck is not actually an island, but it has always been cut off from the rest of southern England. Inland the Isle is protected by the steep chalk escarpment of the Purbeck Hills and by the low, marshy heaths bordering Poole harbour, while its remote coast has a history of shipwrecks and smuggling. In the past bad communications to the north were of less concern, as the main exports of building stone went by sea from Swanage. But today the area's roads are under severe pressure from tourists and industrial development.

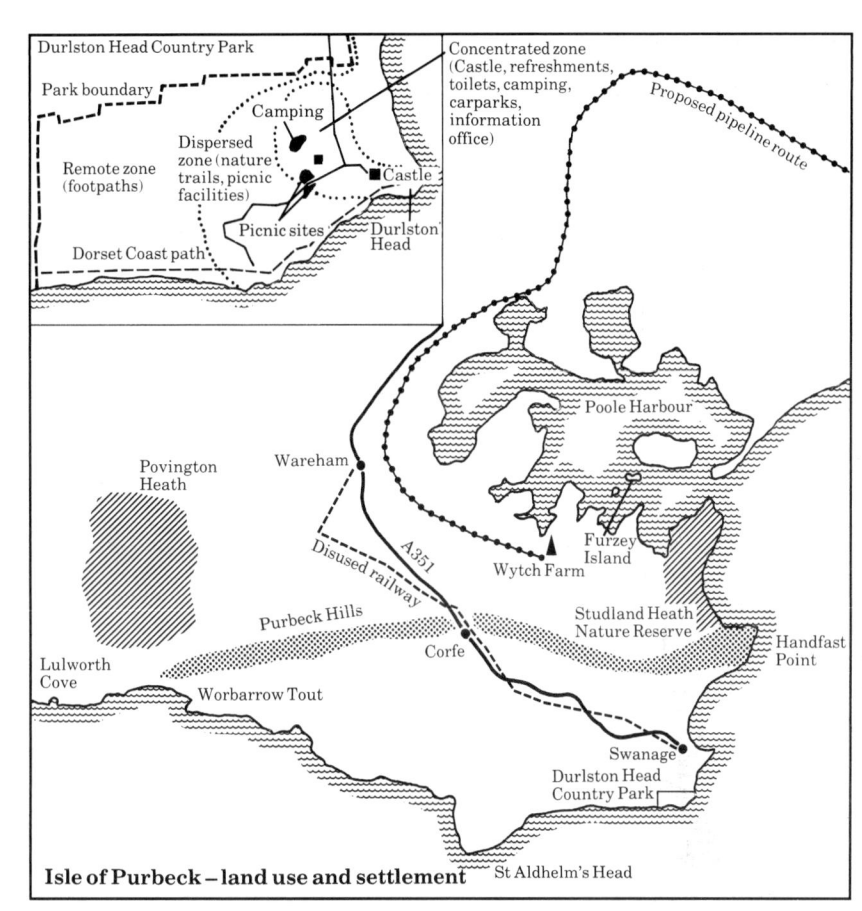

Isle of Purbeck – land use and settlement

- Corfe is one of the most picturesque places on Purbeck, but also in one of only two gaps through the Purbeck Hills. In heavy summer traffic, the village becomes a bottleneck, yet building a bypass is difficult in an Area of Outstanding Natural Beauty surrounded by Sites of Special Scientific Interest.

- The railway line between Wareham and Swanage, through Corfe, has been abandoned. At the Swanage end there is a short tourist railway. Proposals exist for reopening the whole route to ease road traffic.

- On the heathlands to the south of Poole harbour, Wytch Farm oilfield will require a pipeline to take the oil to refineries near Southampton. Farmers, with land on the pipeline route, have negotiated substantial compensation, but naturalists are concerned about the effects of possible oil spillage in Poole harbour. Oil contracts will bring 1400 jobs to the area.

---

1 List six competing forms of land use in the Purbeck area.
2 What damage could each of these inflict on the local environment?
3 List three of the main pressure points, or 'honeypots', that attract tourists to the Purbeck area and give reasons for their attraction.
4 Use an Ordnance Survey Map to suggest three alternative routes for the Corfe bypass:
a) to the west, but avoiding the Corfe Common SSSI and The Rings (an archeological site);
b) to the east, using a tunnel under East Hill but avoiding the railway, which may be reopened; c) to the east, using a dry valley part-way through the escarpment.
5 Write a paragraph giving at least one advantage and one disadvantage of each route. Consider: connections to the A351 on each side of Corfe; the visual impact; the engineering cost; the conservation cost in lost farmland and open space.

LANDSCAPES

National forests

Different sectors of industry produce different uses of land.

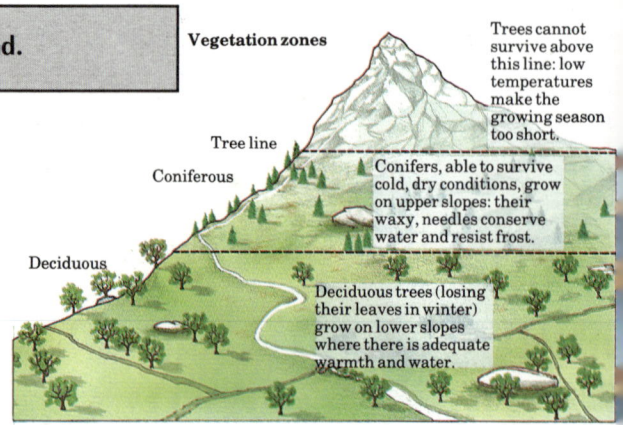

Beauty and the sawmill

Once, much of northern Europe was covered by forests. Deciduous and coniferous trees form the natural vegetation of a warm temperate climate zone.

■ The forests of Europe were progressively cut down to provide wood for fuel and for building houses and ships: one naval vessel took as many as 3000 oak trees. Two hundred years ago, France suffered a severe energy crisis because so much of its natural forest had been destroyed. Then, there were only 8 m ha of forest; today, France has 20 m ha.

Competing uses for forests

Forests for timber

Coniferous forest: fast-growing, straight, softwood trees required for building, furniture and paper products.

Forestry Commission: 400 ha of nurseries produce disease-free seedlings; 22,000 ha planted p.a.

Afforestation: tree-planting combats erosion and, by slowing down run-off, helps prevent floods. Trees supply oxygen to the atmosphere.

Import replacement: UK timber production has trebled since 1959. By 2000 it will meet 11% of all requirements.

Investment: tax concessions encourage private investors to plant forests.

Forests for people

Deciduous forest: attractive landscapes, popular with public, good wildlife habitat. Only 30% of woodland is deciduous.

Forestry Commission: 24,000 employees, mostly in rural areas.

Conifer plantations: alien to most parts of UK; monotonous landscapes; inaccessible for public use; unsuitable for most wildlife and too dark to support undergrowth; 245 ha of conifers planted every year for one ha of broadleaved trees.

Leisure: woodlands, mostly broadleaved, conserved and managed for recreational use. In response to public pressure, more deciduous trees being planted.

Vegetation zones

Trees cannot survive above this line: low temperatures make the growing season too short.

Tree line
Coniferous

Conifers, able to survive cold, dry conditions, grow on upper slopes: their waxy, needles conserve water and resist frost.

Deciduous

Deciduous trees (losing their leaves in winter) grow on lower slopes where there is adequate warmth and water.

■ World War I depleted Britain's forests by 182,000 ha. There was no longer enough wood for pit-props – essential, as industry then relied on coal. So the Forestry Commission was set up in 1919 to plant and manage a strategic reserve of timber. In 1945, after World War II, the government took further action by planning a National Forestry Estate of over 2 m ha. Today nine per cent of Britain is forested. Although this is small in comparison with many countries, the Forestry Commission is the UK's largest landowner.

■ A store of home-produced timber is considered essential by the newsprint industry.

■ Since 1972 forest policy has shifted from strategic reserve to commercial and recreational use.

■ The Forestry Commission now caters for long- and short-stay tourism, educational visits and leisure activities such as hiking. Eight Forest Parks have been created providing campsites, bridleways, footpaths, car-parks and information centres.

Below: *Upland areas of Britain, where the soil is too acid and the climate too cold for broadleaved (deciduous) trees, are used for large-scale conifer plantations. This part-cleared plantation is above Loch Ness. Because conifers mature quickly, in 50-60 years, they are a better investment than broadleaves.*

Below: *Hollands Wood campsite in the New Forest. The New Forest is a Forest Park run by the Forestry Commission. Its woods of deciduous trees (mainly oak and beech) attract walkers, riders and campers. Broadleaved trees, taking 80-120 years to mature, are less commercially successful than conifers.*

Preserving the forests

Today Europe's forests are facing a new threat: air pollution caused by harmful waste gases, especially from car exhausts and power stations. Carried by the wind, these gases seldom fall where they originate making air pollution an international problem. Europe's prevailing winds blow from the south-west. Thus pollutants affecting the forests of Scandinavia mostly come from Britain.

- One effect of airborne pollution has been to raise the acid levels in rivers and lakes. Three-quarters of lakes in southern Norway are now too acid to support fish.
- In Germany 50 per cent of forests are affected by pollution.
- High ozone levels, caused by atmospheric chemical reactions, are also helping to destroy forests.
- In places pollution is bad enough to corrode metal and stone.

Above: *In West Germany, an alkaline fertilizer is blown into forests to protect them against acid rain.*

Sources of air pollution

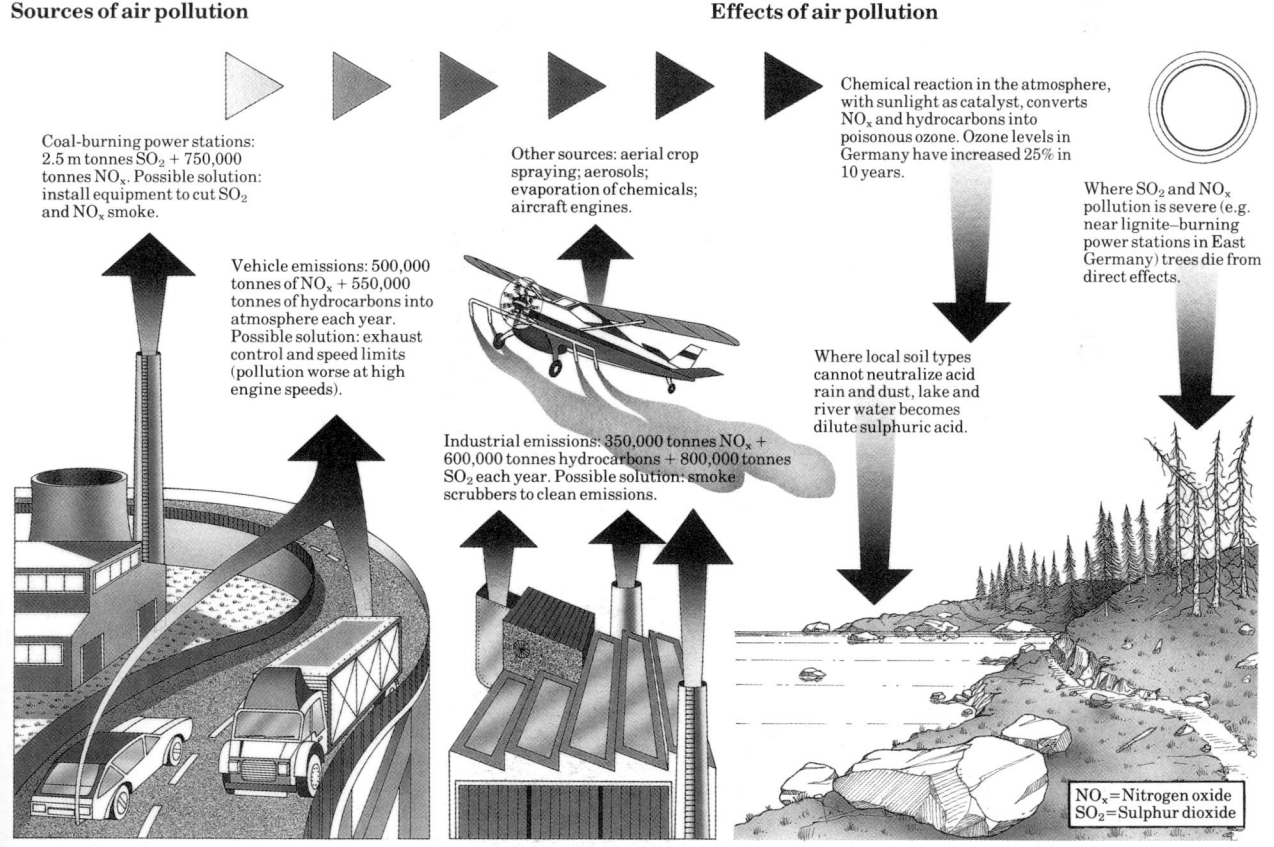

Coal-burning power stations: 2.5 m tonnes SO_2 + 750,000 tonnes NO_x. Possible solution: install equipment to cut SO_2 and NO_x smoke.

Vehicle emissions: 500,000 tonnes of NO_x + 550,000 tonnes of hydrocarbons into atmosphere each year. Possible solution: exhaust control and speed limits (pollution worse at high engine speeds).

Other sources: aerial crop spraying; aerosols; evaporation of chemicals; aircraft engines.

Industrial emissions: 350,000 tonnes NO_x + 600,000 tonnes hydrocarbons + 800,000 tonnes SO_2 each year. Possible solution: smoke scrubbers to clean emissions.

Effects of air pollution

Chemical reaction in the atmosphere, with sunlight as catalyst, converts NO_x and hydrocarbons into poisonous ozone. Ozone levels in Germany have increased 25% in 10 years.

Where SO_2 and NO_x pollution is severe (e.g. near lignite–burning power stations in East Germany) trees die from direct effects.

Where local soil types cannot neutralize acid rain and dust, lake and river water becomes dilute sulphuric acid.

NO_x = Nitrogen oxide
SO_2 = Sulphur dioxide

---

1 What were the main objectives of the Forestry Commission in 1919 and what are they today?
2 Draw simple flow diagrams to show the sequence of events in the life of a coniferous plantation and of a deciduous woodland.
3 What kind of trees would you plant, and why, if you owned:
a) moorland in Scotland?
b) a stately home, open to the public, in southern England?
4 Why is air pollution worse in Scandinavia than in Britain?
5 Fitting anti-SO_2 and -NO_x equipment to power stations will cost over £2 bn in the UK and over £3 bn in Germany. As a result, electricity prices will rise by at least 5 per cent. In your opinion, would this be money well spent?

Two nations

Economic development alters relative levels of prosperity between regions.

Structural change in industry

The Industrial Revolution turned Britain's primary, agricultural economy into a secondary, manufacturing economy. This was the first of many changes that have altered the structure of industry. In the process many small towns in the North and Midlands became prosperous industrial cities, while areas of the South declined.

- Between 1700 and 1800 the population of Lancashire grew from about 150,000 to 700,000, making it the second largest county after Middlesex. At the same time southern agricultural villages suffered poverty and unemployment.

Today's technological advances are reducing the secondary sector, while the tertiary sector grows.

- In 1951 Britain produced 25 per cent of all manufactured goods in world trade. By 1980 this had been reduced to eight per cent. By 1983 Britain was importing more manufactured goods than it exported.
- As a result the centres of heavy industry are declining, with fewer people needed to produce the same or more. This leads to unemployment and poverty in the older manufacturing regions of the North and Midlands. This process is called **de-industrialization**.
- New industries have developed in other regions, especially the South. But these new industries have not created enough jobs to replace those lost in older industries. The result is high unemployment.

Above: *Derelict industrial sites, with closed factories and disused warehouses, have become a feature of many northern towns.*

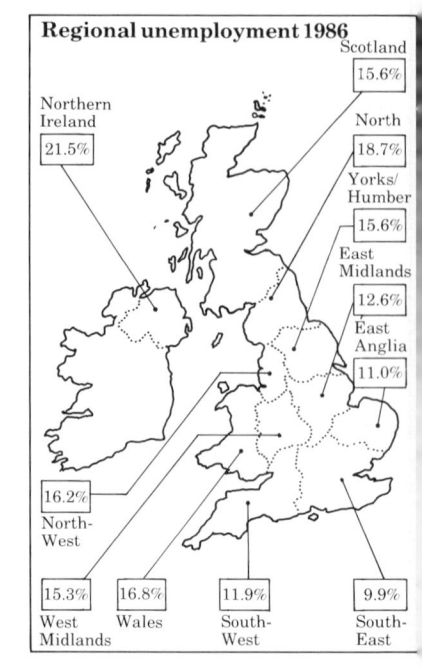

Regional unemployment 1986

- Scotland 15.6%
- Northern Ireland 21.5%
- North 18.7%
- Yorks/Humber 15.6%
- East Midlands 12.6%
- East Anglia 11.0%
- North-West 16.2%
- West Midlands 15.3%
- Wales 16.8%
- South-West 11.9%
- South-East 9.9%

Above: *Britain's 11 economic planning regions, with the level of unemployment in each.*

North-South divide

The effects of de-industrialization have redrawn the economic geography of the UK and exaggerated differences between the regions.

- The better-off regions lie mostly south and east of a line between the Severn and the Wash.
- The regions to the north and west of that line, once Britain's industrial heartland, have suffered most from de-industrialization.
- Exceptions are small pockets of prosperity in the North and pockets of poverty in the South, especially in the deprived inner city areas.

Life expectancy

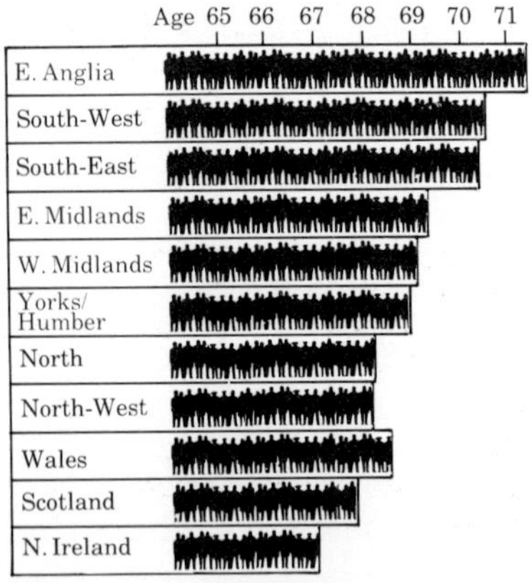

Staying at school after age 16

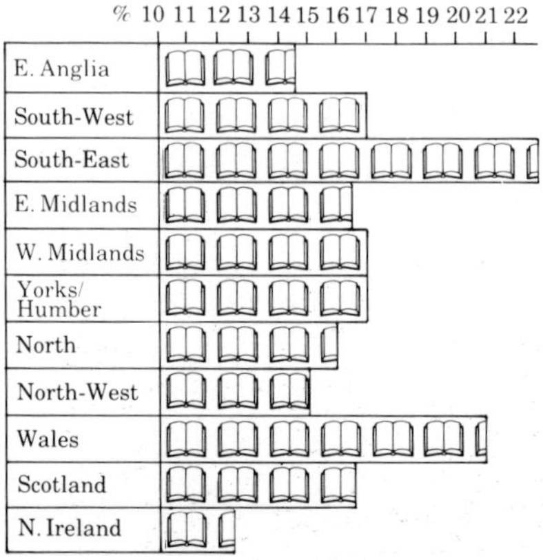

Ownership of cars, central heating, telephones

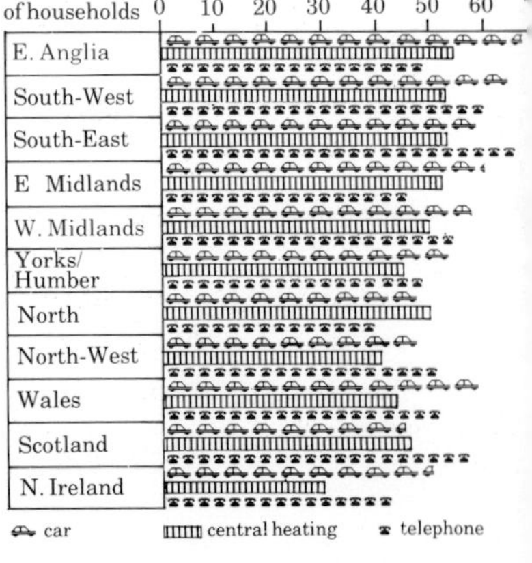

Who loses? Who wins?

The losers

Heavy industry such as steel, coal, textiles and shipbuilding were concentrated in the North and West. Over 2.25 m jobs lost since 1954; 1 m lost 1979-81. → Whole communities often depended on a single mine or mill which was closed leaving little alternative employment. People must move, commute long distances or be unemployed.

Engineering industries, such as car manufacture, declined because of competition. Markets were taken by more efficient producers from Europe and the Far East. → High level of imported manufactured goods; loss of export markets.

Heavy industry employs mostly men. Women in the North were traditionally excluded both from job opportunities and leisure pursuits. → Long-term unemployment of men used to being household heads causes stress, lack of confidence and despair, which may result in violence, alcoholism, and marriage break-up.

Most of the jobs that have gone were for unskilled or skilled manual workers. 2.8 m jobs lost 1961–81. → Unskilled workers are replaced by automation, so jobs will never be available again even in an economic recovery. Millions of people must be trained in new skills.

The Labour Party's main strongholds in the North and West are losing population to the South and East, leaving fewer parliamentary seats in traditional Labour regions. → Labour is becoming increasingly the party of the North and Scotland; the Conservatives represent the South. Each party tends to favour its own region.

With falling employment, trade unions are losing members. → 'Blue collar' unions are losing most members, while 'white collar' unions are becoming more influential.

As industry moved out of cities or closed down, pockets of high unemployment and deprivation have been left in old city centres, like Liverpool and London. → Bitter political conflicts between left-wing local governments and central government. Riots in inner city areas.

The winners

Service sector jobs increased by 3.3 million 1954–82, mostly concentrated on London and the South. → More jobs in industries such as banking and tourism or in government (health and social services).

Skilled and professional people are increasingly well paid. → Shortages of qualified personnel can restrict growth of service industries.

High technology and service industries employ many women, especially in the South-East. → Many women are the main family income earner, although often still not paid as much as men.

Many people made redundant set themselves up in small, flexible, low-cost businesses. → One in 10 Britons is now self-employed.

47,000 small businesses (employing under 200 people) started in 1983. → Small businesses now employ 25% of the workforce and produce 20% of Britain's GDP.

Above: *Political party posters highlight the unemployment issue, one of the major problems caused by de-industrialization.*

The British disease

There are many theories to explain de-industrialization, which has had a more severe effect in Britain than in most competitor countries. Here are some of them.

■ Britain's industrial success was based on a captive market in the British Empire. Now it has gone; so too has Britain's industry.

■ Unlike its competitors, Germany, France and Japan, Britain's industry was not completely rebuilt following World War II.

■ Post-war governments have concentrated on socialist measures to improve health, housing and benefits instead of encouraging business.

■ The British class system perpetuates 'them and us' attitudes between employers and employees.

■ Bad management, lack of investment and initiative have made British industry uncompetitive. Fortunes have been made out of property, rather than manufacturing.

■ Bad labour relations, strikes and restrictive union practices have made industry inefficient.

■ Britain's education system does not produce enough scientists, technologists and managers.

■ Too much has been spent on defence research and arms and not enough on industrial technology.

■ Goods have been imported too freely, so low-wage countries compete unfairly with British industry.

■ Sterling has been over-valued, especially since North Sea oil has given Britain a balance of payments surplus, making goods too expensive to export.

■ Increasingly developed countries are becoming suppliers of services, while LDCs produce heavy industrial goods.

■ As a result of joining the EEC, the South-East is part of the prosperous European core; the North and West are peripheral regions too far from the main markets to be successful.

---

1 What is industrialization?
2 What is de-industrialization?
3 When did each of these processes occur in Britain?
4 Describe and explain the unemployment pattern.
5 Why is the South-East relatively prosperous in comparison with the rest of Britain?
Class Activity: Debate the theories which attempt to explain de-industrialization in Britain. At the end, vote to see which points of view attract most support.

Cosmopolitan Britain

> Minority ethnic groups tend to be concentrated in certain districts.

The new British

For over 2000 years Britain has been a cosmopolitan society, changed frequently by the arrival of new cultural groups: Romans, Saxons, Normans, Irish, Jews and, most recently, Asians and West Indians.

- In 1951 there were about 200,000 people from the New Commonwealth and Pakistan in Britain. By 1981 there was a black and Asian population of 2.2 million (four per cent of the population). Of these some 750,000 were born in Britain.

- Britain's post-war immigrant population is not only from the Indian sub-continent and the West Indies. Many people also came from Italy, Cyprus, Hong Kong and Africa. Then in 1972 the government of Uganda expelled about 40,000 Asians; the majority moved to Britain where some successfully set up their own businesses.

- Most immigrants have settled in urban industrial areas. As a result pupils in London schools now speak 161 different languages. Each language and ethnic group tends to be concentrated in a separate area. In London, for example, Lambeth and Hackney have many people of West Indian origin; Ealing and Tower Hamlets have large Asian populations. By the process of **chain migration**, people from one overseas region followed each other to the same area in Britain. After World War II, the owner of a rubber factory in West London recruited Sikhs from the Punjab, because he had fought alongside them in the war. Others followed, establishing the basis of today's large Sikh community in Southall (Ealing).

England's immigrant population

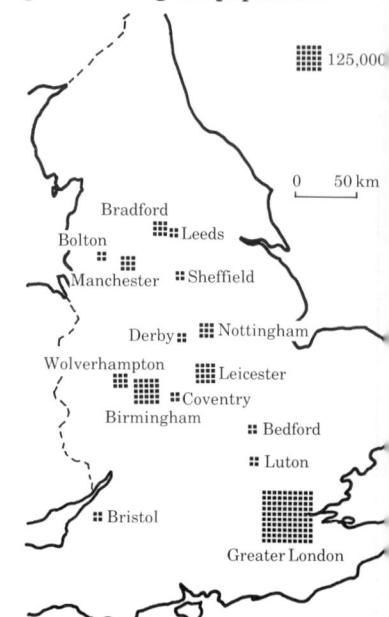

Above: *This map shows where West Indian and Asian people have settled in England, many of them in manufacturing centres which are now in decline as a result of de-industrialization.*

West Indian settlement in London

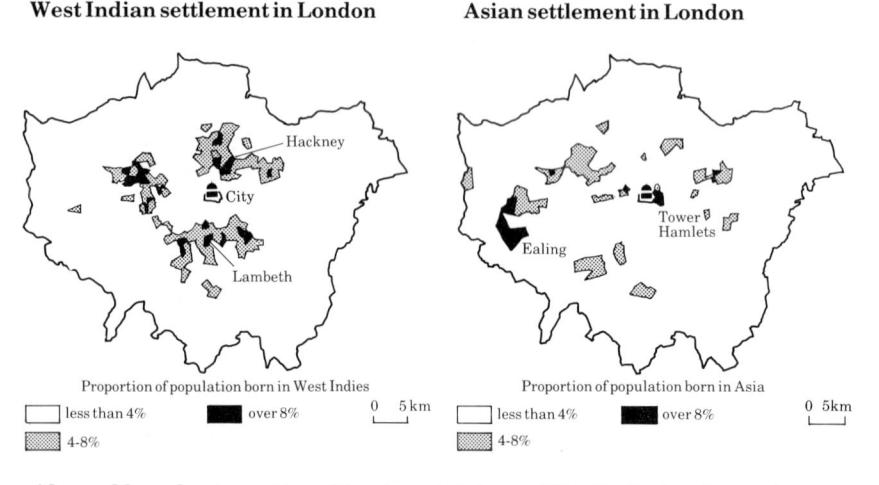

Asian settlement in London

Proportion of population born in West Indies
less than 4%   over 8%   0 5 km
4-8%

Proportion of population born in Asia
less than 4%   over 8%   0 5 km
4-8%

Above: *Maps showing pattern of immigrant (Asian and West Indian) settlement in London.*

Male unemployment rates
House ownership

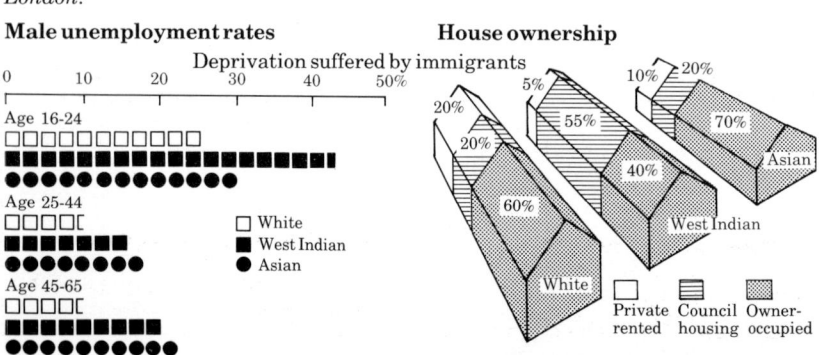

Deprivation suffered by immigrants

Age 16-24
Age 25-44
Age 45-65

□ White
■ West Indian
● Asian

Private rented   Council housing   Owner-occupied

Above: *Among West Indians, many of whom live in low-quality inner city accommodation, over 35% of households are one-parent families. Despite this, a high proportion of West Indian women (74%) go out to work, compared to 46% of whites and 39% of Asians.*

68

Blackburn settlers

Blackburn is a cotton mill town in Lancashire. Out of a population of 142,000, 11 per cent are Asian. There are three different groups within this population: Indians, Pakistanis and East-African Asians. Some are Muslim, others Hindu; between them they speak four main languages: Gujerati, Panjabi, Urdu and Hindi.

Why migrate?
– As a temporary means of accumulating wealth to send back to families, which are generally poor.
– To earn enough money to go home as a richer person, with increased status.
– To take advantage of employment opportunities: in the 1960-70s there was a demand for labour, especially in dirty, low-paid jobs avoided by the British. In Blackburn these jobs were in textile mills.

On arrival
– Early arrivals were mostly men on their own. Over half those in Blackburn went to stay with friends or relatives, who helped with work and accommodation.
– This increased the concentration of migrants in inner city areas where housing, though poor, was cheap.
– Migrants lived frugally. They arrived with nothing and sent much of what they earned home to their families.
– They had difficulty with English.

White attitudes
– Many of the white, host population regarded migrants with intolerance.
– Migrants were resented because they competed for jobs, housing, school places and healthcare.
– Because migrants' culture was different, many whites considered it inferior.

Isolation
– Immigrants were isolated from the host community by: language, culture, religion, white prejudice, the 'myth of return' (the idea that they were only in Britain temporarily), and settlement (concentrated in separate districts).

Settling in
– Once established, immigrants sent for their wives and families, thus creating a more balanced population.
– But the only houses they could afford were in run-down zones.
– Since the 1970s, Asian estate agents, solicitors and banks have set up in Blackburn, making it easier for Asians to establish themselves. Some qualified for council housing.

Finding work
– 60 per cent of Blackburn Asians work in the the textile industry which is subject to fluctuations. Unemployment rates are often high. There is little alternative employment.
– Immigrants were untrained for other work. Many came from rural areas and had no secondary education.
– Only a few firms would employ Asians: 60 per cent were taken on by just eight factories.
– Indians work in different places to Pakistanis.
– Even when unemployed, most are better-off in Britain than at home.

Building a community
– Reunited families with more than one wage earner were now relatively well-off, but preferred to remain close to others of same culture and religion.
– Asian shops, meeting places and mosques (92 per cent of Blackburn Asians are Muslims) helped give a sense of community.
– Hostility from the white population encouraged Asians to stick together for safety.
– By 1981 the central area of Blackburn had an Asian population of over 30 per cent.

Isolation
– With each group living and working in its own community, there was little contact between it and the host population. In a 1981 survey, less than 10 per cent had white friends.
– In central area schools, up to 65 per cent of pupils are from one ethnic group. Lessons are in English, but the main means of communication are Panjabi, Gujerati or Urdu. Because of difficulty with English, Asian children are, on average, one year behind by the age of nine.
– To preserve their own culture, parents send children to mosque schools at night and weekends.

Above: *Most Blackburn Asians are Muslims; these men are outside the mosque.*

Above: *Young Muslims are encouraged to take part in traditional activities.*

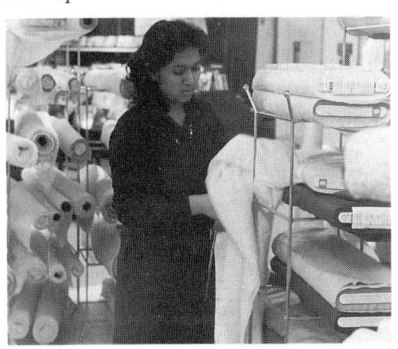

Above: *Many Blackburn Asians work in the textile industry.*

1 What are the attitudes of the host community towards immigrants and how might they change with time?
2 Why did immigration to Britain increase rapidly during 1951-81 and slow down afterwards?
3 Why do immigrants with similar origins congregate in the same areas?
4 Give three examples of deprivation experienced by immigrants and explain why the new British population are often worse-off than the local white population.
5 Make two lists: one of advantages for people coming as immigrants to Britain; the other of disadvantages which they and their families may face.

Nations within nations

Regional minorities often have to struggle to preserve their identity.

People of the Arctic

About 1000 years ago, when the Finns entered present-day Finland from the south, the entire region was inhabited by the Sami. These people, often called Lapps, were gradually pushed north. Their land was taken away from them and they were reduced to virtual slavery for many centuries.

- The harsh Arctic environment made the southerners' advance relatively slow, thus helping the Sami to survive. But in the last 50 years, with the introduction of modern communications, industry and administration, the pace of change has quickened. As a result, the Sami are losing their identity: language, social customs and occupations.

- Traditionally, the Sami were nomadic reindeer herders. Their life followed a seasonal rhythm: as the snow melted in spring they moved north to reindeer calving grounds, then further north to summer grazing; in autumn they returned south and wintered where there was sufficient lichen growth under the snow to feed the herds. The Sami were self-subsistent. Their basic diet of reindeer meat, milk and blood was supplemented by hunting, trapping and fishing; reindeer hide supplied clothes and tents. Most of the hazards they faced were natural: disease, extreme cold, wild beasts and scarcity of winter pasture.

- The intrusion of a majority culture from the south has brought many changes to the Sami lifestyle. There are about 300,000 of them in northern Scandinavia, but most have intermarried with Finns, Swedes and Norwegians; only about 35,000 are of pure Sami descent.

- Widely-scattered tent communities have been brought together into government-built housing with electricity. Education is compulsory for Sami children; they are taught in Sami, but learn Finnish as well. Traditional migration tracks and land-holding rights have been rationalized to fit the new pattern of administration, settlement and industry. Lumbering, mining, hydro-electric schemes, even defence establishments, have brought migrants from the south to Lapland.

- In order to survive, the Sami are adapting to the new culture. Reindeer herding has become semi-nomadic reindeer farming. Half of all Sami income still comes from reindeer, much of it from craft items in hide and bone, made for the tourist market.

- Although the growing season is very short (under 120 days), hay and vegetables are cultivated and wild berries are gathered for sale as delicacies in the south.

- Sami suffer a high unemployment rate. Many take low-status, part-time jobs in government, military and mining operations. But state benefits ensure that Sami family income is only ten per cent below the average for northern Finland. Although co-existence is diluting Sami culture, the remoteness and marginality of the land on Europe's periphery helps them preserve some measure of identity.

North polar projection

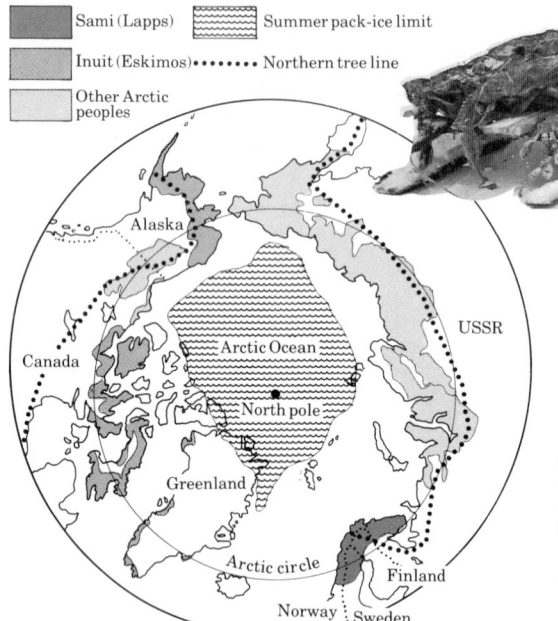

- Sami (Lapps)
- Inuit (Eskimos)
- Other Arctic peoples
- Summer pack-ice limit
- Northern tree line

Above: *Mechanization has brought changes. Here a Sami uses a snowmobile, or skidoo, to pull his sledge rather than a reindeer.*

Left: *About two million people live in the hostile environment of the Arctic circle. But in Alaska, Canada and Scandinavia, oil and mineral developments are threatening their traditional ways of life.*

Below: *Tourism is a new, and important, source of income for the Sami. This woman is selling handcrafted souvenirs: reindeer-skin slippers and bone knives. Sami also work as drivers on reindeer safaris – sled trips into the Arctic.*

Right: *There are roughly 200,000 reindeer in Lapland providing a livelihood for some 800 Sami families.*

The struggles of Euskadi

About 750,000 Basques live in northern Spain and another 150,000 live over the frontier in south-west France. They are a Celtic people, 650,000 of whom still speak Europe's oldest living language, Euskerra. Traditionally, they are hard-working, thrifty and jealous of their independence from Spain.

■ At the turn of the century, Basque enterprise made Euskadi – the Basque country – Spain's first industrial region. Local mines produced coal, copper, wolfram and mercury. Bilbao became the centre of Spanish banking, steel making and shipbuilding – all in the control of just 30 Basque families. In the early 1920s fine mansions were built outside the city while the industrial magnate, Ramon de la Sota, was reported to be wealthier than the Spanish government.

■ Today, the Basque region has a number of natural advantages – such as mineral deposits, a skilled workforce and a location nearer to the European core than the rest of Spain – which would make independence possible. But politically this is unacceptable to the country as a whole.

Above: *The Basque separatist organization, ETA, often uses violence in its campaign to win independence from Spain. Since Franco's death in 1975 and the restoration of democracy, Spain's 17 regions, including Euskadi, have gained a large measure of self-government. ETA, however, continues to fight for full independence: its bombings and shootings make funerals like this one depressingly common.*

Right: *Basque wealth, independence and Republican allegiance made the region a prime target during the Spanish Civil War. In 1937 a German air-squadron, supporting General Franco, bombed the Basque market-town of Guernica: during the three-hour attack, 2000 civilians died. Picasso immortalized the tragedy in his famous painting, shown here on a commemorative stamp. Subsequently, Basque nationalism and culture were heavily suppressed by the Franco regime.*

Left: *Euskerra is now an official language, taught in half of all primary schools and used in street signs, advertising, books and films. The Basque parliament controls issues like economic development and social security and also has the right to form its own police force.*

1 In what ways can minority groups be oppressed by majorities?
2 How are the situations of the Basques and the Sami similar? How are they different?
3 How have the Sami responded to modernization pressures?
4 Describe Basque reaction to the refusal, by the government, to grant full independence.
5 Write a paragraph to explain how Europe might become a federation of small regions, rather than the group of large nations it now is.
Class activity: Form two groups. One group takes the part of an ethnic minority, whose culture, territory and way of life is being threatened. The other group represents the majority. Work out non-violent ways of adapting to each other's cultures.

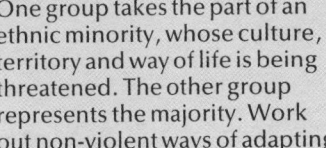

The European ideal

Neighbouring countries join together in trading blocs to promote regional growth.

Aftermath of war

In 1945, at the end of World War II, Europe was in ruins and had to be rebuilt. The new Europe was to be very different from the old.
- European empires were disintegrating as former colonies such as India and the Belgian Congo gained independence.
- The countries of Europe were no longer the world's most important political powers. They were caught in the middle of a new struggle, between the capitalist, democratic USA and the communist USSR.
- The work of reconstruction began with two international agencies: the United Nations Relief and Rehabilitation Administration (UNRRA), which fed, clothed and housed refugees, distributing 22 million tonnes of supplies in five years; and the Organization for European Economic Co-operation (OEEC), which distributed American aid under the Marshall Plan to any country suffering from 'hunger, poverty, desperation and chaos'.
- From 1948–51 the USA contributed $12,000 m in aid to Europe: as a result industrial production rose 65 per cent, farm output by 35 per cent.
- The Soviet Union refused to allow East European countries to accept US aid, thus increasing their isolation from the west.
- The governments of France, Germany, Italy, the Netherlands, Belgium and Luxembourg – realizing that co-operation worked – moved towards a more formally united Europe. In 1957 they signed the Treaty of Rome, which set up the European Economic Community (EEC), now known as the European Community.

Above: *Bomb damage in Hamburg. World War II devastated Europe: in 1946, industrial production was only 30% of the prewar level, farm output just 50%.*

Below: *The French economist, Jean Monnet, is considered the founder of European unity. The culmination of his ideas was the Treaty of Rome, signed on 25 March 1957. It established the EEC, 'to promote harmonious development of economic activities, a continuous and balanced expansion, an increase in stability, a raising of the standard of living and closer relations between the States belonging to it'.*

Above: *The first sector in which all trade barriers were removed was iron and steel. This first 'free' coal train crossed the French-Luxembourg frontier in May 1953. The European Coal and Steel Community grouped France, Benelux, Germany and Italy.*

Above: *The Berlaymont building, in Brussels, is the Community's headquarters; about 19,000 people work there.*

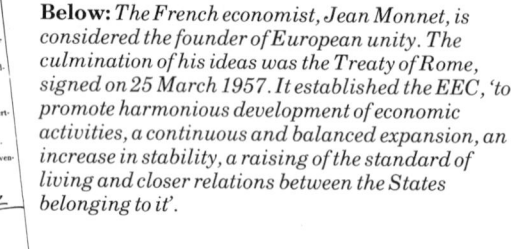

A growing Community

The six nations which signed the Treaty of Rome saw it as the first step towards political union. For this and other reasons, such as Commonwealth ties, Britain did not then join the EEC. Instead, in 1959, the European Free Trade Association (EFTA) was set up by Britain, Austria, Switzerland, Norway, Sweden, Denmark, Iceland and Portugal as a purely economic, non-political measure.

- The EEC's economic success in France and Germany made British governments reconsider their position. In 1963 Britain applied to join, but General de Gaulle of France saw that British membership would weaken the strong economic and political partnership between France and Germany. Britain was refused entry.
- Meanwhile the EEC was developing fast: the Parliamentary Assembly and Court of Justice were set up in 1958; the Common Agricultural Policy (CAP) in 1962; customs union and free movement of labour in 1968.
- After de Gaulle's fall, Britain reapplied, and joined with Eire and Denmark (both heavily dependent on UK trade) in 1973.
- Progress with common EEC policies has been slow, but achievements include: the Lomé Convention, an agreement on co-operation with Third World countries (1975); the Regional Development Fund to reduce economic differences between areas of the EEC (1975); direct elections to the European Parliament (1979); Common Fisheries Policy (1983).
- Since 1973 the EEC has been enlarged twice: Greece became a member in 1981, Spain and Portugal in 1986.

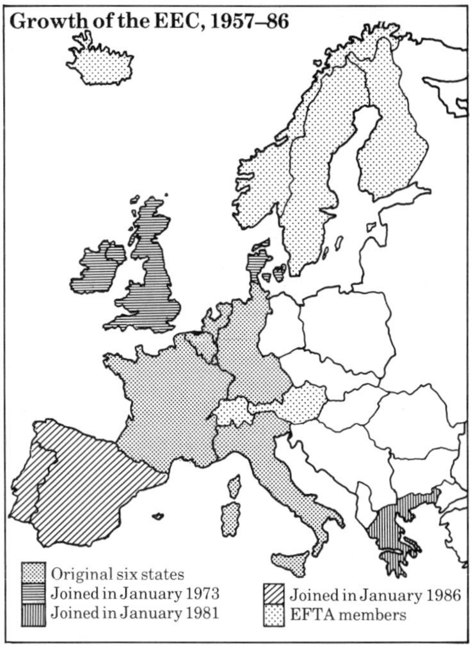

Growth of the EEC, 1957–86

Original six states
Joined in January 1973
Joined in January 1981
Joined in January 1986
EFTA members

How the EEC works

European Council: Heads of government meet three times a year to address major problems.

The Council: Ministers from each member state meet regularly and decide Community policy.

Commission: 17 Commissioners initiate new policies, administer affairs and make sure agreements are respected.

European Parliament: 518 directly-elected MEPs debate Commission proposals and vote on the annual budget.

Court of Justice: Interprets Community law and hears cases involving possible breaches.

Economic and Social Committee: 189 members representing employers, workers and other interests advise on policies.

Above: *Mobility of labour within the EEC means that children may grow up outside their own country. To help them retain their home language, the Community funds 'mother tongue' projects. These Greek story books, produced in Britain, are for Greek children living abroad; the Community contributed £301,000 to this scheme.*

Achievements: the EEC...
– is now the world's largest trading bloc and has greatly increased the standard of living in member states.
– has broken down barriers between countries, making the movement of people and goods easier.
– encourages both political and economic co-operation between member nations (with 320 m inhabitants), for example in the EUREKA high technology project (1986).
– is self-sufficient in most food products and has reduced food prices in real terms.
– promotes development in peripheral areas, thus reducing inequalities between regions.
– has common policies on agriculture, fishing, steel, ship-building, energy, transport, tourism, research and the environment.
– has trade agreements with other countries to encourage freer trade worldwide.
– uses its influence to help solve world problems.

Problems: the EEC...
– produces surpluses in agricultural products, which are sold abroad at subsidized prices, so depriving Third World and other countries of export markets.
– was devised to integrate the economies of northern Europe, yet a third of its people now live on the Mediterranean, and have different problems.
– should promote unity, yet member states still put national priorities first, making policy decisions difficult.
– has a vast budget, 70 per cent of which is spent on CAP subsidies; little remains for social, environmental and industrial projects.
– exerts only limited authority through its Parliament.
– has no real common currency, which would avoid fluctuations in the value of each member state's money.
– has made little progress on issues such as energy, the environment, consumer protection, freer competition in services like insurance and air transport, or further political integration.

---

1 Outline the main factors that led to the creation of the European Community.
2 Describe the institutions which have been established to run the Community. Why are they necessary?
3 Refer to the Community's successes and outstanding problems and discuss to what extent the Treaty of Rome's aims have been achieved.
4 How has the membership of Greece, Spain and Portugal affected the Community's orientation?
5 Put forward reasons to say whether, in your opinion, the Community is a good idea or not.

The Soviet bloc

A region can fall within the sphere of influence of one economic or military power.

The East is red

After World War II, American Marshall Plan aid helped to rebuild western Europe. In response, the Soviet Union formed the Council for Mutual Economic Assistance, COMECON, in 1949.
- COMECON is a trading bloc. All its member nations come within the Soviet Union's political and military sphere of influence. All have communist governments.
- COMECON promotes economic co-operation through a central secretariat in Moscow. It has research institutes, banks and holds regular conferences. There are 22 separate industry commissions to encourage specialization in each country: buses and computers in Hungary; cars, chemicals and optics in the GDR; nuclear reactors and machine tools in Czechoslovakia.

This centrally planned system is bureaucratic and inefficient.
- Decisions take a long time, both to make and to implement.
- Each country tries to protect its own interests (as in the EEC).
- The lack of competition means supplies are uncertain, quality is low and there is no reliable way to price goods. As a result much trade is done by barter, exchanging one product for another.
- The dominant position of the USSR, which supplies raw materials to eastern Europe in return for industrial goods, discourages trade between other partners and also with the West.

Members of COMECON (with joining date)

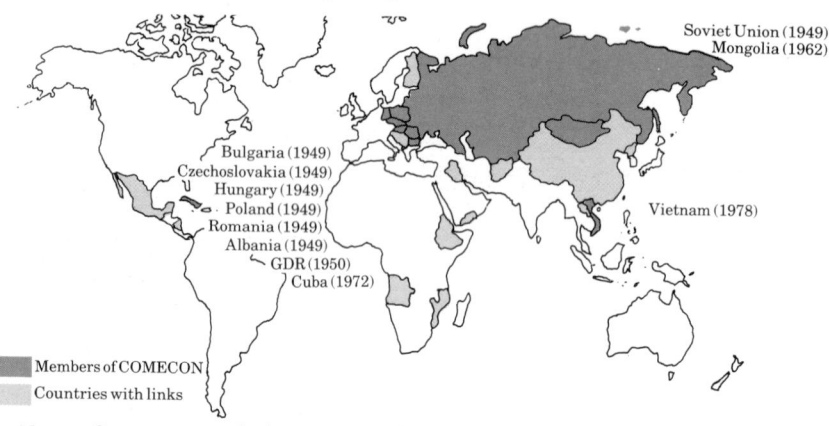

Bulgaria (1949)
Czechoslovakia (1949)
Hungary (1949)
Poland (1949)
Romania (1949)
Albania (1949)
GDR (1950)
Cuba (1972)
Soviet Union (1949)
Mongolia (1962)
Vietnam (1978)

Members of COMECON
Countries with links

Above: *Communist and other countries play various roles in COMECON. Albania has taken no part since 1961. Yugoslavia has been involved in some programmes since 1964. Afghanistan, Angola, China, Ethiopia, Laos, Mozambique, North Korea and South Yemen have observer status, but China has not attended since 1964; Nicaragua has been invited to conferences. Finland, Iraq and Mexico have co-operation agreements.*

COMECON/World population

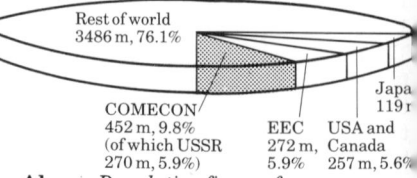

Rest of world 3486 m, 76.1%
COMECON 452 m, 9.8% (of which USSR 270 m, 5.9%)
EEC 272 m, 5.9%
USA and Canada 257 m, 5.6%
Japan 119 m

Above: *Population figures for COMECON and other major trading blocs; also shown as percentage of world population (approx. total 4586 m).*

COMECON/World exports

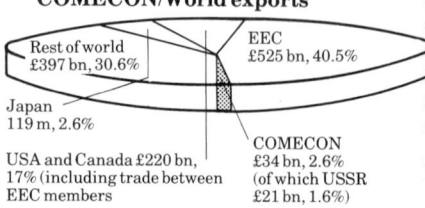

Rest of world £397 bn, 30.6%
EEC £525 bn, 40.5%
Japan 119 m, 2.6%
USA and Canada £220 bn, 17% (including trade between EEC members)
COMECON £34 bn, 2.6% (of which USSR £21 bn, 1.6%)

Above: *COMECON's share of world exports (total £1297 bn).*

Soviet domination

Joint development of USSR raw materials and energy systems have been among COMECON's most successful ventures:
- For example, through COMECON's investment bank, east European countries provided 40 per cent of the funds for a major cellulose plant at Irkutsk. In return, they obtain cheap supplies.
- Transcontinental oil and gas pipelines and a vast power grid are other joint achievements.
- Eastern Europe is dependent on the USSR for 80 per cent of energy input and 90 per cent of oil supplies. This enables the Soviet Union to exert both political and economic control over its allies. However, the USSR must also sell oil to the West to generate 60 per cent of its hard currency earnings.
- COMECON aids its less developed partners: Cuba, Mongolia and Vietnam. The USSR, for instance, buys 80 per cent of Cuba's exports (mostly sugar). In return, Cuban soldiers have supported the left-wing regime in Angola.

Left: *The 2750-km Soyuz (Union) gas pipeline runs from the Urals to the Czechoslovak border and supplies 15,000 m^3 of Soviet natural gas annually to eastern Europe. Other COMECON energy mega-projects include the 5500-km Druzhba (Friendship) oil pipeline and the Mir (Peace) power grid.*

Military domination

COMECON was established in response to American aid to western Europe. Similarily, the Warsaw Pact military alliance was set up in 1955 in response to the formation, in 1949, of NATO (North Atlantic Treaty Organization).
- At the end of World War II Soviet forces occupied eastern Europe. At the 1945 Yalta conference Premier Stalin of Russia, President Roosevelt of the USA and Prime Minister Churchill of Britain agreed to let all countries liberated from the Germans set up their own democratic governments. In spite of this Stalin created a series of puppet regimes in eastern Europe behind a frontier that Churchill named the 'Iron Curtain'.
- All opposition to Soviet-backed governments has been fiercely dealt with: Soviet tanks invaded Hungary in 1956 and Czechoslovakia in 1968; while Poland's Solidarity trade union was banned by a military government in 1982.
- The Warsaw Pact permits the stationing of Soviet troops with nuclear weapons in eastern Europe.

Right: *A Czech student waves the national flag defiantly during the Soviet invasion in 1968. The USSR occupied Czechoslovakia to prevent its leaving the Warsaw Pact.*

Below: *Warsaw Pact and NATO members; France withdrew from NATO in 1966, fearing US domination.*

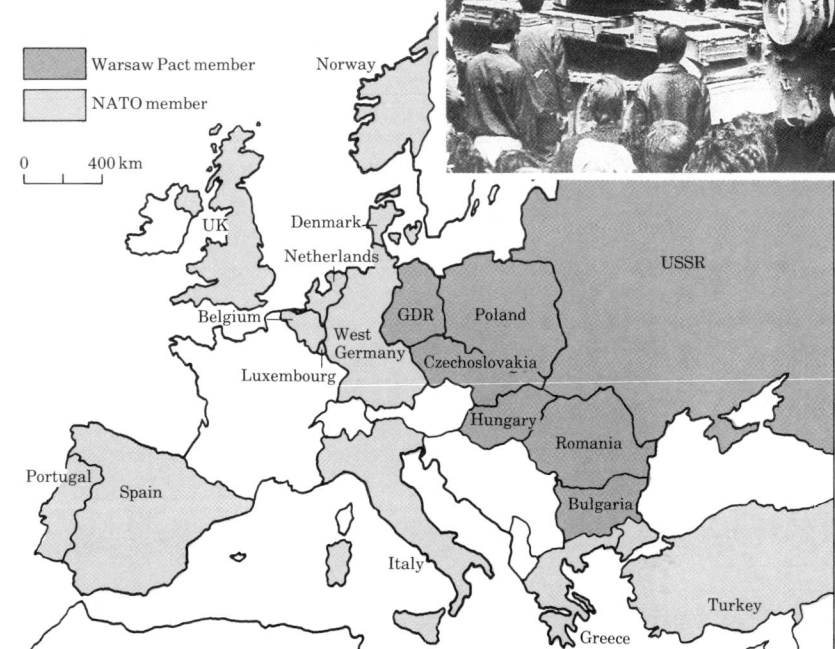

West in the East

After World War II Germany was divided into four occupied zones. Soviet forces, advancing from the east, took eastern Germany, including the capital Berlin. The larger, western part was occupied by the USA, Britain and France. Berlin, in the Soviet zone, was eventually divided into four parts.
- Relations between the allies soon became very strained. In 1948 the Russians cut off land access to Berlin, isolating its two million inhabitants. For ten months everything from carrots to coal, had to be airlifted in.
- Although the western sectors of Berlin remained isolated within the Soviet sphere of influence, movement inside the city was fairly easy. During the 1950s 2.2 million East Germans, most of them young and skilled, defected to the West through Berlin.
- In 1961, the GDR authorities decided to halt this migration and built a permanent concrete wall between East and West Berlin.
- For political and economic reasons West Berlin, isolated inside the GDR, is heavily subsidized by West Germany to prevent its decline.

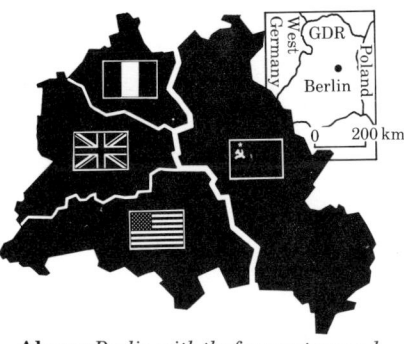

Above: *Berlin with the four sectors and dividing East-West wall. Inset: the GDR.*

Left: *US soldiers patrolling the wall in the American sector. Forty-six km of wall separate East from West in Berlin. In many parts there are several walls, with barbed wire and floodlit minefields between. In addition, a 120-km fence encloses West Berlin inside the GDR.*

1 Why was COMECON formed?
2 What do all COMECON member countries have in common?
3 How does the Soviet Union exert its economic power over the countries of eastern Europe?
4 Why does COMECON have such a small share of world trade, compared with, for example, West Germany?
5 Which came first, the formation of NATO or the Warsaw Pact? Why is this significant?
6 In what ways does the relationship between the USSR and eastern Europe resemble that of the USA and western Europe?
7 Why does West Germany subsidize West Berlin?

Aid to the regions

Government policies attempt to correct regional imbalances.

Coping with structural change

The economic depression of the 1930s persuaded the British government to aid those regions hardest hit by unemployment. Since then there have been various schemes, all aimed at helping regions of industrial decline to keep up with areas of growth.
- Incentives for regional development began in 1934. Trading estates were set up in south Wales, north-east England and in Scotland, where new industries became eligible for grants, tax concessions and training assistance.
- This was only a partial success and, after World War II, a 'carrot and stick' policy was introduced, with incentives and controls to encourage industrial location in Special Areas rather than in already prosperous regions.
- A hierarchy of aided areas has since been established. Those with the most severe problems were made into Special Development Areas (with up to 22 per cent grants for buildings and machinery, no taxes to pay in the first year and reduced rates); next came Development Areas (with grants up to 15 per cent); and then Intermediate Areas (with no grants, but selective aid based on jobs created). At various times the area boundaries have been redrawn to account for industrial change.
- In the 1970s the government set up the Scottish and Welsh Development Agencies (SDA and WDA). Their job is to encourage development in their own regions and act as venture capitalists, taking the risk of investing in new and expanding companies.

The price of a job

In the 1980s the way in which regional aid is organized has changed.
- The controls on development in better-off regions have been discontinued.
- A new hierarchy of assisted areas has been set up; the top category of Special Development Area was abolished. Boundaries have been drawn more precisely, so that only the most needy regions are eligible for maximum assistance.
- Grants are allocated more carefully. In the past companies, such as North Sea oil operators who have located in Scotland anyway and employ relatively few people, have claimed major grants. Grants are now calculated according to the number of jobs created.
- In assisted areas, the government provides factories and workshops if the private sector cannot fund them.
- Twenty-five Enterprise Zones, ranging in size from 50 to 450 ha, were set up to renew derelict industrial areas. They offer a simplified planning system for new developments and financial incentives, such as low rates and tax allowances, over a 10-year period. During their first three years, 8000 new jobs were created in these zones.

Assisted areas in the UK

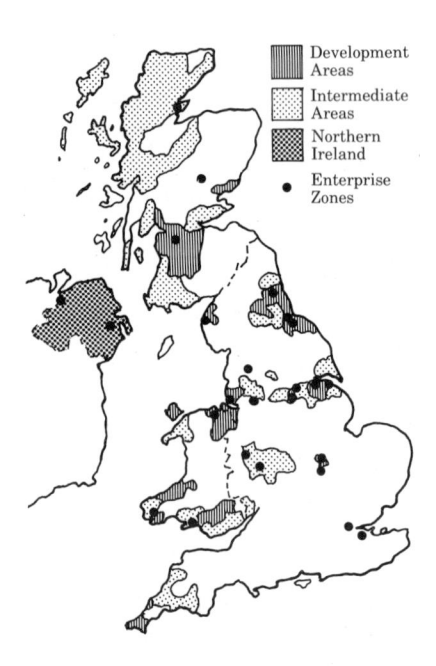

- Development Areas
- Intermediate Areas
- Northern Ireland
- Enterprise Zones

Above: *Development Areas, such as Strathclyde, Merseyside and the North-East, account for 15% of the population of Great Britain. A further 20% live in Intermediate Areas. Enterprise Zones are not officially part of regional aid policy.*

A special case

Northern Ireland ranks as a separate development area.
- In the UK Northern Ireland has the lowest: income per person; output per head of population; level of consumer goods purchased.
- It has the highest: unemployment (22 per cent); birth rate; record of illness.
- Northern Ireland has serious community problems, with divisions between Catholics and Protestants; there are frequent outbreaks of violence, often directed at the security forces.
- It is an area of major structural change in industry. Once Northern Ireland grew flax which supported a large textile industry. Since 1951 66,000 textile jobs have been lost; almost all flax is now imported. In 1950 Harland and Wolff shipyard employed 23,000 people; today it employs 4900.
- UK government development programmes in Northern Ireland run at £340 m a year. They include: grants for buildings, machinery, equipment and rent; industrial training schemes; a small fuel subsidy.

Below: *SWOPS (BP's single well oil production system for use on small offshore fields) is being built by Harland and Wolff in Belfast. Although employment in the shipyard has fallen by almost 80% in the last 35 years, Harland and Wolff still has 6% of Ulster's workforce and ranks as Northern Ireland's second-largest employer (after Short Brothers, the aircraft builders).*

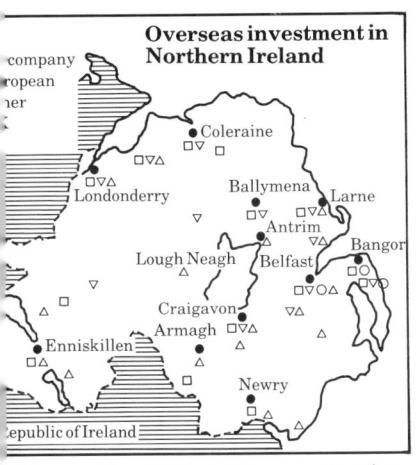

Above: *Since 1980, 1400 new companies have set up in Northern Ireland and 500 have increased their workforce. Many are from the US, attracted by subsidies and by access to the EEC market. 48% of manufacturing employment is now in government-sponsored firms.*

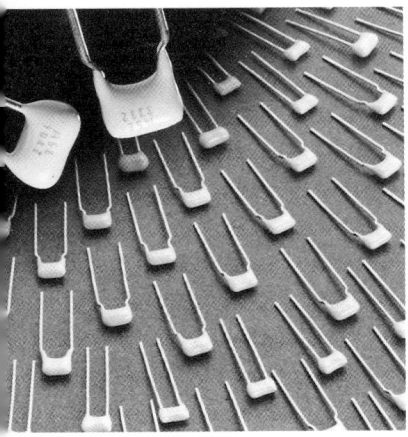

Above: *AVX Ltd is just one of many US companies that, attracted by government incentives, have located in Northern Ireland. With plants at Coleraine and Larne, it is expanding its workforce to 1800, so becoming the largest manufacturer of multi-layer ceramic capacitors in Europe.*

Aiding Europe's regions

Above: *The main regions assisted by the ERDF are: peripheral farming areas of Ireland, the Mezzogiorno (southern Italy) and western France; declining industrial areas such as South Wales, north-east England, and the northern coalfield in France; mountainous and remote regions, such as Corsica, the Scottish Highlands and Greenland, which is part of Denmark. This dam, part-funded by the ERDF, is in Sardinia – included in the Mezzogiorno.*

The 1957 Treaty of Rome, which set up the EEC, contains a commitment to: '. . . reducing the differences between the various regions and the backwardness of the less favoured regions'. However in 1970 the ratio between poorest and richest regions was 3:1; when Greece joined in 1981 this became 5:1; in 1986 Spain and Portugal raised the ratio to 6:1.

In 1973, when Britain, Ireland and Denmark joined the Community, the European Regional Development Fund (ERDF) was set up. Regions with high unemployment, low average incomes and net outward migration qualified for help.

- In 1985, the ERDF distributed over £1300 m. Six per cent of that money can be spent anywhere in the Community. Typical uses include: improving the economic/social situation in border areas (East-West Germany, Northern Ireland-Eire); encouraging small business, especially crafts; helping regions worst hit by structural change, such as the ex-steel towns of Wales and Lorraine.
- Each EEC state is given a quota: in 1985, the UK received £283 m.
- About a third of Britain's quota is used for industry and services, such as tourism. In order to qualify a project must be in a region already assisted by its own government and create at least ten jobs.
- Two-thirds of ERDF money goes into infrastructure: improvements to roads, water, gas, electricity, schools, hospitals and shops.
- The aim of the ERDF is to correct economic imbalances between different parts of the EEC. The best it can hope to achieve is to narrow the gap between rich and poor regions. Many problems of the poor regions are complex and deep-rooted, often accentuated by harsh environment and peripheral location.

---

1 Why do some regions receive government aid, and others none?
2 Why are some regions poorer than others?
3 Describe the different strategies used to reduce economic imbalance between various parts of Britain.
4 How can infrastructure projects paid for by the EEC help poor regions to develop new industries?
5 'The only advantage that Northern Ireland can offer against its disadvantages is the greater size of the bribes on offer.' What did the writer mean by 'bribes'? Is this true?

Supply and demand

Trading networks are created by supply and demand.

The laws of trade

People everywhere have certain needs, such as food and transport. There is a **demand** for these goods and services. As people also produce these goods and services, there is a **supply** of them. But supply may not equal demand.

The link between supply and demand is the price people are prepared to pay for goods and services. Price is the mechanism which adjusts supply and demand, rather like a thermostat which raises or lowers temperature in a building. The way this price mechanism works is not accidental: it follows certain rules, called the laws of supply and demand.

- If there is a given level of demand – for example, 100 items – and an equal supply, supply and demand are balanced.
- If demand remains the same, but supply increases to 150 items, then the price per item falls.
- If demand remains the same, but supply decreases to 50 items, then the price rises.
- If supply remains at 100 items, but demand increases to 150, then the price rises.
- If supply remains the same, but demand falls to 50, the price falls.

When these laws are applied to trade in goods and services, they have certain effects.

- A rise or fall in price is a signal to the producer of goods and services. If prices rise, it means that demand exceeds supply, so he should produce more. If prices fall, it means that supply exceeds demand, so he should produce less.
- The way in which prices, supply and demand alter is not the same for every product. For some products, such as branded foods, a small price cut creates a large increase in demand. This is called **elastic** demand: it stretches easily. Other products, such as electricity, have **inelastic** demand: small price changes hardly affect consumption.
- It is rare for the laws of supply and demand to work freely, without government interference.

A light in the dark

In developed countries homes, offices, factories and hospitals all depend on electricity. If power supply workers go on strike in the middle of winter, when demand is at its highest...

...everyone needs candles. But supply is very limited. The longer the strike goes on the greater the demand for candles. Gradually manufacturers produce more candles to meet the demand.

When the strike ends...

...no one needs candles any more. But by now manufacturers have stepped up the supply and shopkeepers are left with huge stocks of candles which they cannot sell. So they try to clear their stocks.

1 What happened to candle prices during the electricity strike?
2 What happened to the price of candles at the end of the strike?
3 How might the candle-sellers' problems have been avoided?
4 Can you name similar cases of shortage (scarcity of supply) and glut (surplus of supply)?
5 What would have happened to the price of candles at the end of the strike, if manufacturers had not stepped up production to meet the extra demand?

Market controls

New Zealand has 3.2 m people, 70 m sheep and 9 m cattle. Internal demand for meat and wool is very small, so New Zealand must export them.

- In the 1950s Britain bought 60 per cent of New Zealand's farm exports; as Britain was unable to feed itself there was a large demand. Efficient New Zealand suppliers were able to meet this demand in spite of the cost of transporting goods 17,500 km.
- New Zealand's exports to the UK have fallen drastically. Since 1973 Britain has been a member of the EEC, which produces a surplus of beef and lamb. EEC farm prices are much higher than New Zealand's, so New Zealand should be able to beat the competition on price. But New Zealand is prevented from competing in the European market by import restrictions.
- New Zealand has had to find new markets, such as Iran, for its meat exports and develop new products, such as kiwi fruit, for which there was less competition.
- The EEC produces a very large surplus of butter, which is another important New Zealand export. In order to get rid of its surplus, the EEC sells butter abroad at subsidized prices. This surplus supply forces down the price that New Zealand dairy farmers can get for their produce in world markets.

Dangling the carrot

Below: *New Zealand sheep. In 1983, 93% of New Zealand's wool, 85% of lamb and dairy produce and 75% of beef were exported. Altogether, exports account for 24% of New Zealand's GDP (Japan's exports represent 14% of GDP).*

Normal supply and demand

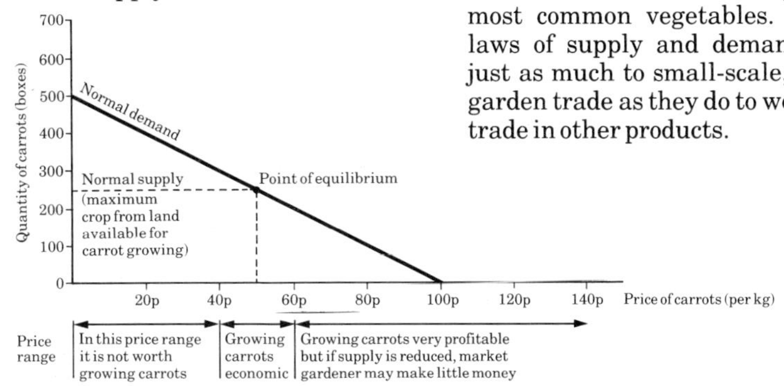

Carrots are one of the cheapest and most common vegetables. Yet the laws of supply and demand apply just as much to small-scale, market garden trade as they do to worldwide trade in other products.

Increased demand and reduced supply

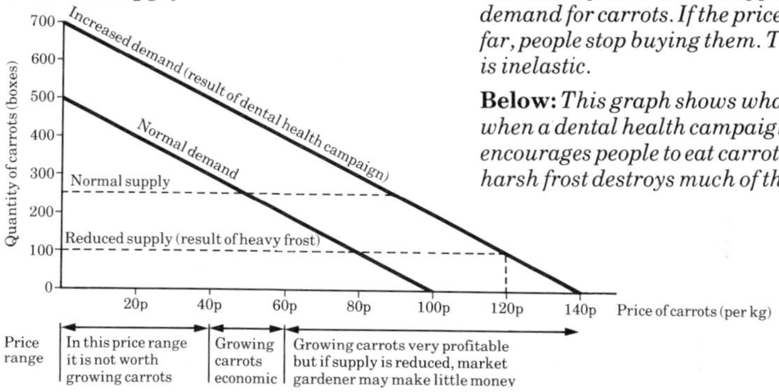

Above: *This graph shows the relationship between the supply and demand for carrots. If the price rises too far, people stop buying them. The demand is inelastic.*

Below: *This graph shows what happens when a dental health campaign encourages people to eat carrots, but a harsh frost destroys much of the crop.*

New Zealand's trade

1969: EEC (excluding UK) 12%, Japan 9%, USA 18%, Australia 7%, Others 12%, Britain 39%, Canada 3%

1985: Japan 14%, USA 15%, Australia 15%, EEC (excluding UK) 10%, Britain 9%, Others 35%, Canada 2%

Increased demand

Reduced supply

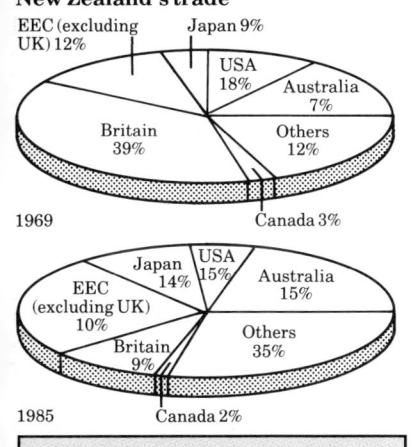

1 In the 1950s and 1960s, why was Britain New Zealand's chief customer for agricultural exports?
2 Why did this relationship change in the 1970s?
3 How did New Zealand respond to the loss of Britain as its chief customer?
4 With which countries has New Zealand increased its trade since the 1970s? What countries might be included in 'others' and why? If trade with these countries is not large enough to be shown separately on the graph what does it suggest about the numbers of countries involved? Is this good or bad? Why?

1 Look at Graph A: What price are carrots under normal supply and demand conditions?
2 What happens to the price of carrots if demand increases and supply remains normal?
3 What happens to the price of carrots if increased demand continues and the supply is reduced?
4 Look at Graph B: What happens to the price of carrots as a result of the health campaign, if supply remains normal?
5 What happens to the price as a result of the frost?
6 What would happen to the price if the government lifted import restrictions?
7 If the supply remains constant, but the Carrot Growers Association runs a successful advertising campaign, what will happen to the price of carrots?
8 Imagine you are a market gardener. In spite of increased demand the frost limited your profits. Would you still grow carrots next year?
9 What factors in the carrot trade are likely to prevent the laws of supply and demand from operating normally?

Staple foods

Flows through a network vary in intensity.

Below: *More than 100 m tonnes of wheat (21% of the world crop) is traded each year. But less than 12 m tonnes of rice (4% of the world crop) is traded annually. Most rice is grown for domestic consumption.*

Trading in grain

The world has six main staple crops: wheat, rice, maize, potatoes, sweet potatoes and cassava. Wheat is the most important cereal crop, with annual production exceeding 500 m tonnes. Rice comes second, with 460 m tonnes produced each year.

- Wheat is a temperate climate crop, harvested only once a year. Between them, the USA, Canada, the EEC, USSR, Australia, Argentina, India and China grow 80 per cent of the world's wheat. In some years, half the global crop enters world trade. The intensity of flow through the trade network varies according to demand. The USSR is usually the world's largest buyer of wheat and demand increases greatly if the Soviet harvest is poor. Some 20 per cent of the world's wheat is used to feed livestock, not humans.

- Rice is grown mainly in tropical countries. Asia produces 90 per cent of world output (with China and India accounting for over half). The USA, USSR, Italy, Spain and France grow rice for the developed world. There are so many varieties of rice that it can be grown almost anywhere between 50°N and 40°S, from land below sea level to 2500 m above. Many places produce two or even three crops a year. Almost all rice is for human consumption: it is the staple food of over one third of the world's population. As with wheat demand fluctuates. Thailand is the top rice exporter. But Indonesia which until 1980 was the largest importer, now produces a surplus.

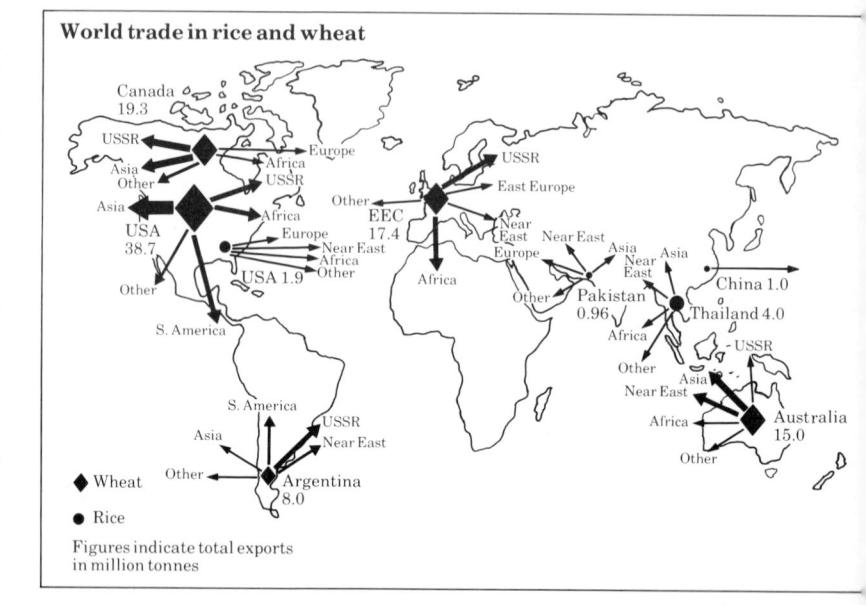

World trade in rice and wheat

Canada 19.3; USSR; Asia; Africa; Other; Asia; USSR; USA 38.7; Africa; Europe; Near East; Africa; Other; USA 1.9; Other; S. America; S. America; Asia; USSR; Near East; Other; Argentina 8.0; USSR; East Europe; Other; EEC 17.4; Near East; Europe; Near East; Asia; Asia; Near East; Africa; Other; Pakistan 0.96; Thailand 4.0; China 1.0; USSR; Other; Asia; Near East; Africa; Australia 15.0; Other

♦ Wheat
● Rice

Figures indicate total exports in million tonnes

Miracle rice

Since 1960 there have been dramatic improvements in rice production.

- Between 1960 and 1980 rice yields increased by 40 per cent. Overall production rose by 60 per cent. The population of Asia grew by 54 per cent during that period, so there is now more food available per head than there was in 1960.

- Increased production is largely due to the introduction of new high-yield rice varieties. These were developed at the International Rice Research Institute (IRRI) in the Philippines. They are short-stemmed and able to withstand high winds: plants make food most efficiently when they stand upright. The new varieties are also disease-resistant and grow quickly, so allowing more crops each year.

- Irrigation, too, has helped boost production. In the southern Indian state of Tamil Nadu, almost 30,000 new wells are sunk each year. These permit farmers to plant rice without waiting for the monsoons, which are erratic both in timing and in the amount of rain they bring.

- These improvements in plant varieties and agricultural methods are often called the Green Revolution. Because of the Green Revolution almost every Asian country has been able to grow more food and reduce imports. In India, cereal production has risen on average by 2.3 per cent a year since 1969. In some states, such as Punjab, it has grown by 7 per cent p.a. Bangladesh has an annual population increase of 2.6 per cent, yet it has managed to cut rice imports by 2 per cent a year. In Malaysia, it has been found that every extra dollar's worth of rice output generates 75 cents' worth of demand for other products, so benefiting the entire economy.

IRRI's 13 week rice system

Week

1	Pl	2	3	4	5	6	7	8	9	10	11	12	H
2	H	Pl	2	3	4	5	6	7	8	9	10	11	12
3	12	H	Pl	2	3	4	5	6	7	8	9	10	11
4	11	12	H	Pl	2	3	4	5	6	7	8	9	10
5	10	11	12	H	Pl	2	3	4	5	6	7	8	9
6	9	10	11	12	H	Pl	2	3	4	5	6	7	8
7	8	9	10	11	12	H	Pl	2	3	4	5	6	7
8	7	8	9	10	11	12	H	Pl	2	3	4	5	6
9	6	7	8	9	10	11	12	H	Pl	2	3	4	5
10	5	6	7	8	9	10	11	12	H	Pl	2	3	4
11	4	5	6	7	8	9	10	11	12	H	Pl	2	3
12	3	4	5	6	7	8	9	10	11	12	H	Pl	2
13	2	3	4	5	6	7	8	9	10	11	12	H	Pl

Above: *The International Rice Research Institute has developed a strain of rice that ripens in 13 weeks from planting. This means that by dividing a 1 ha field into 169 plots, it is possible to plant (Pl) and harvest (H) every week of the year. This is the equivalent of four full crops.*

Above: *Harvested wheatlands in Saskatchewan, Canada. North America is the world's bread basket. Productivity on prairie farms is very high but, as there is a world wheat surplus, prices are low and some farmers have been forced out of business.*

Left: *Winnowing wheat in Syria. Wheat, grown for the home market, is Syria's major crop, occupying 35% of cultivated land. Irrigation, from the Euphrates, is increasing.*

Below: *Over 74,000 varieties of rice have been collected and analysed by the International Rice Research Institute at Los Banos in the Philippines. This research has enabled IRRI to develop new strains.*

Above: *Rice fields are terraced to make flood irrigation possible. The small terraces cannot take machines, so harvesting and threshing is done by hand.*

Food but no reform

The Green Revolution has not solved all the food problems of the LDCs.

■ High-yield varieties of rice require fertilizers. These are expensive and many subsistence farmers cannot afford to buy them, so they cannot benefit from increased production. Also many LDCs do not produce their own fertilizers and must import them.

■ Constant high-yield production, with several crops a year, exhausts the land and can lead to pest epidemics and diseased plants.

■ Social change has not kept up with technical change. In India there have been attempts at land reform since the 1950s. But these have been mostly unsuccessful. This case of one wealthy family in Uttar Pradesh is typical of what happens where land is owned by powerful landlords. The family has benefited greatly from improved seeds and methods and has invested in 15 new wells and a tractor. All the other farmers in the village have only four wells between them and no machines. The landowners have been able to buy up more land and consolidate their holdings, while the other 1200 people in the village still have scattered, small plots. As a result, the landowners have become increasingly rich and politically powerful. The government, anxious for their support, has installed electricity for them alone, while the rest of the village has to rely on oil lamps. This type of story is repeated all over India, where only one per cent of land has been redistributed in the last 25 years.

---

1 Describe world trade in wheat and rice under these headings: a) volume; b) origins; c) destinations.
2 Explain the trade flows you have described.
3 Wheat and rice are considered opposite types of farming systems. What evidence can you find to support or reject this viewpoint?
4 What is the Green Revolution?
5 Give examples of its achievements in rice production.
6 What outstanding problems need to be resolved before the Green Revolution can be a total success?
7 Discuss the role of the International Rice Research Institute in improving rice production in Asia.
8 Why are wheat and rice the world's main staple crops?

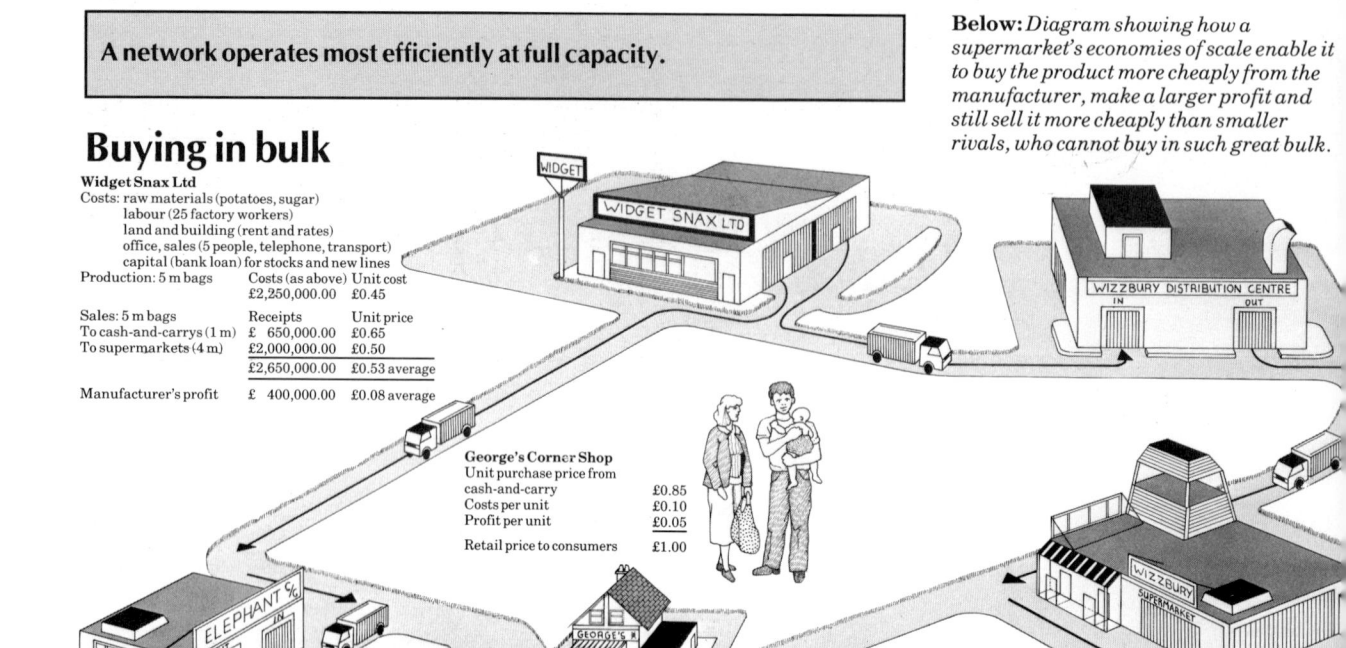

Economies of scale

A network operates most efficiently at full capacity.

Below: Diagram showing how a supermarket's economies of scale enable it to buy the product more cheaply from the manufacturer, make a larger profit and still sell it more cheaply than smaller rivals, who cannot buy in such great bulk.

Buying in bulk

Widget Snax Ltd
Costs: raw materials (potatoes, sugar)
labour (25 factory workers)
land and building (rent and rates)
office, sales (5 people, telephone, transport)
capital (bank loan) for stocks and new lines

Production: 5 m bags	Costs (as above)	Unit cost
	£2,250,000.00	£0.45

Sales: 5 m bags	Receipts	Unit price
To cash-and-carrys (1 m)	£ 650,000.00	£0.65
To supermarkets (4 m)	£2,000,000.00	£0.50
	£2,650,000.00	£0.53 average
Manufacturer's profit	£ 400,000.00	£0.08 average

George's Corner Shop
Unit purchase price from cash-and-carry	£0.85
Costs per unit	£0.10
Profit per unit	£0.05
Retail price to consumers	£1.00

Elephant Cash-and-Carry Ltd
Unit purchase price of Widget Snax	£0.65
Costs per unit	£0.15
Profit per unit	£0.05
Unit selling price to shopkeepers	£0.85

Wizzbury Supermarkets plc
Unit purchase price of Widget Snax	£0.50
Costs per unit	£0.30
Profit per unit	£0.10
Retail price to consumers	£0.90

Economies of scale can be observed all round us, all the time. Whenever a customer buys in **bulk**, he or she is achieving an economy of scale. Buying a larger quantity makes each unit cheaper. The greater the quantity bought, the lower the **unit cost**.

This applies as much to family shopping for soap powder, as it does to a company buying a fleet of trucks. But economies of scale do not work the same way for all products nor for all stages of production and distribution processes. There are practical limits to how much can be bought, or manufactured, at a time.

■ The manufacturer is organized to produce a certain quantity of goods. His plant, operating at full capacity, produces maximum profits. If a manufacturer receives orders for more goods than he can make with his present investment in buildings, people and machinery, he has to decide whether to expand or not. Expansion could be expensive, thus putting up unit costs. Unless he can increase production substantially, profits could be smaller than before.

■ The supermarket might get a better deal from the manufacturer by doubling its order. But managers have to decide if it is worth investing in extra storage space and tying up extra capital in stocks.

■ The consumer can buy in bulk and store perishable goods in a freezer. But if buying a larger freezer adds £200 to the annual food bill, the economies of scale in bulk-buying may be negated.

Cars by the million

Between 1908 and 1927, the Ford Motor Company built 15.4 m of its Model T, the first mass-production car. Between 1945 and 1976, 16.3 m Volkswagen Beetles were manufactured in Germany; although the car is no longer made in Europe, it is still being built in Mexico. These are the kind of success stories all car manufacturers dream about.

■ The largest cost in the production of a new car is research and development, and the establishment of a new production line. These are **fixed costs** – they are the same whether one car is made or one million; small updates to a car's design may add to these. The wider these fixed costs are spread by manufacturing in large volumes, the cheaper the unit cost.

■ If manufacturing costs are kept down by economies of scale, the company can sell its products more cheaply and increase volume further.

■ With low costs and high volume, the company can increase its **margin** – the difference between receipts and expenses. Bigger margins mean more money to invest in new products and larger profits.

Above: The Volkswagen Beetle, conceived in the 1930s as the German People's car, holds the world record for car production; to date almost 21 m have been manufactured.

Above: *The key to profitable car manufacture is high volume. Until recently, this was only possible through employing large numbers of relatively unskilled people. Today high volume can be achieved by investment in automation, like this synchronized robot welding line at Austin Rover's Metro plant. Since the mid-1970s, automation has increased Austin Rover's output by 130%.*

Above: *At its River Rouge plant in Michigan, USA, Ford gains economies of scale by vertical integration: the company owns the coal mines and steel mills that supply River Rouge. Another way to achieve economies of scale is to concentrate production in one place as at Ford's Bridgend plant, Wales, which supplies engines to other Ford factories in Europe.*

Measuring economies of scale

In any business managers have to be able to measure economies of scale in order to find out the **optimum** (most efficient) level of production.

- Volume of production is one way to measure economies of scale. In 1959, 200,000 units a year was the optimum level for Mini production. Today the investment required for a new model is so great (£200 m minimum) that it is necessary to make at least 400,000 a year and preferably 750,000. Beyond this number there is no extra benefit to be gained from producing more: costs and profits are constant. At about 1 m units a year **dis-economies of scale** can set in, making each extra car marginally more expensive to make.
- Another way of measuring economies of scale is by the number of working hours needed to produce one unit. Over the seven-year period 1962-69, Toyota reduced the number of man-hours needed to make one car from 139 to 69. This meant that the same labour force could produce twice as many cars.
- One of the most accurate measures is **value added** per employee. To calculate this it is necessary to know the value of all separate costs that go into a car, compare the total to the value of the finished product and divide that by the number of employees.

Economies at sea

When Japanese manufacturers first exported cars to the USA, they shipped them in ordinary cargo vessels. But the damage was so high they then built their own, special ships. The first Toyota car-carrier began operations in 1968. The largest now carries 4000 cars.

- With ships, largest is not always most economic. In the early 1900s, oil was transported in drums. When demand increased greatly, oil companies built large tankers. The largest are 500,000 tonnes and 500 m long.

- These supertankers are very efficient when operating at full capacity over long distances. But following the 1973-74 oil crisis, consumption in Europe, Japan and the USA fell and there were more very large crude (oil) carriers (VLCCs) than needed. Smaller cargoes could be carried more economically in smaller ships.
- However, if oil prices remain low, countries like the USA and Britain may buy abroad again which would bring VLCCs back into service.

Left: *As world demand for oil fell in the early 1980s, Burmah Oil had to lay up this 450,000 tonne supertanker (seen here towering above the street) at a cost of £500,000 a year. It was brought back into service in 1986 when falling oil prices made its use economic.*

> **1** In the last few years in the UK: a) many small steel mills have been replaced by a few, large integrated mills; b) uneconomic coal mines have been closed; new mines capable of producing 1-10 m tonnes a year have opened; c) football transfer fees have soared to £1 m or more; d) British Rail has introduced special offers such as half price fares to attract passengers; f) London newspaper production has moved out of Fleet Street to Docklands and elsewhere.
> Which of these represent economies of scale? How do they operate? What other information would you need to be sure?
> **2** Write a paragraph to explain the effects of economies of scale on: a) employment; b) retailing; c) office buildings; d) television programmes; e) craft industries.

The road to prosperity

Within a network some routes attract more traffic than others.

The western corridor

The route west out of London has been one of the busiest in Britain's transport network for centuries.
- The Thames valley provided a natural routeway. In the days of horse-drawn traffic, the Great West Road connected the port of Bristol to London.
- In 1841, the Great Western Railway brought prosperity to places like Reading and Swindon.
- The M4 motorway (built in the 1960–70s) made the corridor between London and Cardiff a prime region for industrial expansion.
- This expansion has brought prosperity to the region: in urban areas such as Slough unemployment is about half the national average while house prices are some 30 per cent above; almost all land available for industrial/commercial use in the Thames valley west of the M25 has been used for expanding companies.

Above: Advanced silicon chips are made by Inmos at their Newport plant. Here, a wafer stepper prints the chip circuits on to the silicon wafer. Skilled labour is essential in this type of industry.

Why industry locates along the M4 corridor

☐ Cause ☐ Effect

New manufacturing industries: High-tech firms attracted to South Wales by government grants, low rents, skilled labour and proximity to the M4 include Mitel (telephone systems), Inmos (silicon chips), Matsushita Electric (electronics), Sony (television) and Aiwa (audio).

Government policy: Regional development funds have promoted industrial investment; in Wales, for example, new industries like electronics, have replaced older ones such as coal and steel.

Private sector research: High technology companies have laboratories along the M4 corridor such as Celltech (biotechnology) at Slough, and Hewlett-Packard (computers) at Bristol.

Good rail links: London–Cardiff in 105 minutes; first route for Intercity 125 trains. Rapid, comfortable communications for busy executives.

Defence industries: About 60% of defence expenditure is spent in southern Britain. Half the firms in the M4 area rely on defence for 5–20% of their income: Rolls-Royce, for instance, manufactures military aero-engines near Bristol, employing 8700 people.

Company headquarters: Among the many head offices located in the M4 region are Metal Box (packaging) at Reading, Inmos (integrated circuits) at Bristol, and Honeywell Control Systems (electronics) at Bracknell.

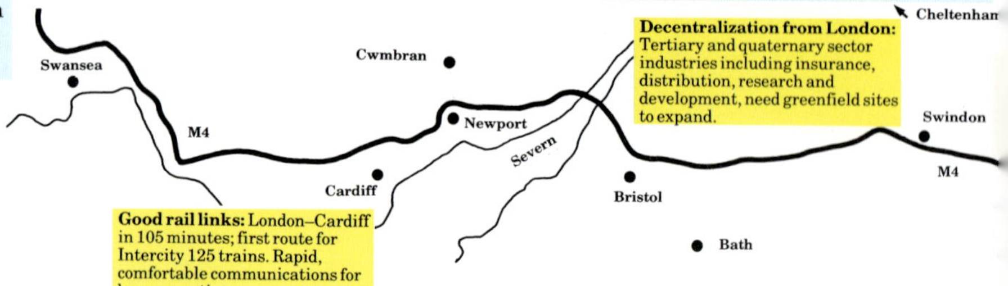

Decentralization from London: Tertiary and quaternary sector industries including insurance, distribution, research and development, need greenfield sites to expand.

Government research centres: Civil research establishments are concentrated in the M4 corridor. They include the Transport and Road Research Laboratory at Crowthorne and the Meteorological Office at Bracknell.

Above: HMS Beaver's computer command system and the radar equipment in the Lynx helicopter were both designed by Ferranti plc. The company's research and development centre for air defence is at Cwmbran, and for naval systems, at Bracknell – both within the M4 corridor.

Above: Turbo-Union RB199 engines for Panavia Tornado all-weather combat aircraft being assembled at the Rolls-Royce Military Engine Group facility at Bristol.

Above: A speeding lorry negotiates the banked bend at the Transport and Road Research Laboratory. The TRRL carries out research into road, traffic and vehicle safety. Its Crowthorne location, well away from densely-populated areas, provides space for a 3800 m circuit with a central area large enough to feature a full-scale junction.

Above: *Windmill Hill, a low-rise integrated business park, is located in the country close to Swindon and the M4. It is designed to serve both business and community needs with office, research, production and storage space alongside shops, banks, car-parks, sports facilities and other amenities.*

Above: *The Head Office of Eagle Star Insurance in Cheltenham. Service industries, such as insurance, must locate where employees wish to live.*

Good environment: Areas of outstanding natural beauty like the Cotswolds attract visitors and residents. High-technology companies prefer attractive environments.

Distribution centres: Easy access to road and rail networks makes the M4 corridor an ideal location for warehouses and national distribution centres. W H Smith, Anchor Foods and Woolworth–all at Swindon, Panasonic at Slough, and BOC Transhield (supplying Marks and Spencer frozen foods) at Newbury, are some of the firms with major storage/distribution facilities in the region.

Highly educated population: 24 per cent more pupils than the national average stay on at school after 16; London, Reading, Oxford, Bath, Bristol, Cardiff and Swansea have universities. A highly-skilled workforce is the main resource of service and research industries.

Availability of capital: Venture capital companies, international banks and the Stock Exchange, all conveniently located in London, provide funds for new projects.

Good road links: M4, M5 and [M]5 motorways connect London [and] the West to other regions. [Dist]ribution companies can serve [the] most prosperous area in the [UK] from centres along the M4.

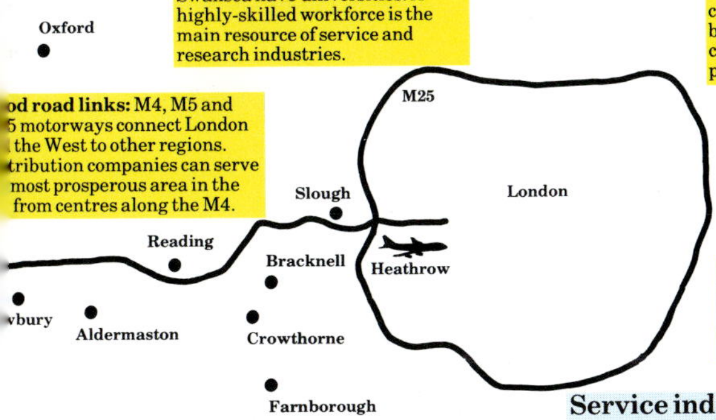

Good air links: Heathrow is the busiest international airport in the world with 31.3 m passengers in 1985. Executives and freight need efficient air connections.

Service industries: The highly qualified, professional people who work in the tertiary sector are well paid and wish to live in attractive environments. Country villages and suburban developments supply the lifestyle they require.

Above: *The RAF's display team, the Red Arrows, in action at the Farnborough Air Show. The Show acts as a shop window for the entire aerospace industry, covering not only aircraft but also equipment such as missiles, radar, flight simulators, communications systems and machine tools. Many of the companies producing this equipment are located along the M4 corridor.*

Above: *Digital Equipment Co Ltd, the UK subsidiary of an American trans-national, manufactures products such as word processors and personal computers. Its spacious headquarters offices are in Reading.*

Incubation and leapfrog

Many firms, newly established in areas of intense economic activity like the M4 corridor, are spin-offs from other companies or research establishments.

■ Often, technologists and entrepreneurs discover an idea with commercial possibilities. The company or laboratory in which they are working at the time constitutes the 'nest' in which the idea is 'laid'.

■ They may leave the nest to 'hatch' or develop their idea elsewhere, either by setting up a new venture or joining another firm. This process is called the incubator theory. Many companies along the M4 (and in California, in Silicon Valley) have evolved in this way.

Another development trend, which also occurs along the M4 corridor, is 'leapfrogging'.

■ Initially, companies decentralize their offices from London and move down the M4, say to Reading.

■ As they expand or set up new companies, the offices are relocated further west where rents are lower. Employees do not have to move house as they can commute along the motorway.

■ PHH International, fleet car management specialists, have had three different locations in seven years: London (13 employees, 140 m^2); Slough (70 employees, 325 m^2); Swindon (560 employees, 6970 m^2). PHH have now moved to a fourth site, a 6.5 ha plot in a Swindon business park.

---

1 Why has the western route out of London been so important for centuries and up to the present?
2 List the various employment opportunities found along the M4.
3 Why are defence related industries, research units and hi-tech firms attracted to the M4?
4 Why do people with new ideas set up business on their own or join another firm?
5 Why do firms tend to move progressively westwards along the M4, away from their original base in London?
6 Write a brief paragraph explaining why main routes are axes of development, whereas the areas in between develop more slowly.

85

Changing world trade

The focus of world trade networks reflects changing political ties.

Trading with the times

Trade has always flowed most freely between places with strong political links. And the centre of world trade has moved as the centre of world political power has changed.

- In ancient times, the Mediterranean was the focus of world political and commercial activity; it retained this position for some 2000 years.
- During the 1500s Latin American wealth made Spain the most important country in Europe. Soon, other countries set up trading colonies: the Dutch in the East Indies, the French and British in North America. The world's commercial centre ceased to be the Mediterranean since all trade now depended on the Atlantic coast ports of Europe.
- By the nineteenth century there was a true global trading network, centred on Europe and the Atlantic. Colonial powers imported raw materials from their colonies and exported finished goods to all parts of their empires. **Colonization** was a process of territorial domination inspired by strategic, material and financial interests and by intense rivalry to extend political control over resources, labour and markets on a large scale.
- In the early 1900s the strength of the US economy pulled the centre of world trade towards New York.
- Since World War II the hubs of world trade have shifted again. The dependence of Europe, Japan and the USA on oil imports from the Middle East made the Persian Gulf a centre of trade and political power. Similarly, the rise of Japanese manufacturing and Californian high technology turned the Pacific Basin into another focal point of world commerce.

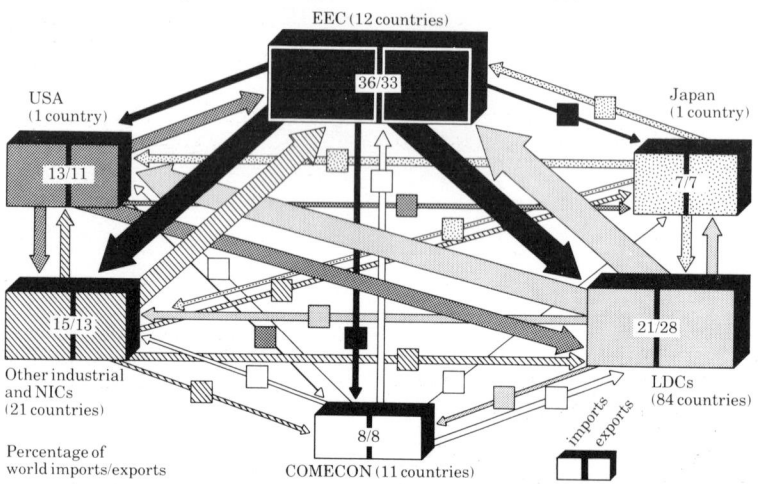

Above: Diagram to show networks between the world's major trading blocks.

World exports and imports (excluding COMECON)

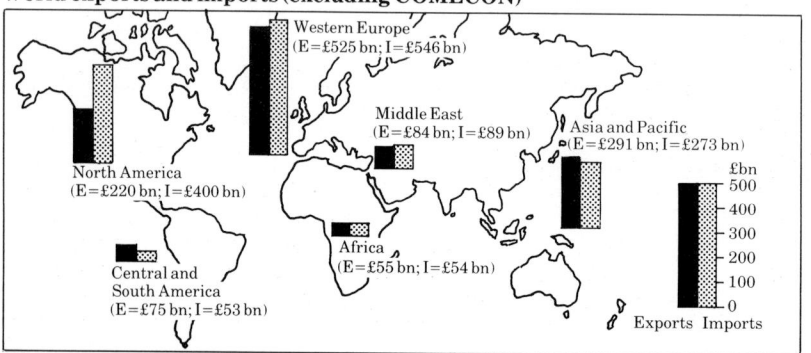

Turbulent tea

Tea, coffee and cocoa – all tropical products – arrived in temperate London in the same year, 1657. The coffee and cocoa trades have had relatively calm histories. But the tea trade began the destruction of ancient Chinese civilization, sparked off the American War of Independence from Britain, brought porcelain to Europe, influenced ship design, and transformed the Indian economy.

Above: For nearly two centuries all tea came from southern China. To pay for it, the East India Company exported opium to China (although the drug was banned there). The British fought and won a war in defence of the opium trade, which eventually had disastrous social effects in China. This contemporary cartoon shows a British Admiral feeding opium to a mandarin.

Above: In their tea ships, the East India Company used porcelain as ballast. But the fine china was so popular that it soon became a major import in its own right. During its first century of tea trading, the Company imported 215 million porcelain pieces to Britain alone. This dish was salvaged in 1985 from the wreck of an East India Company ship sunk in the South China Sea.

Above: *Crisis hit the tea trade in the late 18th century and surpluses were sold to the American colonies. However, a British government tax on imported tea so enraged the traders of Boston that they threw three cargoes of tea into the harbour. The conflict between the American colonists and the London government soon developed into the War of Independence.*

Above: *In the 1850s new, fast ships were built for the tea trade. Clippers raced each other to reduce the voyage home to 100 days.*

Above: *The political instability of China allowed competitor producers into the market. Tea was first grown commercially in India in 1860 and in Sri Lanka in 1890. Today 30% of Britain's tea comes from India and 10% from Sri Lanka (shown here). Other main sources are Kenya (35%) and Malawi (15%).*

Europe's jet

Above: *Airbus hopes to end US domination of civil aircraft manufacture with new, short-haul (TA9) and long-haul (TA11) planes.*

The age of jet transport began with the British Comet in 1952. Since then the jet aircraft industry has been dominated by three American companies, who have built 7100 passenger planes between them – compared with only 1400 built by all other manufacturers together. Boeing alone has built half the western world's jet aircraft.

■ In order to break the US near-monopoly of civil aircraft manufacture, the aviation industries of France, Germany, Britain, Holland and Spain have formed an organization called Airbus Industrie.

■ This was a political decision by European governments. Without vast loans and grants Airbus could never have built an aircraft. It will be many years (if ever) before it is profitable. Yet Airbus has altered the world aircraft market. Sales have also been made to countries outside Europe. Airbus expects to have 20-35 per cent of world sales of all civil jet planes between now and the end of the century.

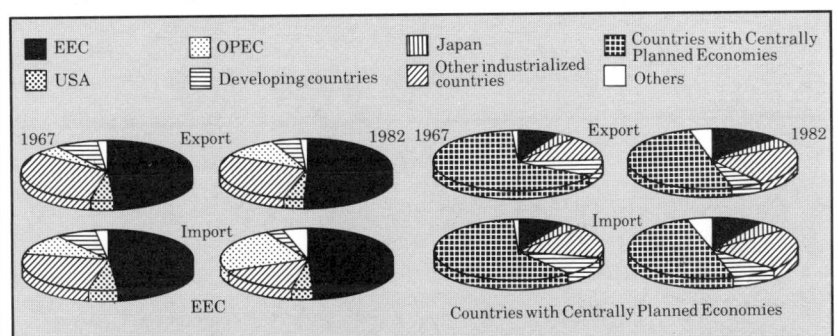

1 Describe what happened to the export trade between members of the European Community between 1967 and 1982. Why did this happen?
2 With which other group of countries did the export trade of the European Community increase between 1967 and 1982?
3 From which group of countries did EEC imports increase between 1967 and 1982? Why?
4 Suggest reasons why EEC imports decreased between 1967 and 1982 from: a) the USA and other industrialized countries; b) developing countries except OPEC states.
5 Suggest what might happen to trade if there was: a) a sharp rise in the price of oil; b) a sharp fall in the price of oil; c) a sustained period of recession in high income countries such as the European Community.
6 With which part of the world do the Centrally Planned Economies trade most? Why?
7 With which other parts of the world have the Centrally Planned Economies increased both their export and import trade between 1967-82? Why?
8 Why has the 'internal trade' between members of the Centrally Planned Economies decreased over the period 1967-82?
9 Why is there virtually no trade between the Centrally Planned Economies and: a) the USA? b) the OPEC countries?
10 From the world map on the previous page, explain which regions have the greatest volume of trade and which the least. Why is it that, apart from North America, imports and exports are more or less equal?

87

Development and change

Within the hierarchy of economic development, the relative positions of different areas are constantly changing.

Subsistence farming

Hierarchies of economic development operate at all scales, from local to worldwide, from rich to poor.
- Subsistence farmers are among the poorest people in the world. They are at the bottom of the economic hierarchy of agriculture. In many countries their farms are plots, smaller than an average garden – with soil so poor that it cannot be cultivated for two years in succession. These farmers cannot afford fertilizers, so when yields fall they are forced to clear new land, often by burning. This is called **shifting cultivation**, or **slash and burn**.

Above: *The Accra plain, Ghana, with vegetation at different stages of regrowth after shifting cultivation; there is new burning on the horizon.*

Subsistence trap

1 Farmer's investment limited to family labour, few tools, poor seed and infertile land (often in scattered plots).

2 Family underfed; lack of resources (skills, energy, finance) to improve land, implements and methods.

3 Crop yields fall, forcing farmer to move and clear new land. Probability of debts from previous bad years.

Shifting cultivation

Zone 1 Zone 2 Zone 3

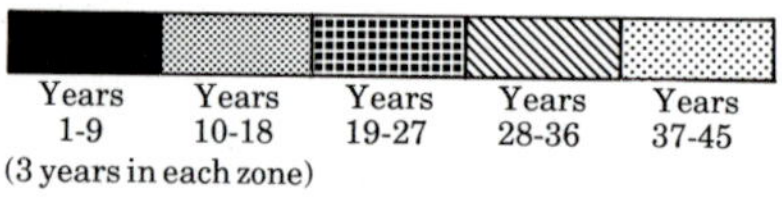

Years 1-9 | Years 10-18 | Years 19-27 | Years 28-36 | Years 37-45
(3 years in each zone)

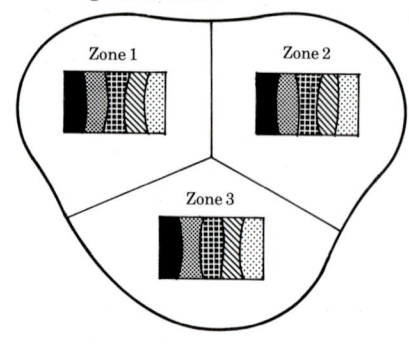

Left: *In parts of Nigeria subsistence farmers 'slash and burn' in a regular cycle, based on three zones. They clear and cultivate a plot in one zone for three years, then move on to a similar plot in the second zone for the next three years; within each zone they ultimately work five plots. The whole cycle lasts 45 years which gives the soil time to recover but, without fertilizer, it remains infertile.*

Above: *Cassava, growing beyond the cleared patch, is the only food crop that survives on badly impoverished soil.*

Singapore moves up in the world

Singapore is a city state. It was founded in 1819 as an East India Company trading post on the route to the Far East. In 1959 the city ceased to be a British colony and became part of the Malaysian Federation. At that stage, Singapore was still a pre-industrial society, low in the world economic hierarchy. Its economy largely depended on the port, which exported rubber, and on British military bases.
- Today Singapore's standard of living is second only in Asia to Japan's. Its port is the fourth busiest in the world and, using oil from Indonesia and Brunei, it ranks as the world's third largest oil-refining centre.
- Yet Singapore still has some problems. Lower oil prices in 1985-86 hit its industries badly, causing an actual fall in GNP. There are also signs of opposition to the one-party government.

Above: *Pulau Bukom refinery. Oil refining is Singapore's main industry; petroleum products account for 31% of all exports.*

Singapore's...

...problems

— Situated in a politically unstable region, threatened by communist infiltration.
— Loss of key role in the trade and communications networks of the British Empire.
— Political disagreements with other members of the Malaysian Federation, leading to Singapore's declaration of independence in 1965.
— High unemployment, serious overcrowding and one of the highest population growth rates in the world (4.4%).
— Internal tensions among three main ethnic groups: Chinese, Malays and Indians.

... solutions

— A modern infrastructure of roads, airport and Jurong industrial estate, the largest in south-east Asia.
— Tax concessions, free trade and other financial incentives to attract trans-national companies.
— New housing schemes to alleviate social unrest: 77% of all people now live in government-built flats.
— A tightly-controlled, cheap labour force: 90% of workers belong to the state-run trade union.
— Improved education to upgrade workforce skills; also re-training for 600,000 people who had only reached primary level.
— Population control: measures include family-planning clinics and tax penalties for couples with more than two children. Growth rate now 1.2%.

... results

— Rapid industrialization: in 1959 only 4% of Singaporeans worked in industry, mostly in textile and leather manufacture; today 29% work in industry, mainly petroleum products, electrical goods, oil rigs, ship repairs and textiles.
— Investment from overseas: trans-national companies now employ 52% of people, account for 71% of output and 84% of exports. New industry generated 500,000 new jobs between 1965 and 1978.
— High growth rates in the world economy (especially in the Pacific) helped Singapore's development; so did the multi-nationals' demand for cheap labour areas.
— Virtual dictatorship by the (largely Chinese) People's Action Party.

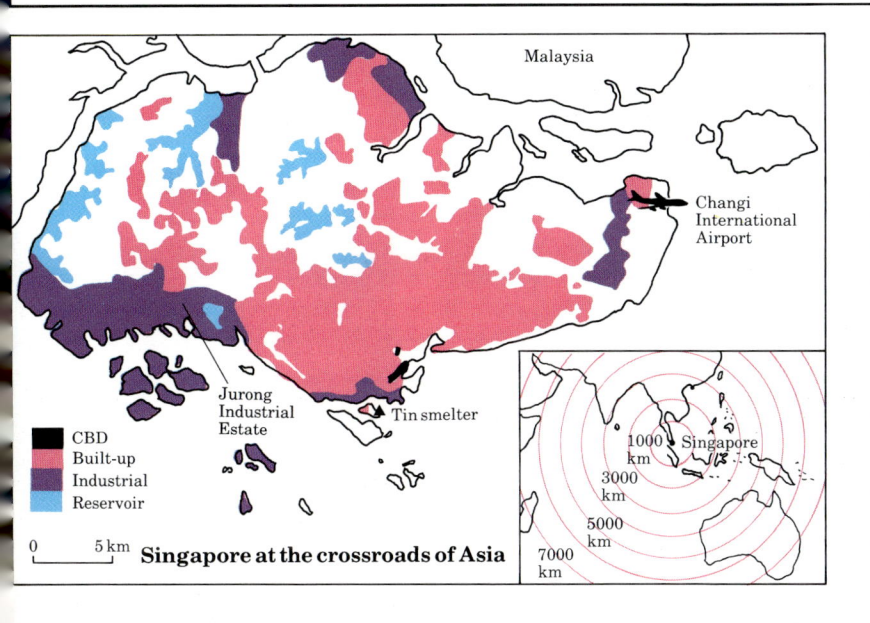

Singapore at the crossroads of Asia

Above: *Singapore's CBD skyline is dominated by the 52-storey Chinese Banking Corporation building (right). Banking and other financial service industries now form the country's leading growth sector.*

Ready for take-off

The way in which countries develop through the economic hierarchy can be plotted on a graph. The time needed for a country to move up from take-off to mass consumption is getting shorter. Britain, the first industrialized country, reached take-off point around 1800; but a mass consumption economy only emerged in the 1930s. In contrast Singapore's development took only 15 years (aided partly by its small size).

The Rostow model

→ Point of take-off   * Point of maturity   ▬ Mass consumption economy

1 What is subsistence farming? Explain how it often involves shifting cultivation.
2 Redraw the subsistence trap diagram showing how the trap might be broken.
3 Singapore is an outstanding example of economic development. Write a brief paragraph summarizing the most important influence in the country's transition.
4 To what extent do you think Singapore could be an example for other LDCs to follow?
5 Describe and explain the Rostow model. Why has it taken countries like Japan and Singapore less time to develop than Britain?

A roof over their heads

HIERARCHIES

> The provision, or supply, of housing is arranged in a hierarchy, according to levels of income or social need.

Living with the past

Reasonable housing is essential to society. But it has never been available equally to everyone. The size and quality of privately owned housing is arranged in a hierarchy according to ability to pay. But the housing market is complicated by many other factors. Among these are:

- The varied nature of housing inherited from the past.
- The idea that society has a responsibility to house everyone decently, even if this means subsidizing public housing.
- The fact that the state owns almost one-third of all housing; in some inner city areas local authorities own three-quarters of all housing.
- Central government policy, such as grants for home improvements and tax concessions on mortgages.
- Competition for land; only agriculture uses up more land than housing.

Above: *For centuries landowners controlled housing in the country, renting cottages to tenants in return for labour or money. In the 1700s a few built model estate villages like Milton Abbas, shown here (often because they wished to destroy the existing village as it spoilt the view from their mansion). Many agricultural workers today still live in tied cottages, owned by the farmer.*

Above: *Georgian town houses in Edinburgh. In the 1800s, as living standards rose, wealthier people bought elegant town houses from developers; such houses were large enough to accommodate a family and servants.*

Above: *During the Industrial Revolution, mill- and factory-owners put up houses in back-to-back terraces and rented them to workers. The houses, like these in Rotherham, were built as cheaply and close together as possible; with just one room on each floor, they had no bathroom, WC or garden.*

Left: *In the 1900s railways, and then cars, improved transport enormously; also, more people could afford to buy their own homes. Between 1920–39 the number of houses in Britain doubled; most were built in suburbia and along main roads. In the London area people were encouraged to move out to properties with gardens in 'Metroland', served by the Metropolitan Railway.*

Above: *In preference to tower blocks (which develop structural and social problems) councils now build low-rise housing estates both in inner city areas and on the outskirts. In inner city zones some councils try to rehabilitate existing housing; also, middle-class families not wanting to commute buy centrally-located homes and improve, or 'gentrify', them.*

Owners and tenants

Most people cannot afford to purchase a flat or house outright as, on average, a house costs seven times more than the annual wage.
- Generally people buy houses on mortgages – long-term loans. Interest paid on these loans is deducted from tax, representing a subsidy to home owners of £2 bn a year.
- The trend towards owner-occupancy has increased rapidly in Britain. In 1919 only 10 per cent of Britons owned their accommodation. Today 60 per cent do. This is a higher rate than in any other European country (West Germany 40 per cent, France 51 per cent) and only just behind the USA with 64 per cent.
- The 1980 Housing Act enabled tenants to buy council houses: over half (three million) have been sold.
- Since 1945 the private rented sector has declined from over 60 per cent to less than 15 per cent. This is largely because new laws have given tenants better conditions, and made housing less profitable for landlords.

Right: In the private sector, the decrease in rented accommodation causes problems for mobile parts of the population, such as students and those moving to find new jobs.

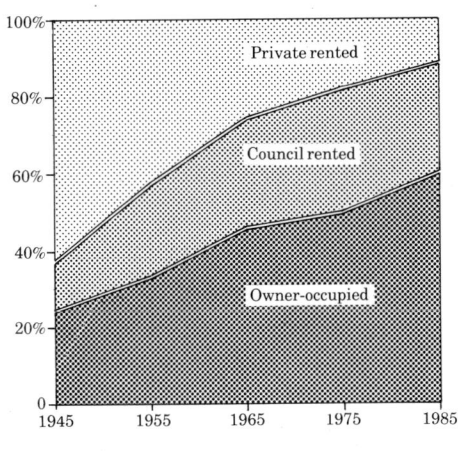

House tenure in Britain

On the housing list

Hull City Council owns 47,000 flats and houses. Each year several thousand are re-let. A points scheme ensures that dwellings are offered first to those on the waiting list in most need. There are two kinds of points:
- Needs points: given to people who lack or share certain amenities (e.g. WC, kitchen) in their existing accommodation; or to people who suffer from stress, hardship or sickness.
- Waiting points: half the value of needs points is added to the total for each year a person is on the waiting list. Extra points are also given to existing council tenants and to the elderly.

Welcome to the Points House

Needs Points
Look at the box which describes your family. Only include the people who will be moving with you.

Waiting Points
Waiting points = half of total needs points.
Waiting points are added every year.
Extra waiting points are given to Council tenants and pensioner families.

Amenities
Inside W.C.
Fixed bath or shower.
Running hot water.
Separate kitchen.

Needs Points + Waiting Points = Total Points

When will I get an offer of housing?
I will be offered this house if I am the person with the most points who wants this kind of house in this area. Only someone moving from a slum clearance area or someone who needs to move because of ill health can take priority over me.

Above: In 1985 Hull Civic News, a free paper distributed by the City Council, described the new points system.

---

1 Imagine you are the Housing Manager responsible for allocating council houses to the applicants described here. Who would you put at the top of the list (priority), who at the bottom, and why? What encouragement could you give the family at the bottom of the list? Here is the points allocation for families with two children:
11 points for each basic amenity (inside WC, bath, hot water, separate kitchen) you lack.
6 points for each basic amenity you share.
8 points if you lack one bedroom.
16 points if you lack two bedrooms.
20 points if you lack 3 bedrooms.
14 points because you have children in a flat or maisonette.

a) John and Jane have two children, Mark aged 10, and Mary aged 14. They live in a two-bedroom flat which they rent privately. They share the bathroom and outside WC, but have their own kitchen. There is no running hot water in the house. They put their name on the council waiting list a year ago.

b) Pam shares her bedroom with her two daughters, Linda (15) and Tracey (16), in rented accommodation in a friend's three-bedroom house. Her friend Sue has two boys, aged six and nine. Pam shares all four amenities with Sue. She has only been on the council housing list since her divorce last year.

c) Esther and Everton have two rooms in her mother's house. They have twins who are now nine. They share all amenities with her mother. They put their name on the housing list when the twins were born.

2 How does housing inherited from the past affect the type of accommodation available today?

3 How is housing affected by local government? By central government?

4 Why are there two different hierarchies of housing provision?

5 Imagine you are a council tenant with the possibility of buying your council house. Explain why you would or would not buy it.

Primate cities

In some countries one city has grown so large that it dominates the hierarchy of settlements.

In order of size

In a hierarchy of settlements the relative size of each city usually follows one of three models.

- **Primate city:** when one city is more than twice the size of the next largest, it is called a primate city. Paris (population 8.5 m) is a primate city, as Lyon has only 1.2 m people.
- **Rank-size rule:** when the largest city is approximately twice the size of the second largest, three times the third largest, and so on.
- **Even distribution:** when no city is dominant, and many cities have approximately the same sized population.

Primate city

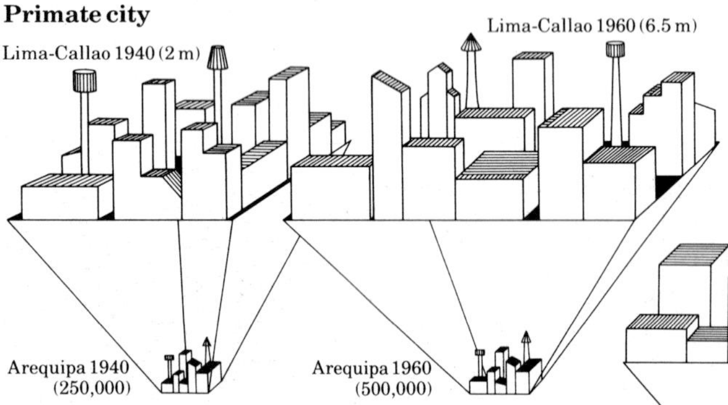

Lima-Callao 1940 (2 m)
Lima-Callao 1960 (6.5 m)
Arequipa 1940 (250,000)
Arequipa 1960 (500,000)

Above: *In South America there is an increasing trend towards primacy of cities. In 1940 Lima-Callao, in Peru, was eight times larger than the next largest city, Arequipa. By 1960 Lima was 13 times larger. In Chile, Santiago increased from four times the size of Valparaiso to 7.5 times in the same period.*

Rank-size rule

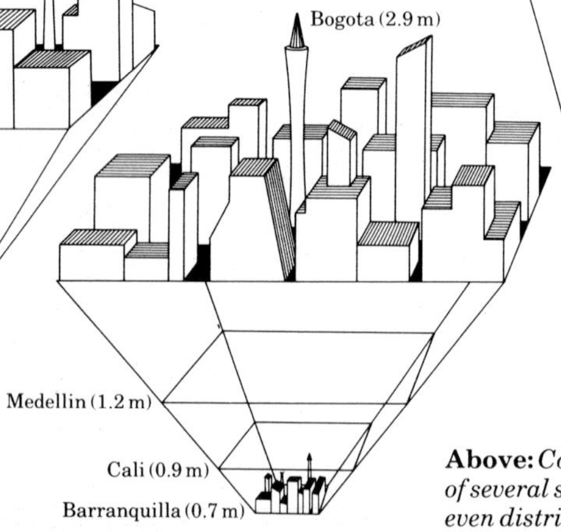

Bogota (2.9 m)
Medellin (1.2 m)
Cali (0.9 m)
Barranquilla (0.7 m)

Above: *The only country in Latin America to follow the Rank-size rule is Colombia. The capital, Bogota, is approximately twice the size of Medellin, three times the size of Cali, and four times the size of Barranquilla.*

Even distribution

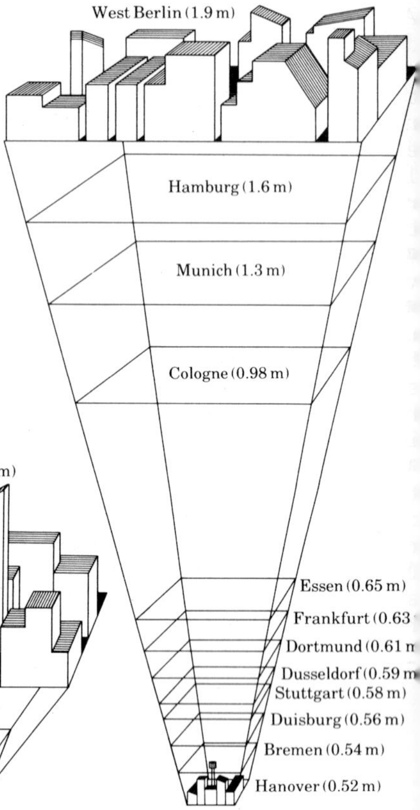

West Berlin (1.9 m)
Hamburg (1.6 m)
Munich (1.3 m)
Cologne (0.98 m)
Essen (0.65 m)
Frankfurt (0.63 m)
Dortmund (0.61 m)
Dusseldorf (0.59 m)
Stuttgart (0.58 m)
Duisburg (0.56 m)
Bremen (0.54 m)
Hanover (0.52 m)

Above: *Countries which are federations of several states are more likely to have an even distribution of city sizes. Berlin was divided in 1945. As a result the German Federal Republic (population 61 m) has no city over 2 m. But it has twelve cities of more than 500,000 inhabitants. There is no dominant city and a relatively even distribution of population.*

How to become primate

Primate cities are found all over the world: in LDCs, developed countries, large and small countries, capitalist and socialist countries. A primate city emerges because of:

- **Centralization:** when all political and economic power has been concentrated in one place for a long time. Louis XIV consolidated the process of centralization that made Paris a primate city.
- **A tributary economy** in the rest of the country: when all contacts with other countries – financial, trade, cultural – pass through one place, often the main port of entry.

Right: *Louis XIV centred all France on himself and his palace at Versailles, near Paris, where 20,000 courtiers and administrators worked and lived.*

Primate of the Nile

Two cities feature prominently on the map of Egypt: Alexandria and Cairo.
- Alexandria, founded in 322 BC, was the former capital. Today, it is the major port on the Nile delta.
- Cairo, the present capital, is just over 1000 years old. A bridging point, it stands where the Nile fans out into its delta.

It was only in 1907, when its population reached twice the level of Alexandria's, that Cairo began to be the dominant, primate city. Since then the difference has been exaggerated, so that today Cairo has a population of 14 m, Alexandria only 2.5 m. Their combined populations represent 33 per cent of the Egyptian total. This trend is likely to increase.
- A hundred years ago 17 per cent of Egypt's population was urban. Today it is around 50 per cent.
- This overcrowding of cities means that slums spring up in the outskirts, while in central areas shacks have been built on top of tenements, and hovels on top of the shacks. Services such as sewerage, refuse disposal, healthcare, education and power supplies are hopelessly inadequate.
- The Egyptian government has attempted to reduce the problem by building new satellite towns about 60 km outside Cairo. Birth control is encouraged; so is development in rural areas to discourage migration to Cairo. Many Egyptians also go to work in richer Arab countries, sending home large amounts of foreign currency, which help Egypt's balance of payments.

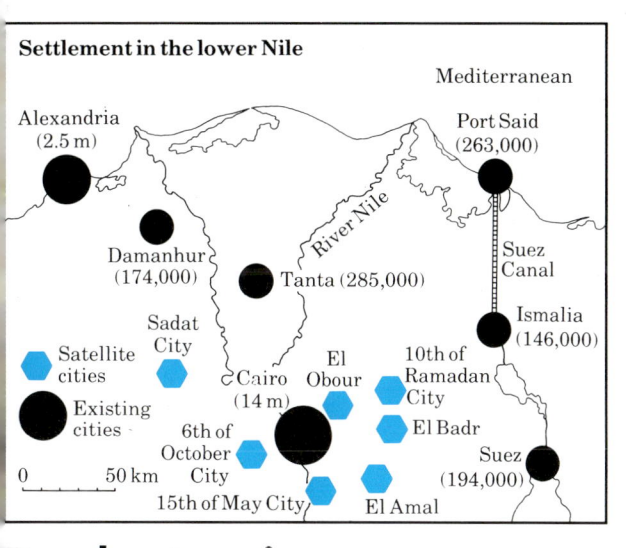

Above: *Cairo, the largest city in Africa and the Middle East, is expanding by over 250,000 people p.a. and, in spite of new building schemes, it still has a severe housing crisis.*

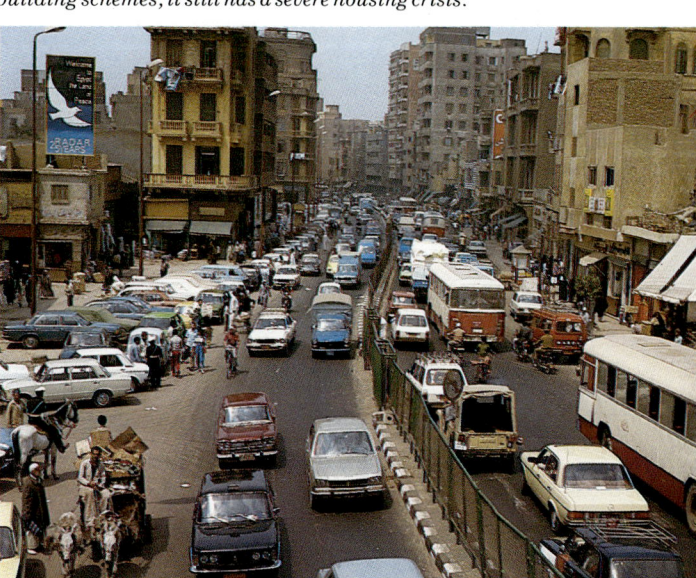

Above: *Traffic is now a major problem. In some parts of the city, elevated expressways are being built to ease congestion.*

Left: *To relieve over-population, seven satellite towns are being developed around Cairo.*

Rural enterprise

Sixty years ago Diyarb Negm was a typical poor village in the Nile delta. Today it is a model of rural development.
- Many villagers went away to work in the oil fields of the Gulf States. For years the £3-5 m they sent home annually bought property or imported consumer goods.
- Eventually 200 people formed the Diyarb Negm Investment Company, investing £10,000 each.
- The company has financed various projects, including: 50 broiler houses to raise 1.5 m chickens a year; a mill producing 10 tonnes of animal feed an hour; a plastics plant making bags for the mill; a sportswear factory providing 2000 jobs.
- With more jobs and increased local prosperity, emigration to the cities has fallen sharply.

---

1 What is a primate city? Give an example.
2 Explain the Rank-size rule. Name a country which has a settlement hierarchy of this type.
3 To which model do Britain's settlements belong?
4 What are the consequences of primacy on:
a) political power and control?
b) headquarters of financial institutions and of industrial firms?
c) information technology?
d) population growth and settlement conditions?
5 Which model of settlement hierarchy do you think is preferable? Write a paragraph giving your opinion and reasons.

Separate development

Some institutions attempt to preserve artificial social hierarchies.

White and black tribes

The word apartheid means 'separateness' in Afrikaans, the Dutch-derived language spoken by the majority of white people in South Africa. In practice apartheid means that whites, who number 4.8 m, have the monopoly of political power and enjoy a high standard of living. Meanwhile the majority, 24.1 m black people – plus 2.8 m coloureds (mixed race) and 900,000 Indians – have little say in the country's affairs and a much lower standard of living.

- South African whites are different from other European colonial populations in several ways. The original Dutch colony – established in 1652 as a supply station for shipping – was taken over by the British in 1815. The fiercely independent Boers, as the Dutch settlers were called, so resented British rule, that they trekked north to find new farmland and set up their own independent states. It was only after two wars that Boer and British territories united to form the Union of South Africa. The Boers had not mixed with the indigenous population (like the Spaniards did in Latin America), nor with British colonists. They remained separate – the so-called 'white tribe of Africa'.

- The black population comes from the nine main tribal groups that originally occupied the land. Many of them, like the Zulus, fought fiercely against white colonization. The coloureds have mixed ancestry while the Asians are mostly descendants of Indians brought in to work on sugar plantations.

- Around 1900, half the white population lived in country areas and only 15 per cent of blacks lived in cities. But as the South African economy developed and its cities grew, more whites and especially blacks moved to urban areas. Today 89 per cent of whites, 79 per cent of coloureds and 46 per cent of blacks live in cities.

Above: *A Boer waggon negotiates a mountain pass during the Great Trek. From the mid-1830s to mid-1840s, thousands of Boers rejected British rule by leaving the Cape and moving north to colonize new territory. In this way the Voortrekkers, as they were called, founded the Transvaal and the Orange Free State and so subjected an increasing number of native Africans to European domination.*

Enforcing apartheid

Above: *So-called 'petty apartheid' has been reduced, but there are still controls stopping blacks using 'white-only' beaches, toilets, buses and restaurants.*

When the Boers were still farmers, owning the land by right of conquest, apartheid needed no laws to support it. Today white domination is enforced by laws that are supposed to allow for the separate development of each racial group. In practice, this means keeping power and wealth in the hands of whites, with Asians and coloureds as second-class and blacks as third-class citizens.

- Blacks are restricted in where they can live, being mostly confined to 'townships', on the outskirts of large cities. From places like Soweto (South West Townships, 12 km from Johannesburg) they commute to low-paid jobs in white areas. Each of the main tribes has also been allocated a 'homeland' in the interior. Most of the land is poor and unproductive; there are few jobs and little industry. Yet three million blacks have been forcibly moved to these areas to live in poverty, often separated from family wage earners working in distant cities.

- Until July 1986, the regulations controlling the movement of blacks were enforced by the Pass Laws. All blacks had to carry identity cards proving they had permission to live and work in certain places. Every year 200,000 blacks were arrested for Pass Law offences.

- Education for blacks is limited, and only 2 per cent of black children complete secondary education compared to 58 per cent of white.

Right: *Some 13 m blacks, 54% of the total black population, live in the homelands. The remaining 11 m are mostly confined to the townships. The two largest tribal groups, Zulu and Xhosa, each has around 6 m people. Lesotho is an independent country within South Africa's borders.*

World against apartheid

Outside South Africa apartheid is generally condemned as a breach of all fundamental human rights. It denies people equal opportunities on account of colour and race. It separates and breaks up families. It maintains an artificial hierarchy, reserving a high standard of living for one small group. It restricts political power to a racial minority.

■ Governments and individuals worldwide detest apartheid, but there are limits to what they can do to change the internal policies of the South African regime. South Africa is no longer a member of international bodies, such as the Commonwealth, and is excluded from many world events like the Olympic Games. Some governments have introduced economic sanctions, restricting trade and communications; while many individuals and companies boycott South African goods.

■ But such measures are relatively ineffective. There are several reasons for this: most large trading nations, particularly Britain, have too much to gain from South African trade to abandon it completely; in the free societies of the West, some people choose either to support apartheid or at least ignore action against it; rich contracts lure international companies, sportspeople and entertainers to South Africa.

■ Recently the pressure for change has increased within South Africa itself. Political unrest, including violent clashes between township-dwellers and white authorities, has claimed almost 1000 victims annually. Much of the opposition is organized by the banned African National Congress party. The economy has been weakened by strikes of black workers, for example in the gold mines which produce 50 per cent of South Africa's export earnings. Blacks have also successfully boycotted white shops.

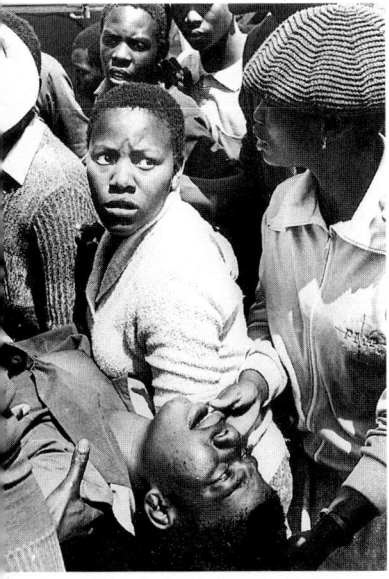

Above: *Rioting is one of the few ways in which blacks can express their frustration. This youth was injured in a confrontation with police. He later died.*

Above: *An anti-apartheid demonstration in London. Many individuals express their disapproval of apartheid by taking part in protest marches and by boycotting South African goods, especially fruit and canned foods.*

Below: *A woman protests at the presence of troops in the township. Over the last few years, violent protest has increased to such a degree that in 1986 the South African government banned international TV coverage and subjected all news reports to censorship.*

South Africa and its black population

1 How did apartheid originate?
2 What, from the white South African's point of view, was the purpose of apartheid?
3 How is apartheid enforced?
4 Imagine that you are: a) a white South African, whose family has been there for many years. You have a large, comfortable house with a swimming pool, two cars and a black maid; you work in an air-conditioned downtown office; b) a black worker living in a township. Your family live in a distant homeland. You get up every morning at 04.00, and ride a bus for three hours to get to work and earn just 25% of a white person's wage. Write two paragraphs explaining each person's view of apartheid.
5 What is your own view about apartheid?

Planning the economy

HIERARCHIES

In some countries new economic and political hierarchies have been imposed.

The Soviet master plan

When Lenin came to power in 1918 Russian industry, agriculture and transport were in ruins. Peasants seized land and workers took over factories. In theory the state took control of everything, but civil war and drought made conditions chaotic. By 1920, famine was so bad that a few people resorted to cannibalism.

■ In 1921 a New Economic Plan was launched which led to some improvements. But it was not until Stalin launched the first Five Year Plan, in 1927, that new factories, mines, dams, roads and railways were built. Despite immense hardship, the USSR was converted from an agricultural economy to a 50 per cent industrialized state within four years (not five).

■ The next Plan focused on peasant farmers. In five years almost all land was collectivized, often at gunpoint. Food shortages, however, continued.

■ Post-war Five Year Plans were less successful. More investment went into industry than into agriculture. Although farm production was increased, it has not kept pace with consumption. Only in years of exceptionally good harvests can the USSR feed itself.

■ Under the twelfth Five Year Plan (1986-90) 27 per cent of all investment is directed into agriculture; a further eight per cent is devoted to processing farm products. A million more tractors will be made. Production from 60,000 state and collective farms, is scheduled to increase by up to 25 per cent.

■ Yet a quarter of all the USSR's food supplies, including 60 per cent of its potatoes, comes from private plots and gardens that account for less than three per cent of all farmed land.

Below: *Moscow's metro was one of many transport schemes carried out in the 1930s. The poster reads: 'First class transport for the proletarian capital'.*

1000 million Communists

Rural administration in China
Pre-revolution / Post-revolution

○ Village
□ Market village
⌂ Administrative town
○ Production team (100–200 people)
△ Brigade (10 Production teams)
◇ Commune (about 6 Brigades)

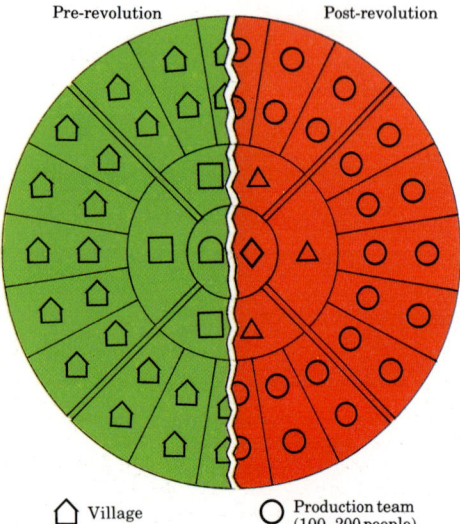

Above: *The rural hierarchy imposed by the Communist government was similar to that which existed before the revolution.*

Before 1949 China was a feudal society with a rural economy. A ruling elite, comprising less than 10 per cent of the population, owned 80 per cent of the land. The peasantry either farmed the remaining 20 per cent, or worked as landless labourers. Cities, such as Shanghai, had economies based on overseas trade.

■ In 1949 after a long struggle, the Communists – led by Mao Tse-tung – came to power. They adopted the Soviet model of a socialist economy. A central bureaucracy was set up to run agriculture, transport, industry and banks and to control all aspects of daily life. Soviet experts were brought in to develop heavy industry.

■ After 1960 Sino-Soviet relations deteriorated. Mao attempted to solve China's internal problems by means of the Cultural Revolution which caused havoc through its severity.

■ Since the death of Mao in 1976, reforms have once again changed rural China. Farmers can now make profits: this has more than doubled the value of farm production. China is now self-sufficient in many crops.

Above: *The commune system gave peasants no incentive. Jobs were allocated by Party officials and all commune workers were paid more or less the same regardless of how hard they worked.*

Above: *Since 1978, the new Responsibility system allows free enterprise once targets have been met. Farmers, now able to sell surplus in local markets, have an incentive to grow more.*

Above: *New rural enterprise includes collectives, like this embroidery factory, which provide necessary employment in country areas. Twenty-five million people earn their living from rural industries.*

Above: *The return of free enterprise has raised standards of living and increased consumer spending. Once, bicycles were a luxury; now people can save for TVs and refrigerators.*

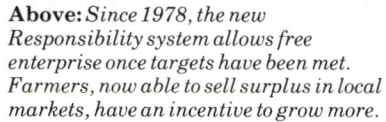

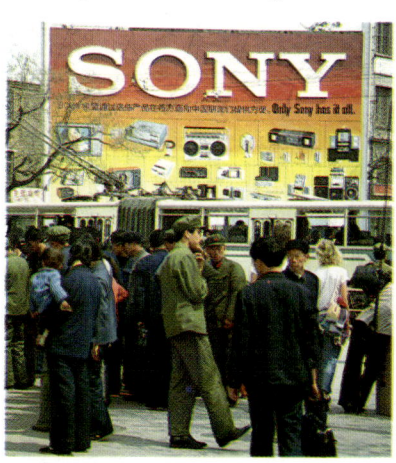

Above: *Foreign manufacturers, especially the Japanese, have now moved into China's expanding consumer market. This Sony advertisement dominates one of Peking's main streets.*

Above: *Peking's second-hand motorcycle market is also free enterprise. Ten years ago there were no private motor bikes in Peking: now there are 14,000 – but a new one costs four years' basic pay.*

Kibbutz community

A kibbutz is a rural enterprise in Israel based on principles of co-operative work and collective ownership of property and land.
■ There are over 275 kibbutzim throughout the country, varying in size from 200 to 2000 people.
■ All kibbutz members benefit from the same services such as food, housing, education and health care. They work without wages but do receive money for personal use.
■ Kibbutzim operate democratically and members accept the communal system voluntarily.
■ Originally farm communities, most kibbutzim now have factories as well and produce seven per cent of Israel's industrial exports.

Above: *Kibbutz farms are highly efficient, accounting for 40 per cent of the country's agricultural output. Many young people from overseas serve in kibbutzim as short-term volunteers.*

1 How was Russia transformed from an agricultural state into an industrialized one?
2 Why is Russia unable to meet its food requirements in most years?
3 Moscow's metro provides cheap, rapid and reliable transport. Why is it necessary?
4 How is China being converted from a feudal society into a modern economy?
5 What is different about the Responsibility system? How does this fit in with communist ideals?
6 How do kibbutzim differ from communist collectives or communes?
7 Why do you think young people from other countries go to live on kibbutzim?

Skyscraper cities

MORPHOLOGY

The intensity of urban land use depends on its proximity to the centre.

Why so high?

City centres (CBDs) are attractive places; not always attractive to look at, but attracting people in large numbers for work, shopping, recreation, education or to obtain professional services, such as legal or medical help. The fact that CBDs pull in so many people has important effects on the way in which city-centre land is used.

- Shops and offices must locate where they can attract most custom.
- Most custom corresponds to the greatest pedestrian flows.
- Pedestrians tend to walk in straight lines, so the best sites are up and down the main streets of CBDs.
- The competition for these sites is very fierce, forcing up the prices of the best positions. Business will pay high prices, if they can attract enough custom to make a profit.
- In order to achieve the high returns needed to pay the price of locating in the best CBD sites, firms have to make maximum use of the land. This usually means building vertically.
- The result of pressure on the limited space available in the CBD is high-rise blocks – skyscrapers in the biggest cities – in the CBD. These are often divided into shops on the lower floors, offices above and sometimes penthouse apartments at the top.
- Alternatively, pressure on the CBD can force businesses to relocate to the city outskirts.

Above: *Some of the world's highest skyscrapers. All are in CBDs, where many floors of revenue-earning space (as offices, shops or tourist attractions) are needed to make a profit from the most expensive land in the city.*

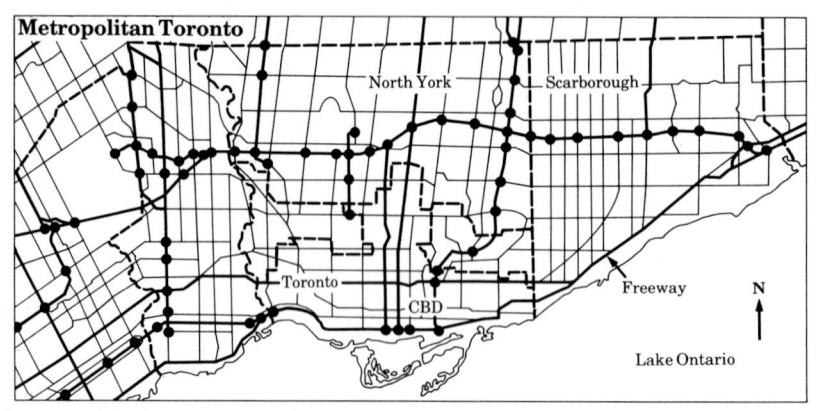

(NatWest Bank Tower, London (183 m), UK's tallest building; Eiffel Tower, Paris (300 m), Europe's tallest building since 1889; Centrepoint, Sydney (305 m) tallest building in the southern hemisphere; Empire State Building, New York (381 m), world's tallest building 1931–73; Sears Tower, Chicago (442 m), world's tallest building)

Above: *Over half Toronto's CBD has been redeveloped in the past 20 years. Major banks and mining companies have built skyscrapers in the middle of the CBD, with hotels, stores and entertainments on the edge, and smaller office buildings and shopping areas in suburban centres, such as North York.*
Right: *Cross-section of property values in the City of London. The most expensive sites are largely taken by banks and other financial institutions.*

What is the price?

The main cost of a property is the rent plus the **rates** – local taxes.

- Rates are calculated on the value of land, the buildings on the land, what facilities are in the buildings and on the use to which the buildings are put. Offices attract the highest rates, followed by other commercial and industrial uses, such as shops and factories. Residential use attracts the lowest rates.
- Land values, and therefore rent and rates, are highest in the middle of CBDs and diminish with distance.

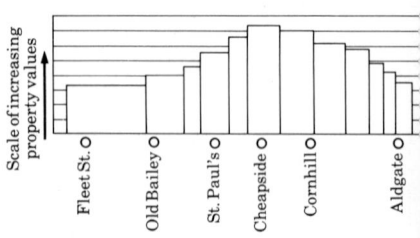

(Scale of increasing property values: Fleet St., Old Bailey, St. Paul's, Cheapside, Cornhill, Aldgate)

Left: *While inner city areas around the CBDs of many North American cities have declined, metropolitan Toronto's population has more than doubled in the last 30 years. The result has been pressure on CBD land values and many skyscrapers. 25% of Toronto's jobs are in the CBD, yet it only occupies 0.2% of the land area.*

At the crossroads

The most accessible points in a shopping area are often where two main streets cross or meet. Shops sited there pay the highest rents.

■ Such key positions are known as **peak land value intersections**. The most expensive of these sites are in the CBD, but at other intersections, such as suburban shopping centres, land values reach a local peak.

■ The further away a shop is sited from the peak land value intersection the smaller the pedestrian flow and the lower the rent paid for the space.

■ Different businesses have different land/price requirements: some, like warehouses, need a great deal of cheap space regardless of pedestrian flow; others, such as department stores, require a high level of passing trade even if the space is expensive.

■ As a result, most towns present a certain degree of uniformity with similar businesses sited in similar positions. Top value High Street locations are often taken by department stores and service companies (banks and building societies), which can afford high rents. Smaller shops are pushed out to the ends of the main street. Doctors, dentists, solicitors and insurance brokers often establish themselves on the fringes of the main shopping area. Residents and small family firms sell and move out because their property rises in value.

Peak land value intersection

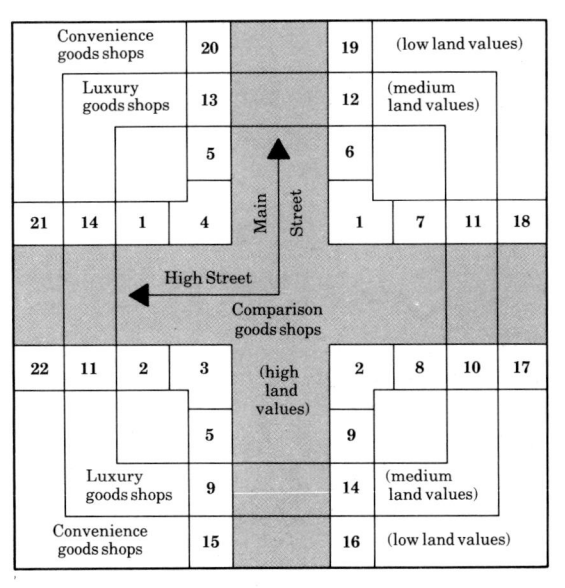

Comparison goods shops (high land values)
1 Department store (chain)
2 Supermarket (chain)
3 Large chemist (chain)
4 Bank 5 Ladies fashions
6 Shoes 7 Furniture
8 Newsagent/books/stationers
9 Building Society
Luxury goods shops (medium land values)
10 Travel agent 11 Men's fashions 12 Antiques
13 Jeweller 14 Estate agent
Convenience goods shops (low land values)
15 Butcher 16 Grocer
17 Hardware 18 Dry cleaner 19 Small chemist
20 Toys 21 Car showroom 22 Café

Left: *Land values create a trend in the location of businesses.*

Below: *From general patterns of urban land use, it is possible to build up a typical picture or urban transect.*

Urban transect

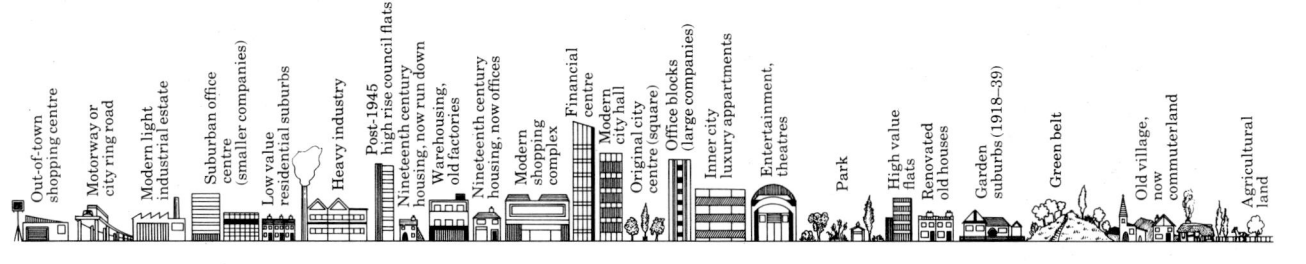

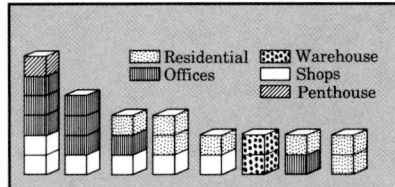

Out-of-town shopping centre; Motorway or city ring road; Modern light industrial estate; Suburban office centre (smaller companies); Low value residential suburbs; Heavy industry; Post-1945 high rise council flats; Nineteenth century housing, now run down; Warehousing, old factories; Nineteenth century housing, now offices; Modern shopping complex; Financial centre; Modern city hall; Original city centre (square); Office blocks (large companies); Inner city luxury apartments; Entertainment, theatres; Park; High value flats; Renovated old houses; Garden suburbs (1918–39); Green belt; Old village, now commuterland; Agricultural land

---

Residential Warehouse
Offices Shops
Penthouse

1 Refer to this rent gradient diagram (above):
a) Which activity occurs most frequently on the lower floors?
b) Which activity is absent from the ground floor? Why?
c) Why is the penthouse only found nearest to the city centre?
d) Why does the overall height of buildings decrease away from the city centre?
e) How does the income generated by each of the land uses relate to where they are found both horizontally and vertically?

1880
1950
Today

2 These diagrams summarize the changes in land use from 1880.
a) Describe what has happened to this piece of land over the past century.
b) Explain these changes in land use. Consider mobility, shopping habits, construction techniques, motives of retailers/property developers, property values.
c) Why did this piece of land become increasingly valuable?

3 Using the diagram of the peak land value intersection (top):
a) Which areas have the highest and lowest rents and rateable values?
b) What happens to the rateable value as you proceed from the crossroads outwards?
c) Why do rent and rateable values vary in this way?
d) What use is made of the zone with the highest rents and rateable values?
e) What uses dominate in the zone with the lowest rents and rateable values?
f) Which single point in the city centre do you think has the highest rateable value/rent? Why?
g) What pressures are there on the houses nearest to the CBD edge?

Plantation agriculture

MORPHOLOGY

> Large-scale monoculture requires large-scale investment.

Crops and countries

Plantations are large agricultural estates, producing a single crop. This is called **monoculture**. Most plantations are in tropical LDCs. Many of them are owned by trans-national companies, which sell the crop throughout the world.

- Plantation agriculture requires a high level of investment. This is possible for international companies, but not for small farmers in LDCs. Heavy investment is needed to process and transport the crop to market. Banana companies, for example, have refrigerated ships, handling equipment in ports, and ripening centres near the market. The cost of a product is mostly in its transport and marketing.

- Plantation agriculture is difficult to mechanize. It is labour-intensive, but as the value of the basic crop is low, the wages of plantation workers are also low. Yet wages account for the bulk of production costs – 76 per cent on tea plantations in Sri Lanka. On some plantations, owners provide housing, schools and hospitals for workers. On others, workers suffer extremely bad conditions.

- In order to recover their investment, plantation owners need the benefit of **economies of scale**. Many plantations are therefore very large. One rubber plantation in Liberia is the size of the Isle of Man and employs 21,000 people. With large-scale monoculture it is possible to train specialists and develop new techniques. But this requires a high level of investment.

- Plantations grow cash crops, which provide much-needed export earnings for the LDC producers. But cash crops use up land that could grow food for the local population. Monoculture also exhausts soils if it is not well managed.

Above: *Picking coffee on a plantation in Indonesia. About 5% of the world's coffee comes from Indonesia.*

Above left: *Pod-breaking on a cocoa plantation in Ghana. The white beans, in the baskets, are then fermented and dried.*

Where the money goes

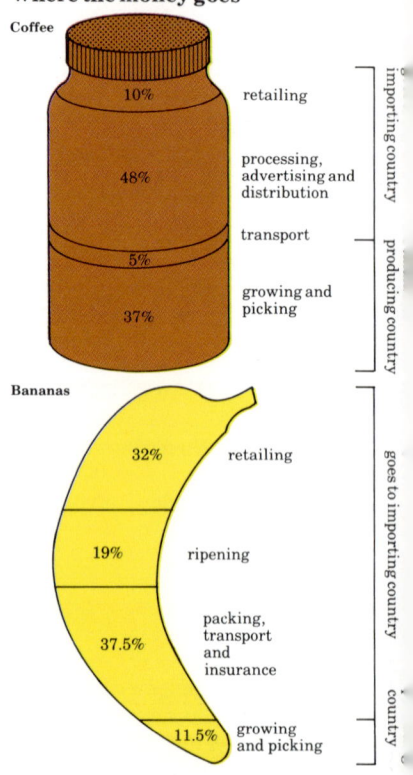

Coffee
- 10% retailing
- 48% processing, advertising and distribution
- 5% transport
- 37% growing and picking

(importing country / producing country)

Bananas
- 32% retailing
- 19% ripening
- 37.5% packing, transport and insurance
- 11.5% growing and picking

(goes to importing country / producing country)

Left: *Cut sisal being tied into bundles, ready for transport, on a plantation in Guatemala.*

The banana story

Bananas were first imported commercially into Britain in 1901. They soon became very popular; there were even songs written about them. Since then bananas have become important cash crops for many LDCs, such as Jamaica, Ecuador, Surinam, Belize and Cameroon. Today, Britain imports 350,000 tonnes of bananas a year.

1 A banana plantation on the Caribbean island of St Lucia. Bananas are not trees but plants. Nine months after planting, they flower and produce the stem that will eventually carry 100-200 bananas.
2 Baby bananas first hang downwards but, as they grow, they turn up toward the sun. About 12-15 months after planting, they are ready for harvesting. Stems are cut green and immediately taken to the cutting and packing station.
3 The fruit, washed and boxed, is quickly taken from the plantation to a refrigerated ship. Throughout the voyage to Britain, cool air is fanned round the bananas to keep them at 13°C.
4 On arrival, bananas are unloaded at special fruit berths and taken by insulated transport to temperature-controlled ripening centres. The ripening process lasts 4-5 days. The fruit is then delivered to retailers or weighed and priced for supermarkets.

Cameroon crisis

Until 1960 the Federal Republic of Cameroon was two separate administered territories, one French, the other British. Before independence both had a flourishing export trade in bananas. Smallholders grew 60 per cent of the crop; the rest came from plantations belonging to the American United Brands Company. Subsidiaries of United Brands exported the bananas to Britain and France.

After independence Britain set a tariff on bananas from Cameroon. As a result, British importers had withdrawn from the trade by 1967. The French subsidiary of United Brands continued to import from Cameroon, but several other factors drastically cut crop size. Diseases and hurricanes hit the growing area. There was increased competition from higher quality fruit from the West Indies and Latin America. Smallholders were too poor to invest in improved farming methods.

By 1975 the French subsidiary of United Brands had abandoned the Cameroon's trade. By the 1980s most smallholders were out of business. Production was down to 30 per cent of the 1950s total. Plantations owned and managed by Frenchmen accounted for 56 per cent of the total, government plantations for another 38 per cent. Yields are only one third of levels achieved in Latin America.

Choices for the government of Cameroon

For banana production
– Bananas produce regular, year-round export earnings.
– New plantations can be brought into production within one year.
– There are people with the necessary skills to grow bananas.
– Many people, such as plantation workers, box makers and aerial crop sprayers, rely on bananas for their livelihood.
– The French government still gives Cameroon a guaranteed import quota at prices above the world market.
– Fruit unsuitable for export finds a ready market as food for local people.

Against banana production
– The world market is saturated. Without a quota from France, Cameroon would lose its major customer.
– Government-run and independent plantations do not produce fruit of high enough quality to compete with other producer countries.
– The marketing and distribution system is not well organized.
– There is a lack of managerial skill, but the government is unwilling to seek the help of a trans-national company, as this would take profits out of Cameroon.
– Banana plantation land could be more profitably used for other cash crops, such as oil palm or rubber.
– Land needed for local market crops.

---

1 What is a plantation?
2 What are the advantages and disadvantages of plantations?
3 What happened to cut banana production in Cameroon by 60 per cent in 30 years?
Class activity: Take the part of one of the following people: a) a French plantation owner; b) a worker on a government-run plantation; c) a smallholder; d) a director of a trans-national fruit company. Write a paragraph supporting or opposing a proposal to halt banana production in Cameroon and convert the land to other plantation crops.

Deciding how to farm

MORPHOLOGY

> Decisions made by farmers are one of the most decisive influences on the use of land.

The farming industry

At whatever scale it operates, from subsistence to highly mechanized farming, agriculture is an industry.

- Crop growing and stock raising require the input of various forms of investment, which must be bought, employed or rented: land, buildings, machines, labour, seeds, fertilizers, animals, energy. Other **inputs** are less within the farmer's control: soil conditions, rain, sunshine. Yet others are dictated by governments: grants, subsidies, planning controls.
- The farmer manages these inputs to make his investment as productive as possible.
- **Outputs** (animals sent to market, crops harvested) generate the farmer's income. If management is successful, the revenue from outputs is greater than the cost of inputs: the farm makes a profit.
- The success of management is helped or hindered by many factors, all of which influence decisions taken by the farmer.

Farmer's decisions

SOCIAL INFLUENCES

Land tenure
Land can be either owned or rented. People tend to put more effort into things they own, or if they have security of tenure.

Traditions/beliefs
Custom and religion have an effect on farming methods, especially in LDCs (for example, sacred cows in India).

Information
Farmers need advisory and information services (farming magazines, TV, radio) to keep them up-to-date with new developments.

ECONOMIC INFLUENCES

Profits
The amount of surplus, or profit, a farm makes dictates how much can be put back into the farm as investment.

Labour
The cost, availability and skill level of labour affects farm production.

Markets
Farmers must have markets in which to sell output. Some markets are risky, others offer secure returns. Some offer higher prices than others.

Capital
Farmers can get grants and subsidies to finance improvements or they borrow from banks.

POLICY

Government policy
Government policy may be to subsidize farmers, encourage them to export, or replace imports. Policies affect what crops are grown and at what prices.

BEHAVIOURAL INFLUENCES

Chance
Some farmers are prepared to take higher risks than others. Some are good risk-takers; others not.

Choice
Some farmers have a wide choice in deciding what to produce; others are limited in what they can do.

Effort
Some farmers are prepared to put in more effort than others.

Management
Some farms are more efficiently organized than others.

Ability
Some farmers are more talented than others.

ENVIRONMENTAL INFLUENCES

Location
Climate, weather, terrain, aspect of the farm and soil type all affect what the farmer can produce.

Conservation
If the farm is in an area of special environmental importance, the farmer or the government may decide that land conservation has priority over agriculture.

TECHNOLOGY

New technology
The latest developments may be: available but, through circumstances, useless (for example, no fuel for tractors); not available; or available and profitable in use.

Decisions, decisions

Senegal: Peanut farmers provide 50 per cent of export earnings of this ex-French colony in West Africa. World peanut prices have fallen, making production scarcely economic. The government encourages continued production to avoid balance of payments problems.

> **1** Does the Senegalese farmer:
> a) continue to grow peanuts?
> b) revert to food production for his family and the local market?

Malaysia: Haji bin Ismail farms 11 ha on the Muda river, where the World Bank has financed a Green Revolution scheme, allowing two rice crops a year instead of one. He bought two tractors on credit and his two sons became contractors, hiring out the tractors and themselves to other farmers. But after five years other contractors set up in competition; rice yields improved; subsidies and free fertilizer made paddy farming more profitable.

> **2** Does Haji bin Ismail: a) buy another tractor on credit and compete? b) get his sons to help him make the most of paddy farming?

Sudan: Khogalab is a village 35 km north of Khartoum, the capital. A water scheme allows fellahin (small farmers) very limited plots of irrigated land, giving them a choice of new crops and markets: a) simple fodder crops for cash sale to other farmers raising meat for Khartoum; b) vegetables that are water- and labour-intensive, but provide food as well as high returns if they can be sent quickly to Khartoum; c) subsistence vegetables and animal fodder plus a small cash crop such as melons.

> **3** Do the fellahin: a) rely on fodder crops making enough money for them to buy all their food? b) grow vegetables and buy some food and all animal fodder? c) grow vegetables and fodder for subsistence, and accept the very low cash returns from growing melons?

Jersey Farm Restaurant and Hotel

EVERYTHING YOU COULD WANT STRAIGHT FROM THE FARM

A unique and memorable evening can be spent in our licensed restaurant within our farmhouse. We serve traditional English country fayre of the highest standard made from ingredients fresh from our home-grown produce

OUR PEDIGREE JERSEY HERD SUPPLY ALL THE MILK, CREAM AND BUTTER ON THE MENU

Above: *Many small farmers supplement their income with alternative activities and outlets such as offering accommodation, selling eggs and fresh produce at a roadside stall or even running a campsite.*

Left: *Modern oasis agriculture, financed by oil revenue, in Saudi Arabia. Although traditional date gardens still form the nucleus, they are surrounded by smallholdings and farms which produce fruit, vegetables, fodder and cereals. These grapes, grown under irrigation, are for table use only since wine is not permitted in Muslim countries.*

Saudi Arabia: For thousands of years the oases of the Arabian peninsula have been self-sufficient, depending on date palms for food, fuel, building materials and animal feed. Small plots of vegtables supplemented diet. The earth is rather salty, but there is water underground. Using its oil revenues, the Saudi government is investing in new water-extraction and irrigation techniques to create large-scale oasis farms. Roads have been built linking them to distant markets.

> 4 Imagine you are oasis dwellers, facing the changes brought about by oil wealth. Take the point of view of: a) an elderly person who has lived the traditional way all your life; b) the elderly person's grandson or granddaughter. Say whether you accept or reject the government initiatives.

Scotland: The isle of Islay, lying off the west coast, has 90 farms, 10,000 cattle and 14,000 sheep. Its farmers are poor but they have fertilized and improved pastures to make them the best in the Western Isles. However, rare barnacle geese also appreciate good grass and winter there in thousands. Under an EEC directive the geese and their habitat must be protected. But the farmers want to reduce the numbers of geese to conserve their pastures.

> 5 Should the farmers of Islay: a) accept a lower income because rare birds happen to spend the winter there? b) provoke a court case (perhaps by shooting some geese) to establish their legal rights, although this could involve years of wrangling in the EEC?

Australia: Before 1969 many farmers in Tasmania made a reliable but modest living from growing peas and potatoes. Then poppies were introduced as a crop: today 700 farmers grow 7000 ha of what they once considered a weed! Since the poppies are of the same family as those cultivated for opium in the Far East, they are produced under strict security, mainly for the pharmaceutical industry to make pain killers. The companies provide the seed, supervise soil preparation, order applications of fertilizer and pesticides and even dictate sowing and harvest times. The end product is low in bulk and weight and high in value.

> 6 As a Tasmanian farmer, do you give up your independence to become a caretaker for a crop of weeds? Poppy growing will give you an assured living, but you can only grow them if you have a clean police record!

England: Jim and Betty Donalson are tenant farmers in the beautiful Yorkshire Dales, renting 30 ha of land which is only suitable for dairy cattle. Since the EEC set quotas on milk output, the Donalsons have had to limit production, thus reducing their income which was never large. They do not own their land, so cannot sell up and do something else with the capital. At 50 Jim feels he is too old to get another job, although Betty could probably find something. Their MP has told them that he cannot do anything, as farm policy is decided in Brussels.

> 7 Jim is in favour of taking a small EEC grant to give up milk production and retiring early to a local town. Betty thinks they would be better to remain in their home and offer bed and breakfast to tourists walking the Dales. Which would you do and why?

Above: *Around 20,000 barnacle geese winter on Islay and are threatening the island's livelihood. Local farmers claim a goose eats five times as much grass as a sheep and also destroys the field with its droppings. For their part, conservationists are anxious to protect the geese and other rare birds.*

Tennessee's new deal

> Political commitment can make possible both economic and environmental improvements.

Hit by the depression

In 1929 the US stock market crashed. By 1933, 13 million people were unemployed. The great depression hit the seven south-eastern states around the valley of the Tennessee river particularly badly. This was already one of the poorest regions of America.

- The per capita income was only 45 per cent of the national average. Many residents of the Tennessee Valley suffered malnutrition; 30 per cent had malaria.
- More than half the region's three million people lived on farms, 50 per cent of them as tenants; most made only a subsistence living.
- Bad farming practice caused widespread soil erosion. Most forest areas were stripped for fuel as only three per cent of farms had electricity.
- The infrastructure of the region was very poor: road and rail networks were sparse while rapids on the Tennessee made water transport almost impossible. Lack of river control meant that homes and lives were lost in regular spring floods.

Above: *A Tennessee Valley tenant farmer with his family in the 1930s. Throughout the region, literacy levels were low and birthrates high: one-third above the national average. Unemployment was also high, with most of the labour force unskilled.*

Creation of the TVA

Proposals to develop the whole 1050-km river basin of the Tennessee Valley had been put forward in 1907. But none of the schemes had sufficient political backing until the election of President Roosevelt in 1932. His New Deal brought a fresh approach to government-funded development. In America almost all the infrastructure, like gas, electricity and telephones, was – and still is – owned by private companies. In 1933 Roosevelt set up a 'Corporation clothed with the power of government, but possessed of the flexibility and initiative of a private enterprise'.

Called the Tennessee Valley Authority (TVA), it aimed to:
- Produce hydro-electric power by building dams on the Tennessee river and to supply that power to farms, industry and towns.
- Control floods with the dams.
- Make the river navigable from Knoxville, Tennessee, to the Mississippi and to encourage freight traffic.
- Replant forest areas.
- Repair soil erosion damage.
- Educate farmers and improve agriculture.
- Promote local industry, beginning with a fertilizer plant.

Above: *Sixty years ago, poor harvests and malnourished animals characterized farming in the Tennessee Valley.*

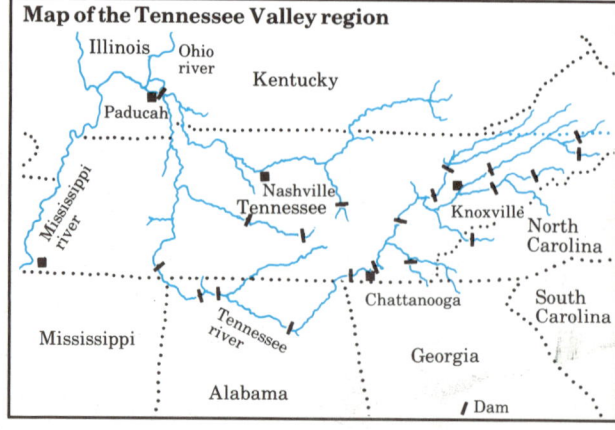

Left: *Bad farming methods – indiscriminate tree clearance, ploughing down slopes instead of across them and the cultivation of crops, such as corn, cotton and tobacco, that left the earth exposed in winter – caused chronic soil erosion. Every rainstorm washed away topsoil and carved deep gullies into the land.*

Map of the Tennessee Valley region

Achievements of the TVA

Within six years the TVA had built five dams and five more were under construction. World War II brought government arms-production projects to the region. By the 1950s half the TVA power production was going to defence establishments. Initial objections to the TVA, mostly from private enterprise opposed to government interference, had been overcome. In the last 50 years the TVA has played a major role in altering the human geography of the region.

Problems

The TVA has become a victim of its own success. It has achieved so many of its original aims that, not surprisingly, it has also made some mistakes in recent years.

■ The political commitment, pioneer spirit and idealism of the New Deal have gone.

■ Like many of America's utility companies which generate electricity, the TVA overestimated future demand for electricity. It ordered costly nuclear power stations: only two are operational. Another five have been delayed, or postponed.

■ The TVA, which began as an agency to repair environmental damage has been accused of causing pollution. Sulphur emissions from coal-fired stations have affected forests. Opencast coal mining in Kentucky creates ugly landscapes. Both problems are now being tackled. But there are still conflicts of interest between various TVA departments.

■ Not everyone agrees with flooding river valleys for reservoirs.

■ Some people feel that the TVA has not really provided an integrated regional planning service. Instead it has concentrated on producing electricity. Only 200 out of 40,000 TVA employees work on planning and community development.

Above: *Over 8.5 m hectares are now forested, including 750,000 ha that had been badly eroded. Previously, fire destroyed 10% of all woodlands but prevention measures have reduced the annual burn to 0.5%. Forestry and wood-using industries provide 53,000 jobs.*

Above: *The Tennessee river has become a 1050-km long highway, open to year-round traffic from Knoxville to Paducah – where it flows into the Ohio and so into the Mississippi. Freight traffic has risen from 1 m to 31 m tonnes annually and, together with waterfront industry, employs 45,000 people. The leading river port is Chattanooga.*

Left: *South Holston Dam, one of 39 dams that now straddle the Tennessee and its tributaries. Many of the dams – and their lakes – are multi-purpose: they are used for flood control (to date, preventing over $2 billion's-worth of damage), water storage, recreation and for generating electricity; currently, 15% of TVA power comes from hydro plants. Coal-fired stations produce 65% and nuclear plants 20%.*

Below: *Tennessee Valley farms are, today, twice the size they were fifty years ago and twelve times more profitable. Out of the region's 7.8 million population, only 100,000 are now in agriculture. Improved farming methods include double-cropping, terracing, soil enrichment and limiting hillside use to grazing. The use of fertilizers has been particularly significant. The TVA's fertilizer programme, launched in the 1930s, has grown into a research centre that develops, tests and promotes new fertilizers for use through out the US; it also advises on fertilizer technology to LDCs.*

---

1 Describe the condition of the Tennessee Valley in the early 1930s.
2 Why was the Tennessee Valley Authority set up?
3 What were its aims?
4 To what extent have these aims been achieved?
5 Why has the TVA been criticized in recent years?
6 What lessons have been learned from the TVA's experience which can be applied to other drainage basins with similar problems?

MORPHOLOGY

The third age

Migration and settlement are influenced by demographic trends.

Population explosion

While many LDCs have a population explosion of young people, the developed world is experiencing a population explosion of old people.
- As fewer babies are born and people live longer, the proportion of people over 60 is steadily increasing.

- In Britain pensionable age is 65 for men and 60 for women. In 1986, ten million people, or 20 per cent of the population, were pensioners. By 2025, if present trends continue, 25 per cent will be pensioners and 10 per cent will be over 75.

Proportion of people over 60

1985 average   2025 estimate

World 9% 14%
Africa 5% 7%
Europe 20% 25%

Above: *By 2025 life expectancy in LDCs is expected to increase to 70, just below current averages for developed nations. When that happens the proportion of the LDC population over 60 will increase as it has in Europe, Japan and the USA.*

Left: *On average women live eight years longer than men. From age 80 onwards, women outnumber men by about two to one.*

Retiring to the seaside

As people become more affluent and live longer they are inclined to regard the third age – retirement – as a new beginning. Although most remain where they lived and worked, many move to:
- The seaside, where they may have pleasant memories of holidays.
- The countryside, leaving the cities where they spent their working lives.
- Faraway sunspots, such as the Canary Islands or Spain, which are familiar from overseas holidays.

To Wales: People from Manchester and Liverpool retire either to the coast at Lytham St Annes and Southport, or to the Welsh countryside. People over 60 in Colwyn, Clwyd: 29.8%.

To the South-West: The mild climate and high sunshine record attract people from all over England. People over 60 in Torbay, Devon: 30.6%.

Post-war New Towns have an unbalanced population. Young people who moved to New Towns in the 1940-50s reached retirement age at the same time. During 1971-81 Stevenage's pensionable population increased by 73% and Crawley's by 58%. But New Towns still have few old people by national standards: Crawley 8% and Stevenage 7%.

To East Anglia: People from north London. Flat regions, like East Anglia, are more popular with elderly people than hilly landscapes which make walking difficult. People over 60 in Tendring, Essex: 30.2%.

To the South-East: Many Londoners retire to the south coast; those from south-east London tend to go to Brighton, Bexhill and Eastbourne; those from south-west London go to Worthing and Bognor Regis. People over 60 in Worthing, Sussex: 38.8%.

Right: *Within the UK there are a few regions that have attracted disproportionately large concentrations of elderly people.*

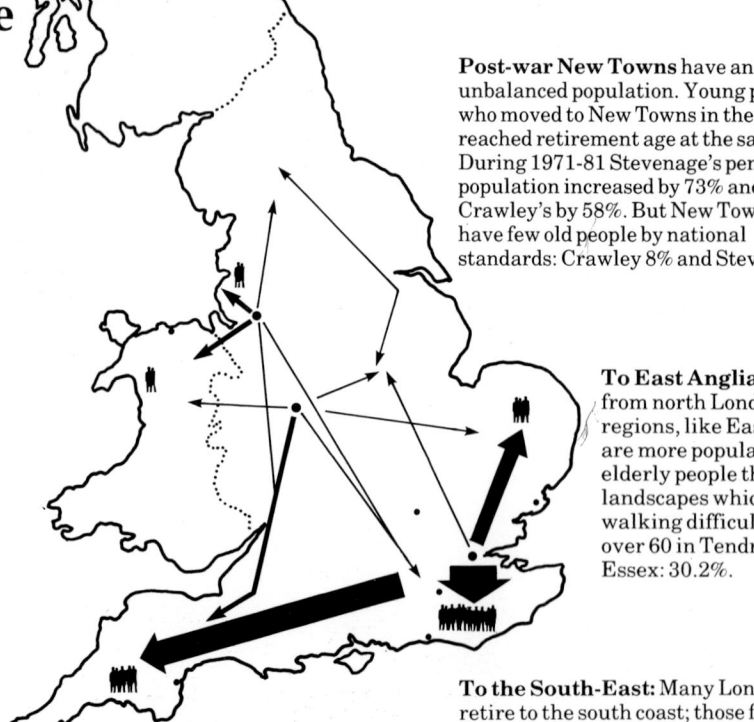

Migration of approx 50,000 people over 60

Some older than others

The migration of older people significantly affects the host regions. The effects, both economic and social, have advantages and disadvantages.

■ People are retiring earlier and move when they are still fit. At this stage they are an important human resource, either working or helping in their new communities.

■ As they get older they require greater care and represent a major item on local social service budgets.

Benefits
Retired people have regular incomes, which they mostly spend locally, on shopping and entertainments. They often have savings, which they invest with local building societies and banks.

Retired people create jobs. Many improve their retirement homes, with the help of builders and decorators. They employ gardeners and domestic help, requiring more assistance as they get older.

Senior citizens support local businesses. If they cannot drive they use public transport, or take taxis. Towns with high pensioner populations have more solicitors, estate agents and undertakers than elsewhere.

Retired people use private and state medical services, generating jobs in nursing homes and sheltered accommodation. More rest homes are being built to cater for increasing numbers of people too infirm to live alone.

Costs
Older people become ill more frequently, putting a strain on local hospitals, doctors, clinics and paramedical services, such as physiotherapy and district nursing.

If a resort becomes known as a place for elderly people, younger holiday-makers are put off. A resort can seldom cater for both old and young, as their needs are not compatible.

Retirement areas tend to have a limited range of housing; much of it single storey. This ties up land in one use, leaving less available for family houses, industry and commerce.

Retiring to Bognor

In the same way that people retire to specific regions, so too they tend to be concentrated in particular parts of those regions. Bognor Regis (Sussex) is in the Arun District, which has the fifth highest concentration of people over 60 in the UK: 32 per cent. Within Bognor itself there are even heavier concentrations of old people.

■ Aldwick and Pagham are residential areas close to the sea. More than 44 per cent of people are over 60.

■ In West End there is an overwhelming concentration of elderly women. There are 44 rest homes and a large sheltered housing scheme there. As women outlive men, most rest home residents are female.

■ Central Bognor has many old people but also many students. Both groups are flat dwellers. The elderly tend to have lived there a long time, choosing to stay in the central area or trapped there, unable to afford to move to the more expensive suburban areas.

Main migration patterns of people over 60

Above: *Map of Bognor Regis with population graphs for some of the wards.*

Below: *Retirement accommodation and rest homes account for a significant share of land use in areas with a large elderly population.*

1 Why is retirement sometimes called the third age?
2 Why do so many people migrate to the south coast when they retire?
3 Describe the age structure of Aldwick, Pagham and West End. Do these wards have balanced or unbalanced populations?
4 Weigh up the costs and benefits to a particular settlement of having a large population of senior citizens. Is it an advantage or disadvantage to the community?
5 Can you explain why care for the elderly, once a family responsibility, must now be provided by the state? Do you think this is correct, given the increasing elderly population?
6 Would it be an advantage or disadvantage to be old in a town with a large elderly population?

One world

MORPHOLOGY

Using the information on these pages, make up a suitable concept.

Space age in Gabon

A spin-off from the US space programme is providing energy for basic community services in remote villages in Gabon, West Africa. The American space agency NASA pioneered the use of photovoltaic cells to power satellites in space. In developed countries these solar cells are already in commercial use operating products such as pocket calculators and farm electric fences. To demonstrate their potential for the developing world, NASA has set up photovoltaic systems in four Gabonese villages. The electricity powers: a refrigerator for medicines, an air fan in the dispensary; a water pump for the well; a television and VCR in the school; and street lighting. The solar cells will last 20 years with little maintenance, but their cost is high.

> 1 What are the advantages and disadvantages of photovoltaic power systems to developing countries?

Above: *At Donguila, Gabon, solar cells (converting sunlight into electricity) provide power for water pumps and distribution system.*

Abandoned island

Tiny Kastellorizo is the remotest of all the Greek islands. It is eight hours by ferry (115 km) from the nearest main centre, Rhodes; yet less than 2 km from the shore of Turkey, which has long disputed Greece's claim to many islands; its case, regarding Kastellorizo, is strengthened by the fact that so few people now live there.

In 1911 there was a population of 17,000. But after World War I, the island was under Italian rule and cut off from its natural hinterland on the Turkish coast. With no markets and no work, most of the people emigrated – many to Australia. By 1943 there were less than 2000, and they were all evacuated by the British after heavy fighting with the Germans. Today only 200 people live on the island, yet the local newspaper prints 5000 copies, of which 4000 go to Australia (where Perth is Kastellorizo's twin town!). The Greek government tries to encourage people to return to the island, with transport subsidies and 80 per cent grants to expatriates who come back and rebuild family homes.

Left: *The entire population (in about 1950) of Kastellorizo in one photograph.*

> 1 Why do local people want to leave places like Kastellorizo, while tourists want to go there for holidays?
> 2 Why do people who emigrate often go to the same city or region as other people from their home area?

Smokestack politics

The world's atmospheric circulation ensures that the effects of pollution go far beyond national frontiers. Nowhere suffers more from this than Scandinavia. Since prevailing winds blow from the west and south, Scandinavia is downwind of Europe's most heavily industrialized zones. In 1985 there were moves to stop Norway's annual gift of a Christmas tree for Trafalgar Square, because pollution from Britain is killing so much of the Norwegian forest. European industry, especially coal-burning power stations, put approximately 30 million tonnes of sulphur into the atmosphere every year. Britain, the USSR and eastern European countries are the worst offenders.

About one-third of the reindeer slaughtered in Arctic Norway and Sweden in 1986 were unfit for human consumption because of radioactive fallout from the Chernobyl nuclear plant accident in Russia. Up to 80 per cent of the lakes in southern Norway may be too acid to support fish life. Acid rain also affects buildings and may be seriously weakening structures such as dams. But, unless Norway and Sweden can persuade their neighbours to control airborne pollution, there is little they can do about it.

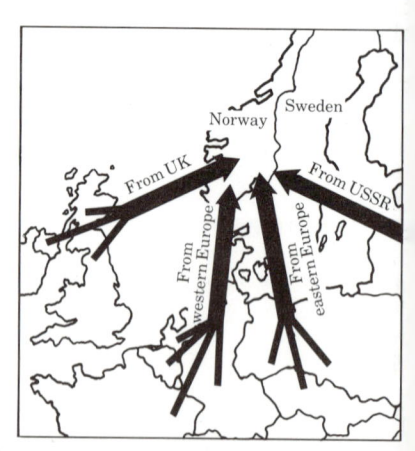

Above: *Sources of airborne pollution affecting Norway and Sweden.*

> 1 Where does the airborne pollution affecting Scandinavia come from?
> 2 Why does Scandinavia suffer from pollution that originates in other countries?

Continent of peace

Eighteen countries, including the USSR, USA, Australia, New Zealand, Britain, Norway, Argentina and Chile, conduct research in the hostile environment of Antarctica. But since 1961, when the Antarctic Treaty came into force, the world's coldest continent has been a demilitarized zone. Although the Soviet Union and the United States both have bases there, they are for scientific purposes only and neither claims any territory. The Americans have a station actually at the South Pole, while the Russian Vostok base recorded the world's lowest known temperature: −88.3°C. Much important research can only be carried out in Antarctica. For example, layers of ice made up from snowfall over millions of years allow scientists to study changes in world climate and perhaps predict the next ice age. The ice also holds a record of atmospheric pollution levels, enabling them to see if present day pollution is likely to damage the atmosphere. Certain kinds of damage to the atmosphere could cause the world's climate to become hotter. If this happened and the Antarctic ice melted, the world's sea level could rise by about 60 m.

Above: *The UK biological research station on Signy Island (60°43'S). Here scientists study plant and animal life, in particular bird and seal populations.*

> **1** Antarctica may contain reserves of oil, natural gas and useful minerals. Should these be explored and exploited? If so, by whom?

Water shortage

In the western part of North America one of the scarcest resources is water. The whole of the south-west US and northern Mexico is an area of water deficit. In theory, California has enough precipitation to provide water for its population of 25 million. However water supplies are not evenly distributed: 70 per cent of supply is in the northern one-third of the state; 80 per cent of demand is in the southern two-thirds – which includes 4 million ha of irrigated farmland mainly in the Central Valley, and the SanSan megalopolis (accounting for 80 per cent of the state's population). Already there are many aqueducts bringing water from north of Sacramento to the Central Valley and San Francisco area, and from the Colorado river to the Los Angeles area and Imperial Valley. But supply is inadequate and demand is growing. Plans exist for transferring water south from the Columbia and Fraser rivers and even from the Mackenzie river, which flows into the Arctic. The Columbia is already dammed along most of its length. Conservationists are trying to prevent this happening to the Fraser.

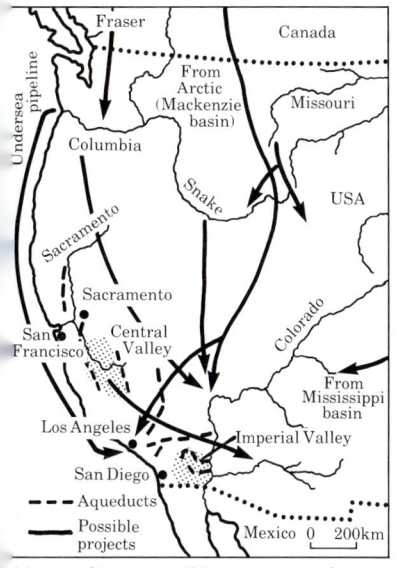

Above: *Some possible water transfer schemes in North America.*

> **1** The Fraser and Mackenzie rivers are entirely on Canadian soil; the Columbia flows through Canada for much of its length. Imagine you are:
> a) a US senator for California;
> b) a member of the Canadian Parliament for British Columbia;
> c) a member of the Mexican government planning to use water from the Colorado to develop Mexico's northern desert. What arguments would you use for and against water transfer schemes?

World view

In the early 1980s a group of international statesmen, eight from developed nations and ten from developing countries, made a special study of the uneven distribution of the world's wealth. The group – known as the Brandt Commission after its chairman, Willy Brandt, (ex-Chancellor of West Germany) – issued two reports. The main conclusion was that instead of concentrating on the military and political rivalry between East and West, world leaders should be more concerned with the social and economic barriers dividing the richer countries of the North and poorer countries of the South. The Commission explained that developed and developing nations have many mutual interests; and are inter-dependent.

In the North 30-40 million people are unemployed; northern industry could produce £500 bn worth more goods a year than at present. For its part, the South needs the goods that the North could produce. It also has to find ways of boosting agricultural output, producing more energy, and tackling social problems.

Many nations of the South are hampered by huge debts. The Brandt Commission suggested several solutions: massive new credits so that the South can buy goods from the North; easing of trade restrictions, to allow the North to import the South's products more freely; individual efforts with contributions to development and relief programmes.

> **1** What are some of the mutual interests of developed nations of the North and LDCs in the South?
> **2** Can you think of any way in which the Brandt Commission's ideas have been followed up?

Index

CONCEPTS are in capital letters
Major themes are in bold
Place names are in italics

A
Accessibility 16, 28, 29
Afforestation 55, 60, 64
Afghanistan 74
Africa 27, 34, 43, 60, 61, 68, 86, 93
Agriculture 22, 31, 32, 46, 60, 63, 72, 88, 96, 99, 100, 102, 103, 104, 109
Aid 44, 47, 72
Albania 74
Algeria 44
Alps 24, 35
Angola 74
Antarctic 26, 109
Apartheid 94, 95
Arctic 26, 39, 70
Area of Outstanding Natural Beauty 43, 63
Argentina 2, 41, 80, 109
Asia 24, 80
Aspect 56, 102
Atlantic Ocean 8, 47, 86, 95
Australia 10, 11, 27, 28, 37, 42, 47, 53, 58, 59, 80, 103, 108, 109
Austria 72

B
Balance of payments 31, 33, 50
Bangladesh 48, 57
Barbados 13, 30, 31
Belgium 72
Belize 101
Berlin 75, 92
Biomass 5, 60
Botswana 95
Brandt Commission 109
Brazil 32, 39, 41
Britain 4, 6 10, 13, 14, 16, 17, 23, 25, 26, 28, 29, 30, 32, 33, 39, 42, 44, 47, 50, 52, 63, 64, 65, 67, 68, 69, 72, 75, 76, 77, 83, 84, 86, 87, 89, 90, 95, 101, 106, 108, 109
Brunei 88

C
Cairo 93
California 4, 5, 12, 13, 25, 27, 85, 86, 109
Cameroon 101
Canada 8, 11, 44, 80, 81
Canals 7
Capital 32, 44, 47
Caribbean 101
Central Business District (CBD) 16, 19, 28, 29, 89, 98
Centralization 92
Chernobyl disaster 43, 108
Chicago 18, 19
Chile 92, 109
China 5, 11, 15, 30, 55, 57, 74, 80, 86, 87, 96
Cities 16, 18, 57, 92, 96, 98
Class activity 6, 9, 31, 37, 67, 71, 101
Climate 56, 57, 64, 102
Coal 19, 42, 43, 62, 65, 67, 72, 77, 104, 108
Coasts 8, 26, 30, 86, 108
Colombia 92
Colonization 41, 44, 72, 86, 88, 94
Common Agricultural Policy (CAP) 22, 23, 72
Commonwealth 68, 95
Communications 15, 33, 46, 47, 63, 70, 95
Commuting 19, 29, 99
Companies 84, 89, 100, 101
Computers 12, 47, 85
Conservation 42, 43, 58, 59, 60, 63, 102, 103, 109
Consumers 10, 23, 38, 39, 42, 47, 76, 82
Conurbations 16, 18, 19
COMECON 74, 86
Crops 9, 80, 81, 100, 101, 102, 104
Cuba 74
Cyprus 68
CYCLES 16, 18, 20, 22, 24, 26
Czechoslovakia 43, 75

D
Dairy farming 22
Decentralization 9, 84
Decolonization 41
Defence 41, 44, 70, 75, 84
Deforestation 59, 60, 61
Denmark 5, 39, 72, 77, 79
Deposition 55
Desert 60, 61
Development 20, 29, 30, 31, 40, 43, 44, 45, 47, 48, 58, 60, 66, 76, 88, 94, 102, 109
Drought 37, 60

E
Earthquakes 14, 15, 25, 36, 46
East African Rift Valley 14
East Germany 32, 74, 75
Eastern Europe 43, 72, 74, 75, 108
Eco-systems 34, 59
Economies of scale 82, 83, 100
Ecuador 101
Edinburgh 20, 90
Education 17, 47, 64, 67, 69, 70, 84, 89, 94, 97, 98
Egypt 93
Electricity 4, 5, 43, 58, 77, 104, 105, 108
Electronics 12, 20, 33, 40, 47
Employment 8, 12, 17, 32, 33, 40, 46, 48, 58, 67, 83, 93, 98, 107
Energy 4, 38, 42, 43, 58, 72, 108, 109
England 6, 10, 23, 29, 43, 63, 65, 68, 76, 77, 103
Entrepreneurs 13, 47, 85
Environment 13, 17, 21, 28, 29, 42, 58, 60, 63, 70, 72, 77, 84, 102, 104, 109
Equator 4, 26
Erosion 24, 59, 60, 61, 104
Ethiopia 60, 61, 74

Ethnic minorities 19, 70, 71
Europe 4, 8, 13, 22, 23, 28, 29, 30, 38, 44, 47, 48, 52, 64, 65, 67, 70, 74, 83, 86, 106, 108
European Community (EC/EEC) 17, 22, 23, 38, 48, 72, 74, 76, 78, 80, 86, 103
European Free Trade Association (EFTA) 72
European Parliament 23
European Regional Development Fund (ERDF) 77
Euskadi 71
Exports 8, 10, 11, 17, 23, 32, 39, 41, 42, 66, 67, 71, 83, 87, 95, 97, 101

F
Famine 45, 60, 96
Farming 22, 34, 57, 60, 77, 88, 96, 102
Faults 25
Fertilizer 5, 23, 27, 40, 60, 81, 102, 103, 104, 105
Finland 70, 74
Fishing 26, 27, 57, 72
Floods 55
Folds 25
Forests 8, 25, 37, 46, 57, 59, 64, 70, 104
Fossil fuels 4, 42, 43
France 5, 13, 22, 23, 29, 30, 39, 42, 44, 48, 49, 64, 67, 71, 75, 77, 87, 90, 101
Frankfurt 29, 33, 40, 92
Fuel 5, 10, 60, 61, 102

G
Gabon 41, 108
Geology 24, 43, 62
Geothermal energy 5
Ghana 88, 100
Glasgow 20, 21
Government 7, 9, 20, 23, 30, 31, 33, 37, 43, 44, 45, 49, 52, 59, 70, 71, 75, 76, 77, 84, 87, 89, 90, 93, 95, 101, 102, 104
Greece 23, 51, 72, 108
Green Revolution 45, 80, 81, 102
Greenland 24, 77
Gross Domestic/National Product (GDP/GNP) 30, 40, 45, 79, 88
Guatemala 100

H
Hazards 59
Health 17, 51, 97, 107
Himalayas 24
Hinterland 16
HIERARCHIES 88, 90, 92, 94, 96
Hong Kong 33, 68
Hostile environments 39
Housing 17, 19, 20, 21, 29, 43, 52, 68, 89, 90, 93, 97, 107
Hungary 43, 74, 75
Hwang Ho, river 55
Hydro-electric power (HEP) 4, 58, 70, 104

I

Ice age 109
Iceland 5, 72
Immigration 48, 49, 68, 69
Imports 33, 41, 44, 64, 66, 67, 78, 80, 81, 101, 109
India 5, 24, 45, 48, 57, 68, 80, 81, 86, 87
Indian Ocean 31, 95
Indonesia 57, 80, 88, 100
Industrial Revolution 10, 16, 20, 32, 66
Industrialization 89
Industry 6, 9, 10, 12, 13, 16, 20, 32, 42, 43, 64, 66, 67, 70, 76, 77, 83, 84, 96, 102, 104, 107, 109
Infrastructures 31, 43, 44, 77, 89, 104
Inner cities 17, 19, 20, 21, 28, 29
Investment 21, 29, 40, 47, 64, 76, 83, 89, 96, 100, 102, 103, 107
Iran 38, 78
Iraq 38, 74
Ireland (Eire) 77
Irrigation 34, 68, 80, 103
Isle of Purbeck 62
Israel 13, 38, 97
Italy 22, 23, 68, 72, 77

J

Jamaica 101
Japan 5, 11, 13, 15, 19, 32, 33, 38, 41, 44, 45, 46, 67, 79, 83, 86, 106

K

Kenya 87
Korea 11

L

Lakes 8
Laos 74
Lapland 70
LANDSCAPES 56, 58, 60, 62, 64
Leisure 30, 64, 98
Less Developed Countries (LDCs) 4, 5, 13, 18, 19, 23, 30, 32, 35, 39, 40, 41, 44, 45, 47, 60, 81, 86, 89, 91, 100, 101, 102, 106, 108, 109
Liberia 100
Livestock 22, 34, 35, 61, 102
Locations 29
London 6, 10, 21, 29, 30, 32, 33, 52, 67, 68, 84, 85, 86, 90, 95, 106
Los Angeles 16, 18
LOCATIONS 4, 6, 8, 10, 12, 14

M

Malawi 87
Malaysia 11, 13, 80, 88, 102
Mali 32, 33, 49
Management 12, 47, 52, 83, 101, 102
Manufacturing 13, 17, 39, 44, 46, 66, 84
Markets 10, 11, 28, 41, 47, 61, 67, 72, 86, 101, 102, 103
Mecca 51
Mediterranean 4, 14, 15, 22, 30, 48, 72, 86, 109

Megalopolis 18, 109
Melbourne 11, 37
Mexico 15, 30, 74, 109
Mezzogiorno 77
Middle East 38, 42, 86, 93
Migration 18, 19, 34, 48, 68, 106, 107
Mining 59, 70, 71
Mississippi, river 54
Modified Mercalli Scale 15
Mongolia 74
Monsoon 57
Morocco 44
Moscow 74, 96
Motorways 28, 29, 84, 85, 99
Mountain-building 14, 24, 25
Mozambique 74, 95
MORPHOLOGY 98, 100, 102, 104, 106, 108

N

Namibia 95
National parks 31
Natural disasters 15, 27, 36, 37, 44, 55, 59
Nepal 45
Netherlands 39, 44, 72, 87
New Towns 20, 21, 106
New York 18, 33, 86
New Zealand 5, 11, 24, 79, 109
Newly Industrializing Countries (NICs) 32, 39, 40, 41, 86
NETWORKS 78, 80, 82, 84, 86
Nicaragua 74
Niger 4, 61
Nigeria 34, 88
Nile, river 93
Niugini (Papua New Guinea) 9
Nomadism 34, 60
North America 4, 25, 27, 28, 38, 43, 86, 109
North Atlantic drift 26
North Atlantic Treaty Organization (NATO) 75
North Korea 74
North Sea 39, 42
Northern Ireland 50, 66, 76, 77
Norway 39, 65, 72, 108, 109
Nuclear power 4, 42, 104

O

Ocean currents 26, 27
Oceans 26, 57
Offices 16, 32, 83, 85, 98
Oil 19, 38, 42, 58, 62, 74, 76, 83, 87, 88, 93, 103
Organic farming 23
Organization of Petroleum Exporting Countries (OPEC) 38, 39, 44, 49, 87
Out of town shopping centres 20, 99
Oxfam 45

P

Pacific basin/rim 15, 47, 86
Pacific islands 30
Pacific Ocean 14, 25, 26
Pakistan 48, 68
Pangaea 25

Paris 33, 49, 92
PATTERNS 48, 50, 52, 54
Peak land values 99
Peking 97
Peru 26, 27, 92
Philippines 13, 80
Plantations 44, 100, 101
Plate tectonics 24
Poland 75
Politics 38, 44, 47, 52, 67, 71, 72, 81, 89, 93, 96, 105, 108, 109
Pollution 4, 13, 59, 65, 104, 108, 109
Population 17, 18, 20, 32, 46, 60, 61, 69, 76, 84, 89, 107, 108
Portugal 23, 48, 72
Primary industry 32, 66
Primate cities 92
Pyrenees 24

Q

Queensland 10, 11, 53

R

Railways 19, 21, 84, 90, 104
Raw materials 9, 10, 41
Relief 24
Research 10, 12, 72, 84, 109
Resources 6, 34, 40, 41, 44, 46, 47, 58, 84, 86
Retailing 28, 83
REGIONS 66, 68, 70, 72, 74, 76
RELATIONSHIPS 38, 40, 42, 44, 46
Rice 46, 47
Richter scale 15, 36
Ring of fire 36
Rivers 2, 6, 7, 8, 9, 54, 55, 104, 105, 109
Roads 77, 104
Rocks 24, 54, 55
Ruhr 20, 28

S

San Francisco 12, 13, 18, 19, 25
Saudi Arabia 44, 103
Scandinavia 8, 25, 65, 70, 108
Scotland 4, 5, 10, 20, 23, 25, 50, 65, 66, 76, 103
Scottish Development Agency (SDA) 76
Sea 26, 109
Secondary industry 66
Senegal 102
Service industry 77, 84
Settlements 16, 18, 63, 92, 93, 106
Shanghai 96
Shops 20, 28, 69, 77, 82, 95, 98, 99
Silicon Valley 12, 19, 85
Singapore 8, 11, 13, 89
Skills 10, 12, 13, 17, 20, 21, 32, 44, 47, 52, 67, 84, 101, 102
Soil 8, 34, 56, 59, 60, 61, 65, 88, 102, 104
Solar energy 4, 108
Somalia 61
South Africa 94, 95
South America 26, 92, 101
South West Africa 42
South Yemen 74

111

South-East Asia 30
Soviet Union 7, 11, 43, 44, 72, 74, 80, 96, 108, 109
Space 47, 108
Spain 22, 23, 30, 71, 72, 86, 87, 106
Sri Lanka 87, 100
St Lucia 101
Steel 19, 67, 71, 72, 77, 83
Subsistence farming 88, 104
Suburban areas 16, 19, 21, 28, 84, 90
Sudan 60, 61, 102
Sun belt 13
Supermarkets 28, 82
Supply and demand 78, 79
Surinam 101
Swaziland 95
Sweden 8, 42, 44, 72
Switzerland 35, 42, 72
Sydney 11, 33, 98
Syria 81

T
Taiwan 13
Tanzania 30, 32
Tasmania 58, 59, 103
Technology 13, 41, 47, 67, 93, 102
Tenants 90, 104
Tennessee Valley Authority (TVA) 104, 105
Terracing 55, 60, 61
Tertiary industry 32, 33, 52, 66, 67
Textiles 17, 40, 41, 67, 69, 76
Thailand 80
TIME-DISTANCE 30, 31, 32, 33, 34, 35, 36, 37
Tokyo 33, 46
Topography 47, 56
Tourism 30, 31, 50, 58, 62, 70, 72, 77, 98, 103, 108
Trade 16, 19, 38, 50, 72, 78, 86, 95
Trades unions 13, 67
Trans-national companies 20, 40, 41, 44, 85, 89, 100
Transhumance 35
Transport 10, 16, 28, 29, 30, 42, 47, 50, 51, 72, 84, 96, 100
Tunisia 44
Turkey 32, 48

U
Uganda 68
Unemployment 31, 44, 49, 66, 69, 76, 84, 89, 109
United Arab Emirates 44
United Nations (UN) 44, 72
Urban areas 29, 57, 84
Urban decay 16
Urban renewal 16
Urban transect 99
USA 5, 6, 8, 11, 12, 17, 18, 19, 30, 33, 36, 40, 42, 44, 46, 47, 80, 83, 86, 87, 104, 105, 106, 108, 109

V
Vietnam 74

W
Wales 6, 14, 50, 51, 66, 76, 77, 106, 109
Warsaw Pact 75
Washington D.C. 18, 19
Water 6, 7, 57, 58, 77, 103, 109
Weathering 24
Welsh Development Agency (WDA) 76
West Germany 22, 28, 29, 30, 39, 40, 42, 44, 48, 49, 51, 65, 67, 82, 87, 90, 92
West Indies 13, 30, 101
Winds 5, 26, 37, 56, 61, 65
World War I 64
World War II 31, 38, 46, 48, 64, 67, 68, 72, 74, 75, 76, 86, 104

Y
Yugoslavia 74

Z
Zaire 45
Zimbabwe 41, 95